MARSHAL ZHUKOV

Zhukov and granddaughter Alexandra shortly after the war.

MARSHAL ZHUKOV

THE MAN WHO BEAT HITLER

ALBERT AXELL

In Europe the war has been won and to no man do
the United Nations owe a greater debt than to
Marshal Zhukov ...
US General Eisenhower, June 1945

PEARSON
Longman

London • New York • Toronto • Sydney • Tokyo • Singapore
Hong Kong • Cape Town • Madrid • Paris • Amsterdam • Munich • Milan

PEARSON EDUCATION LIMITED

Head Office:
Edinburgh Gate
Harlow CM20 2JE
Tel: +44 (0)1279 623623
Fax: +44 (0)1279 431059

London Office:
128 Long Acre
London WC2E 9AN
Tel: +44 (0)20 7447 2000
Fax: +44 (0)20 7447 2170
Website: www.history-minds.com

First published in Great Britain in 2003

© Pearson Education Limited 2003

The right of Albert Axell to be identified as Author
of this Work has been asserted by him in accordance
with the Copyright, Designs and Patents Act 1988.

ISBN 0 582 77233 8

British Library Cataloguing in Publication Data
A CIP catalogue record for this book can be obtained from the British Library

Library of Congress Cataloging in Publication Data
A CIP catalog record for this book can be obtained from the Library of Congress

10 9 8 7 6 5 4 3 2 1

Typeset by Fakenham Photosetting Ltd, Fakenham, Norfolk NR21 8NN
Printed and bound in Great Britain by Biddles Limited

The Publishers' policy is to use paper manufactured from sustainable forests.

CONTENTS

Acknowledgements   vii

Introduction: A Search for the Real Zhukov   1

1   The Shaping-up Years   13

2   A Tsarist Cavalryman   21

3   A New Regime   30

4   The Great Madness   44

5   Zhukov in Mongolia   50

6   Hitler Goes to War   63

7   Moscow in Danger   78

8   'We Were *Eating* the Park . . .'   90

9   'A Pocket Edition of Hell'   100

10   Kursk: the Nazis' Waterloo   113

11   The Partisans of Belarus   122

12   Berlin: Defeat and Revival   135

13   Hitler's Marriage and Death   150

14   'Bastards and Plotters'   156

15   Stalin and Zhukov   171

16   Beria: Arrest and Death   184

17   Big Brother and Zhukov   191

18   The Eisenhower–Zhukov Friendship   197

19   Wives and Daughters   213

20   Falling in Love – the Second Time   223

21   In Memoriam   229

Epilogue: A Grateful Posterity   232

Select Bibliography   243

Index   248

LIST OF MAPS

1   Barbarossa   70
2   Russian Counter-attack at Moscow   86
3   The Battle of Stalingrad   108
4   The Battle of the Kursk Bulge   119
5   Operation Bagration   123
6   The Berlin Operation   143

ACKNOWLEDGEMENTS

During the last quarter of the twentieth century the author interviewed more than thirty Russian generals, admirals and air marshals who had crossed swords with Adolf Hitler's armed forces. Many of them had fought alongside or under the command of Georgi Zhokov between 1941 and 1945. Some of them had also fought in the Russian Civil War, the Spanish Civil War and the war against Japan in 1945. Some, like Zhukov, were ex-cavalrymen. Many were in Berlin at war's end. They included Air Marshal Sergei Rudenko, Admiral of the Fleet Sergei Gorshkov, Generals Ivan Shavrov, Afanasy Beloborodov, M.I. Belov, I.G. Pavlovsky, L.S. Skvirsky, Semyon Krivoshein, Alexei Zheltov, David Dragunsky, S.P. Vasiagin, Boris Vyashin and Admiral M.M. Ivanov. As might be expected in that bloodiest of all wars, many of these generals carried the scars of the battlefield; some had been wounded two, three, even four times. Not a few of these men were highly articulate and well-read. The six or seven who invited the author to their homes had rooms filled with book shelves, including whole collections of those Russian classics: Pushkin, Gogol, Dostoevsky, Tolstoy, Turgenev and Chekhov.

In 2002 two members of Russia's Academy of Sciences kindly assisted the author in his research on this book, Professor Oleg Rzheshevsky, President of the National Committee of Russian Historians and the Association of the Second World War Historians; and historian Dr Mikhail Myagkov. Special thanks must also go to Marshal Zhukov's two eldest daughters, Ella and Era, who good-naturedly fielded endless questions about their father when the author visited them in Moscow. In addition they provided him with dozens of family photographs, even taking some off their living-room walls so that the author could make copies of them.

German reaction to Zhukov's major victories is provided mainly by the articles and memoirs of Wehrmacht generals who saw service on the Russian front. The generals include Heinz Guderian, Hasso von Manteuffel, Kurt von Tippelskirch, Franz Halder, Gunther Blumentritt and Hans Doerr.

Various archives and libraries were indispensable in researching Zhukov's life. The author wishes to thank the staffs of the Russian State Military Archive and the Central Archive of the Ministry of Defence; and, in London, the British Library (including its admirable Newspaper Library), the Imperial War Museum, the Society for the Cooperation in Russian and Soviet Studies, and the Swiss Cottage and West Hampstead libraries.

A number of specialists in Great Britain, Ireland, Russia and Germany were kind enough to read the typescript and offered their comments and suggestions.

The author's sincere thanks go to friends and colleagues for their continued support and encouragement. To name a few: V.V. Makarov, Ann Pavett, Janet Q. Treloar, John Hale-White, Nicholas Gibbs, Ronald James Wren, Barry Holmes, Dmitry Shaklanoff, Jay Axelbank, Dominique Le Frapper, Martin Blakeway and Paul Colston, the editor of *Russian Mirror*.

Finally the author wishes to thank Casey Mein, Anna Vinegrad and Magda Robson, members of the highly capable editorial staff at Longman (Pearson Education) in London, and to my copy-editor, Pendleton Campbell.

INTRODUCTION: A SEARCH FOR THE REAL ZHUKOV

My father suffered a lot of hardship and deprivation in his childhood and youth. But this life taught him a lot and hardened him.

MARIA ZHUKOVA

The man who inflicted more defeats on Hitler's Reich than anyone else is also the least known in the West. A recent look at library catalogues showed there were more than 65 books available on the life of Montgomery, 190 on Eisenhower, 79 on MacArthur, more than 20 on Alanbrooke, 30 on Wavell and 45 on Patton. (On the German side there were, for example, 8 books on Manstein, 16 on Guderian and more than 50 on Rommel.) But there were only 3 books available on Georgi Zhukov, the Russian marshal who was hailed by US General (later President) Dwight 'Ike' Eisenhower, as the man to whom the United Nations owed a greater debt than to any other military figure for his triumphs against the Wehrmacht.

Who was this man to whom the West is indebted?

Georgi Zhukov is hardly known in the West, but for many years he was a virtual non-person in his own country, unmentioned by the media, his great role in the victory over Hitler's Germany diminished or overlooked by official histories. Historian Vasily Morozov says Zhukov was during this period 'emotionally battered by monstrous injustices' carried out by enforcers of the official line. Another historian, Viktor Anfilov, refers to 'the evil designs of the political censors' under Stalin and Khrushchev. Now, however, Zhukov (1896–1974) is on the way to becoming a 'people's hero' as the country regards folk heroes like Minin and Pozharski in the seventeenth century, Suvorov in the eighteenth and Kutuzov in the nineteenth.

Zhukov is often accused of being severe. . . . No doubt he was. Here is what Viktor Anfilov says:

He was indeed severe, demanding and strict. To bring about the rout of the enemy, he gave not only his mind but his heart, not fearing to look death in the face. He often expected the troops to stand fast, not only with strict orders but at times by request. On the 21st of November [1941] during the battles for the town of Rogachov, he sent the following telegram to the commander of the 8th Tank Brigade, who was P. A. Rotmistrov: 'I request that you hold Rogachov for at least another 24 hours.'[1]

Needless to say it was more than a request. Anfilov says that 'Here you have a lesson in the art of being a commander and knowing about human psychology.'

Throughout his military career Zhukov was attacked for being too demanding, for being guilty of 'excessive exactingness'. By the latter was meant Zhukov's insistence on the highest levels of performance in all military activities. But as historian N. Badiakin says, the marshal set the highest standards for himself and 'this gave him the moral right to demand it from others'. Badiakin mentions Zhukov's attention to detail. He speaks of his own postwar military duties when as a young officer he had to continuously write annual reports of combat training which were sent to the commander of the military district (Zhukov) for approval. 'Usually we got them back after two weeks. You can hardly imagine it. . . . The reports were covered with Zhukov's notes and comments and directives. And there was an enormous number of these reports connected with the military district.' Zhukov, he says, didn't delegate anything. He considered it was 'part of his job'.

Zhukov was almost fanatical on the subject of historical truth. He is quoted in the military newspaper, *Krasnaya Zvezda* (Red Star) as saying: 'Time will put everything in its place and judge everybody. . . . You can only properly serve your people by telling them the truth and fighting for it.' Anfilov explains: 'Zhukov said you need to look the truth in the eye and not be embarrassed to admit [for example] that at the beginning of our war with Nazi Germany the enemy was significantly stronger and more experienced than us, was better prepared, trained and armed.' And he preferred the truth, such as saying 'rapid retreat' of our troops rather than calling it 'forced withdrawal'.

Zhukov was not one to give in to adversity. Maria Zhukova, his youngest daughter, says her father taught his daughters not to surrender to difficulties. 'A difficult life is life's best school. Indifference, father said, was the most dreadful thing. In his childhood and youth he had suffered a lot of hardship and deprivation. But that life taught him a lot and hardened him.'

Zhukov is often accused of wasting lives. . . . This is not an easy question to address because there were no Queensberry Rules on the Eastern front and the Nazi invader was one of the most callous in history. (One of Hitler's generals, Franz Halder, entered this cynical remark in his diary: 'In the East harshness is kindness toward the future.') No doubt many a wartime commander can be criticized for not caring about the loss of lives. And Zhukov is doubtless open to criticism. But there were also instances when he took pains to save lives, when he argued with Stalin about the timing of an operation, or called for its cancellation as it would only result in casualties. (See chapter 15.) Added to this was the sheer length of Russia's front lines. At Stalingrad, for example, millions of troops were involved, spread along a continuous front equal to the distance between New York and Florida, or twice the distance between London and Aberdeen.

Thick-set, with handsome features, pale blue eyes peering through rimless glasses, a social drinker, fine dancer and non-smoker, Georgi Konstantinovich Zhukov was regarded by many colleagues as brusque, coarse, arrogant, profane. A future marshal, K.K. Rokossovsky, who knew Zhukov well, described him back in 1930 as 'strong-willed and decisive' but also 'demanding' and 'insufficiently sensitive'. A year later, Zhukov was accused of being excessively harsh and coarse by a superior officer, S.M. Budenny, a popular Cossack hero of the Civil War. The same criticism – excessive severity – would frequently be levelled at him during the Great Patriotic War, the Russian name for the Second World War. There is no doubt that Zhukov was ruthless and frequently pitiless. Reflecting on such claims, Zhukov admitted them but said they were justified. He also admitted being sharp-tongued at times but he excused himself, saying that, when thousands of lives were in the balance and a big operation was underway, there was little time for delicacy.

Zhukov had his shortcomings and he was criticized in books and articles both at home and abroad. He was attacked for being ill-tempered, vain, arrogant. One Western writer said Zhukov was 'vicious and 'vindictive', but none of his Western colleagues or his compatriots, who knew him intimately, ever detected such nastiness.

But there was more subtle criticism from a British source. Sir David Kelly, a former Ambassador to Moscow, wrote of Zhukov: 'He incarnates the military doctrine of the Red Army which is based on . . . the necessity of a despotically planned economy, the conviction that military art is the application of the party line in military matters, and the certainty that all wars spring from class warfare and are therefore totally unavoidable until the last capitalist society has been liquidated.'[2]

All these criticisms aside, there was another Georgi Zhukov, one more accessible, more friendly, more human. British General Sir Francis de Guingand, Montgomery's Chief of Staff, described Zhukov as having a 'friendly and cheerful personality'.[3] American author John Gunther, after meeting him several times in the postwar era, said Zhukov had 'the friendliest, heartiest smile of any of the Russian leaders we met'. And US General Dwight Eisenhower's son, John, called Zhukov 'congenial', even 'effervescent'.

Off the battlefield, Georgi Zhukov was a loving father to his daughters. When he was able to come home for a day or two (usually after a breakthrough over the enemy had been achieved) he would relax and enjoy chattering about trifles with his wife and daughters, or put on a mock-serious air and play a traditional Russian song on the accordion.

What sets Zhukov apart from many of his compatriots was his strong independent spirit, keen sense of history and consistent desire for postwar friendship, even unity, between the former fighting Allies in order to prevent future perils to global peace. Zhukov died in 1974 at age 77. Russia, it will be remembered, did not shed its Communist cloak until many years later.

General Eisenhower who worked closely with Zhukov for a year in the administration of postwar Germany, said the differences in their creeds – which they would speak of candidly when they were together – never got in the way of their official business. In the postwar period one occasionally heard it said that Zhukov was the 'best man in the Soviet Union'. Speaking to journalists, a foreign diplomat in Moscow gave this opinion as to what set the marshal apart from others: 'Zhukov is the only man high up who tells the truth. He may evade a question, but he will not lie.'[4]

But in his difficult retirement Zhukov had to struggle with the Kremlin authorities not to emasculate his voluminous memoirs, still considered the best of the war memoirs published by the celebrated generals and marshals. It was never easy for him to compromise with the truth.

It is no surprise that during the heavy doctoring of the manuscript by the Party censors for the earlier editions of Zhukov's memoirs – first published in Russia in the late sixties – some observers were reminded of Big Brother from the novel *1984* by British author George Orwell (see chapter 17). The analogy is apt. In Orwell's classic, there is a Ministry of Truth engaged in making clean copies of the past to please Big Brother who has a super aim in mind: By calling lies the truth, by rewriting pages of history, Big Brother can hold back at least for several millennia the forward march of history.

Who was Georgi Zhukov?

During the war, the daily combat toll on the Russian side was nearly 10,000 lives, and the figure doubled if you included civilians. Zhukov was being sent to every sector of the front where the situation was critical. And his talent for extricating armies out of crisis situations won him medal after medal. There were endless stories about the marshal's florid vocabulary and his habit of giving an ultimatum to recalcitrant commanders. Typical (it was said) was this one to frontline officers: 'Either carry out the order by tomorrow morning or you will be shot for treason.' A Zhukov tactic was to issue a seemingly impossible order on the telephone and hang up without giving the commander a chance to argue.

Zhukov was implacable towards cowards and panic-mongers in the ranks, and in extreme cases he was fully capable of introducing the firing squad. In September 1941, during the siege of Leningrad, he issued an order that anyone who abandoned his post without written permission would be shot.

In 2002 a best-selling book by British author Antony Beevor crammed with allegations of wickedness by Russian soldiers in Germany in 1945 was published in London (*Berlin, the Downfall, 1945*). The book was immediately attacked by the Russian Ambassador in London, Grigory Karasin; and later by Professor Dr Joachim Fest, one of Germany's senior historians. Mr Karasin called publication of the book 'an act of blasphemy, not only against Russia and my people, but also against all countries and the millions of people who suffered from Nazism'. Dr Fest, an expert on Hitler and on Berlin at the end of the war, described the book as 'patchwork history', and also a book that is peppered with factual inaccuracies. Serial rape and looting, vengeance and atrocities – these are central to Beevor's book and he indicates that all this took place on Marshal Zhukov's watch; that is, during the first year after the collapse of Hitler's regime when Georgi Zhukov was Commander-in-Chief of all Soviet forces in Germany. There is a sentence (on page

413) which says that 'many people' think the Russian troops were given two weeks to do as they pleased with the German population before any discipline was enforced. But Beevor does not know Zhukov, especially his swift reaction to lack of troop discipline. A careful reading reveals lacunae, or missing statements in the book, from five or six top Russian generals and others (including Zhukov) who were in Berlin in May 1945 during the allegations of wanton misconduct, even insinuations of atrocities on a level with the Nazi regime, who spoke directly to the German people about security and discipline, and recorded these conversations in their memoirs.[5] (On the subject of crimes – real or blown out of proportion – by an occupation army, it may be mentioned that another book which appeared much earlier (in 1958) not only touches on the issue of rape and pillage in Germany but makes the spurious claim that Marshal Zhukov himself was involved. The marshal, it said, 'issued the order' [*sic*] that allowed the Red Army to commence its debaucheries against the German people for *three* weeks. The book, put out by a religious organization in America, went through 14 editions.)

Zhukov's talent as a strategist caught the attention of an American expert on military affairs, Hanson W. Baldwin, an editor of the *New York Times*. Baldwin observed that, during his first important assignment, to crush a Japanese invasion force in Mongolia in the summer of 1939, Zhukov had handled, for the first time in actual war, mass armoured formations, and had proved the practicability of applying the old cavalry tactics to armour – deep penetrations, wide outflanking encirclements, shock, mobility and firepower.[6]

In June 1945 Zhukov was chosen to take the salute on a white stallion in the Victory Parade on Moscow's Red Square. (Historically the conqueror would ride a white horse.) Looking back, Zhukov called it an 'unforgettable day' in his life. Thousands of Zhukov's officers, including air force pilots and tank troops, rejoiced when the marshal decreed that they could march past without sabres, spurs and other accessories. Many who have seen the parade captured on film say it is probably one of history's greatest parades. Near its close, 200 veterans in shiny new uniforms, to the roll of drums toss 200 of Hitler's banners onto the rain-soaked cobblestones in front of the Lenin Mausoleum. A number of British and American historians (including William J. Spahr and Otto Preston Chaney of the USA and Antony Beevor of Britain) repeat the story that Stalin wanted at first to take the salute himself, riding the same white Arab stallion, but when he mounted the horse it bolted, throwing him to the ground, bumping his head and shoulders after which he gave up and said, 'Zhukov's an old cavalryman, let him take the parade.' Is it a true story? Would Stalin (he was 66 at the time, did not ride, was in poor health, and could hardly mount a horse unaided), risk falling off a horse in front of tens of thousands of military men and women and thousands of spectators? The historians all use the same source: Stalin's son, Vasily, who turns out to be a less than reliable source. Vasily was, says Air Marshal Sergei Rudenko, his sometime superior officer, 'often blind drunk'. He also says that Vasily was habitually 'nervous from booze and unrestrained from permissiveness'. Russian expert Roy Medvedev goes further, describing Vasily as a 'coarse, semi-illiterate alcoholic'. Not only was the son of Stalin often in his cups, but because of his violent temper and the tales he spun he (according to Rudenko) 'ruined many people's lives'. His drinking habits and dissolute life led to his premature death in 1962 at the age of 42.[7]

Wherever he went in his own country after the war Georgi Konstantinovich was cheered. Soon, however, Stalin (and later Khrushchev) were unable to contain their jealousy of Zhukov's immense popularity. They also perhaps justifiably feared his dominant influence within the armed forces. Another demerit in the eyes of the party was his deep resistance to the system of having political officers wield power at all levels in the military. His British, American and French counterparts in Germany on the Allied Control Council could sense the burden he carried, trying to socialize with his foreign friends when even these innocent contacts were being recorded by Beria's spies as possible grounds for suspicion of disloyalty.

After Zhukov was recalled from Berlin, after a short period as Deputy Minister of Defence, he was exiled to relatively unimportant military districts, first to Odessa in the Ukraine and then to the Urals. At that time Zhukov's enemies within Stalin's secret police – including Lavrenti Beria and Viktor Abakumov – were trying to implicate him in shrewd frameups of 'treasonable' relations with British and American friends. The last twenty years or so of Zhukov's life were difficult ones with few joys. For some years the old war hero's name almost totally disappeared from the newspapers. He also suffered from heart trouble. Meanwhile he started work on his famous memoirs, entitled *Reminiscences and Reflections*.

Zhukov's name is associated with spectacular triumphs, a half dozen of which appear in this book. Zhukov was consistently victorious; the

Nazi beast, after initial huge advances, was in due time thrashed or held back, licking its wounds. However, at least one prolific American expert has challenged conventional wisdom, setting out to prove that Zhukov lost one 'great battle' called Operation Mars in front of Moscow in the autumn of 1942. An examination of other expert military and historical opinion shows the detailed argument of the author (David Glantz, *Zhukov's Greatest Defeat*, 1999) does not hold water; that the statistics he uses are highly exaggerated. Zhukov himself explains in clear terms the circumstances that made him move, temporarily, from the Stalingrad field of battle to the one in front of Moscow. Two Russian historians, among others, have gone far to puncture the book's thesis. (Professor Dr Oleg Rzheshevsky and Dr Mikhail Myagkov.) Briefly, Operation Mars was more of a diversionary tactic than anything else, where Zhukov had the task of preventing the Germans from shifting large forces from the Central Front to the Stalingrad Front where one of the greatest battles of all time was shaping up. As each side knew, the events at Stalingrad would have a decisive influence on the course of the war. Zhukov, who was coordinating two fronts in the Mars operation west of Moscow, was at the same time deeply involved in the operations of the Stalingrad counter-offensive which he had helped plan.[8]

Western and Eastern experts have attempted to appraise Zhukov's military talent.Thus, British historian John Keegan says Zhukov combines all the qualities of great generalship. These include, he says, strategic know-how and tactical brilliance, the highest degree of courage, superb leadership and political influence. The Briton also mentions (as do other writers) Zhukov's 'apparent insensitivity' to casualties.

Another expert, the Indian military historian, Colonel A.L. Sethi, says Zhukov's conduct of battles between 1939 and 1945, including offensives against Japan (in Mongolia), at Moscow, Stalingrad, Kursk and Berlin all 'bear the stamp of military genius'. Zhukov, he says, was not only 'outstanding' in his field but Sethi places him 'above all others' as leader in the art of mass-warfare in the twentieth century. Sethi acknowledges that there are much better known military men outside of Russia. (He lists Montgomery, Rommel, Guderian, Eisenhower, MacArthur, Patton, de Gaulle, Giap.) He also calls Zhukov's rise from a cobbler's son to the highest military rank in Russia the 'most phenomenal rise' that any human could achieve.[9]

With an eye on the immortals, American expert Phil Grabsky, author of *The Great Commanders* (1993), says that, while Alexander the Great commanded an army of less than 100,000 men, Zhukov led a force of millions. A 'brilliant general', he says, 'must have a clear-cut strategy, steady supplies, rabid determination and great strength of character'. Zhukov in his view was a master of all four.

Almost from the early disastrous setbacks for the Red Army, it didn't take long for Zhukov's fame to penetrate German lines. Russian officers say that when German POWs were asked what in their opinion were the most formidable features of the victorious enemy, they usually replied: Russian tenacity and ... Marshal Zhukov. Sometimes the POWs also mentioned the T-34 tank which experts said was one of the best ironclads in the war. But it became clear that the man behind the mammoth victories was the ex-cavalryman Georgi Zhukov.

The radical nature of the war against Hitler's regime was discussed by General Eisenhower in a speech in 1945. He concluded: 'This was a holy war and had to be won regardless of cost.' Since Hitler and his generals had an extermination policy ready for the Slavic peoples, including the Russians, Zhukov and his comrades-in-arms had made up their minds to fight to the end, giving no quarter. But one cannot doubt the sincerity of Zhukov and his commanders who ruled out acting like the Nazis did on Russian soil with the razing of thousands of villages and creating concentration camps and crematoriums. Here is what Zhukov writes about Nazi crimes: 'There was never any thought of punishing the German working people for the crimes the Nazis committed in our land. Our people took an unequivocal stand with regard to the common German people: they needed help in realizing their mistakes and uprooting the vestiges of Nazism.'

Not surprisingly, all kinds of human dilemmas would crop up during Zhukov's administration of Berlin, sometimes requiring his on-the-spot attention. Here is one in which Zhukov's Solomonic solution was pleasing to one and all.

While driving through the outskirts of Berlin one day, the marshal saw an unusually motley crowd in which there were some Russian soldiers. There were many women and children in the crowd. Zhukov ordered his driver to stop the car, got out and approached the crowd. Apparently the marshal thought that they were Russians who had been released from Nazi concentration camps. But they proved to be Berliners.

As I stood there watching [recalls Zhukov] I heard one of our soldiers, who held a fair-haired boy of about four in his arms, say:

'I lost my wife, my little daughter and son when my family was evacuated from Konotop. They were killed when the train was bombed. The war is ending. Why should I live alone? Give me this boy. The SS [Nazi special guard unit] men shot his mother and father.'

Somebody said:

'By the way, the boy looks like you.'

A woman standing beside him said in German:

'No, I can't give him to you. He's my nephew and I shall bring him up myself.'

Somebody translated what she said and the soldier's face fell.

I intervened:

'Listen, friend, when you return home you'll find yourself a son: we have so many orphans now. Still better if you take a child with its mother!'

The soldiers laughed and the German boy smiled. Our soldiers opened their kit bags and distributed bread, sugar and tinned meat among the women and children. The little boy whom our soldier held in his arms received chocolates besides. The soldier kissed the boy and sighed sadly.

Zhukov went up to the soldier and shook his hand.

Zhukov was without his insignia and wearing only a leather jacket. Soon, however, he was recognized and had to stay for another half hour answering many questions. 'I wish I had written down the names of these soldiers. All I remember is that they were from General Nikolai Berzarin's 5th Shock Army.' (Berzarin, who became the first Commandant in Berlin, said of his time on the front lines: 'Throughout all these four years I have been unable to get used to destruction, tears and dead bodies either in our own or in the enemy's land.')

In the author's research he found a number of similarities between Zhukov and Alexander Suvorov, the eighteenth century field marshal who came to be called 'the pride of Russia'. Suvorov is said to have fought sixty battles and won sixty victories. Apparently no one has counted how many large and small battles Zhukov won, but Western experts including Eisenhower have expressed admiration for his major victories.

Asked about himself, Suvorov once said: 'I am a soldier. I know neither my origin, nor stock.'

Zhukov dedicated his memoirs to the soldiers, to the men under him who 'knew how to face mortal danger, and displayed great valour and heroism'. Zhukov also hails his soldiers who, when peace returned, had the onerous work of restoring thousands of towns and villages that had been levelled to the ground.

Suvorov's troops learned from experience that the harder they trained the easier it was for them in battle. Similarly, Zhukov did not spare his officers and men in training exercises, spending days and weeks with his commanders and NCOs until he was satisfied with their combat readiness.

Suvorov invariably displayed humaneness towards the civilian population and prisoners of war and he punished his men for pillage. He was fond of saying: 'Strike at the enemy with humane treatment as effectively as with weapons.' Zhukov is unequivocal: 'There was never any thought of punishing the German working people for the crimes the Nazi committed in our land.'

Even as late as the 1990s some Western observers depicted Georgi Zhukov as merely a 'cutout picture' of a hero, as one who lacked a third dimension. Since then a good deal more material about Zhukov has become available, from books, newspaper and magazine articles, archive sources, and from Zhukov's daughters. This book attempts to add a missing human dimension to Georgi Zhukov and to stimulate new interest in this remarkable if contradictory son of Russia.

Notes

1. Viktor Anfilov in *Krasnaya Zvezda* (Red Star), 26 December 2001; *Stalin's Generals*, Tr. by Harry Shukman, 1993; W.J. Spahr, *Zhukov, The Rise and Fall of a Great Captain*, 1993.
2. *Observer*, 7 July 1957.
3. Major-General Sir Francis de Guingand, *Generals at War*, London, 1972.
4. John Gunther, *Inside Russia Today*, London, 1957.
5. For the lacunae in his book see chapter 12. But one omission may be cited here: the network of death camps with their high-capacity crematoriums and gas chambers. If one raises the question of comparative evil in May–June 1945, then it is natural to expect details about Hitler's 'factories of death' which have been called the most vivid manifestation of the essence of Nazism. (The camps, mainly in Germany and Poland, were liberated in April 1945). For example, many of these camps had special crucibles for melting gold teeth extracted from dead prisoners' mouths. They yielded an average of 12 kilograms of gold daily. The crematoriums' attics were used for drying the hair of the dead. The ashes were used for filling bogs or fertilising cabbage patches. Some of these camps had the largest cemeteries in the world.
6. *New York Times*, 20 June 1974.
7. Interview with Air Marshal Sergei Rudenko in *Soviet Soldier*, No. 6, 1990. Also, A. Axell, *Russia's War, 1941–45*, London, 2001, contains author's 1985 interview with Rudenko.

8. Countering the claim of US military historian David Glantz that Zhukov suffered a major defeat in Operation Mars outside Moscow in the autumn of 1942, an internationally recognized authority on the Nazi–Soviet War, Professor Rzheshevsky, who is President of the Association of Second World War Historians, says: 'Operation Mars had two aims: first, to prevent German forces from being transferred from the central part of the front to the South; and second, to prevent a possible surprise German blow from the Rzhev bulge (250 km west of Moscow) towards the capital. The two tasks were interchangeable, and the priorities changed during the planning and preparation of Mars. Moscow was never in the same danger in 1942 as it was in autumn, 1941; and Stalingrad was a huge Russian success.' To sum up, Professor Rzheshevsky says 'the book (*Zhukov's Greatest Defeat*, 1999) and its concept remain outside the limits of sound historical science.' Dr Myagkov points out that Operation Mars not only facilitated a successful outcome of Uranus (the counter-offensive at Stalingrad) but on its own terms was a great achievement as it put off an unexpected blow by the enemy in the direction of Moscow. Further, he says that Uranus and Mars were conceived as a single whole to sharply change the situation on the Soviet–German front in 1943. Both historians handed materials to me when I visited them at the Russian Academy of Sciences in Moscow in 2002. Zhukov himself makes the telling point that the plan of the Supreme Command in the summer and autumn of 1942 was actually to disorient the enemy, making him think that a huge winter operation was beginning in front of Moscow with the westward thrust of Russia's armies against Hitler's Army Group Centre. Thus in October the Nazi Command began building up large forces precisely in this area.

9. In 1987 the author met a group of generals at a round-table in Moscow (they had all fought in the Great Patriotic War) and asked them how they rated Zhukov. General of the Army I.G. Pavlovsky, gave this reply: 'Zhukov was a great military leader, we may say the best among the best.' He added, 'But we had 12 Front commanders at the end of the war. All of them were excellent military commanders. However, Zhukov was outstanding among them. They recognized this themselves.' A Russian military historian, General Dr Mikhail Belov, who has written dozens of articles about Zhukov, said the marshal was 'unequalled' as a military commander. He told the author what in his opinion were the special abilities of an outstanding commander like Zhukov: the ability to prepare a big operation and carry it out in extremely difficult conditions, to predict the enemy's intention and move fast to stop it, to use deception at a crucial stage to fool the enemy.

1

THE SHAPING-UP YEARS

The young Georgi showed an early aptitude for reading and self-education.
PHIL GRABSKY, *The Great Commanders*

Georgi Konstantinovich Zhukov was born in 1896 in Tsarist times in the tumbledown village of Strelkovka, some 160 kilometres south of Moscow. In his parents' modest dwelling there was hardly space for both living and cooking for his family of four: Zhukov's mother, father and older sister. As for the cramped quarters, Zhukov quotes a Russian proverb: 'To be crowded isn't to be buried.'

His father, Konstantin, a shoemaker ('he earned a miserable pittance cobbling'), was adopted from an orphanage at the age of two. Zhukov's mother, Ustinia, also born into poverty, was physically strong, being able, it was said, to lift a 90-kilogram sack of grain. At an early age Zhukov demonstrated his own physical prowess, as well as other lifelong traits: stubbornness and the determination to excel.

Zhukov was too young to know the details but, when his father had found a job with a shoemaker in Moscow, the incendiary events of 1905 occurred, and his father along with many other workers were 'sacked and deported' from the city for taking part in demonstrations. In those years agitators and malcontents were often dealt with harshly by the Tsarist authorities who frequently exiled the offenders to Siberia to work in mines or salt works, or on the Trans-Siberian Railway. Some of the convicts, including women, were kept in chains. As a punishment for rebelliousness, men were often flogged. (The authorities sometimes put a straightjacket on some offenders, moistening the material so that, drying, it tightened, causing unbearable suffering.)

Zhukov remembers that the autumn of 1902 when he turned six was a difficult time for his family.

The crops had failed and we had grain to last only till mid-December. All that our parents earned barely sufficed to buy bread and salt and to pay our debts. We had our neighbours to thank for helping us out now and again with a pot of cabbage soup or porridge. The principle of helping one's neighbour was not an exception but rather a tradition of friendship and solidarity that reigned among poverty-stricken Russians.

When spring came they fared better thanks largely to the fish in nearby rivers which teemed with perch and tench. Georgi says that on 'lucky days' he could repay the neighbours with fish for their soup and porridge. The road to the good fishing areas led through dense groves of lime trees and thickets of birch which abounded in strawberries and, towards late summer, in mushrooms. Folk from nearby villages came to these thickets to strip the trees of bark to make bast shoes which were known in local parlance as 'the latest in checkered footwear'.

Zhukov, who wrote about these times two decades after the war, said the groves and thickets were gone: Hitler's Wehrmacht had chopped them down during the war; and after the war a collective farm had put the land under the plough.

The young Zhukov helped his family in haymaking and reaping. But he also attended a parish school a mile from his village. As happens in youth, Zhukov saw that some of his friends had store-bought leather bags to carry their books and other belongings. His was a handmade burlap bag.

'I told mother that these were the kind of bags beggars carried and I would not go to school with it,' says Georgi.

'When father and I earn enough money,' mother replied, 'we'll buy you a satchel. Meanwhile, you'll have to make do with the hand-made bag.'

Although Zhukov says he adored his father, he was often punished in the old-fashioned way, his father whipping him with his belt and demanding an apology. Says Georgi: 'I was stubborn and no matter how hard he thrashed me I bit my lips and never asked for pardon.'

One day however the flogging he received was so severe that he ran away from home, spending three days in a neighbour's hemp field. Only his sister knew his hiding place. She kept it secret and brought him food parcels. Finally a neighbour found him and took him home. 'Father gave me one more licking, then took pity and pardoned me.'

At this time in Zhukov's life, a tavern waiter named Prokhor, who was his godmother's brother, showed a liking for the young boy and often took him along to hunt wild duck in summer and hares in winter. Georgi became adept at flushing out hares and retrieving duck from the water.

One day, Georgi's father left for Moscow again. Before he left he told his wife that factory workers in Moscow and St Petersburg, driven to desperation by unemployment, were going on strike more and more often.

'Better keep out of it, mother said, or else the cops'll have you!' Georgi remembers her saying.

For a long time they heard nothing from him and were full of anxiety. Soon they learned that in St Petersburg on 9 January, Tsarist troops and police had opened fire at a peaceful demonstration of workers from the giant Putilov munitions plant who were headed for the Winter Palace and were being led by Father Gapon, an Orthodox priest. They had come to ask the Tsar to grant them better working conditions. Zhukov mentions strangers arriving in the villages that spring, political agitators who urged the people to take the law into their own hands 'against the moneybags and the Tsarist autocracy'.[1]

In 1906 Zhukov finished at the three-year parish school, getting top marks in all forms and being awarded honours. Everyone in his family rejoiced. His mother presented him with a new shirt and his father made him a pair of leather boots. Meanwhile, in the winters young Georgi built himself up physically, enjoying an outdoor life of fishing, skating (on home-made skates), and skiing in nearby hills. Although he was on the short side he was quite broad in the shoulders.

When he reached the age of eleven the youthful Zhukov was apprenticed to learn the furrier's trade with an uncle in Moscow. Quickly he learned 'the ropes' the hard way. On his first day of work in Moscow he received a blow on the head for not following the unwritten rules: he had straightway fished out portions of meat from the common pot of cabbage soup. His work-mate, Kuzma, told Georgi who now had a swelling on his head to practise subservience: 'Grin and bear it when you're beaten. A beaten man is worth two who aren't.' Georgi does not say what he thought of this advice.

On Saturdays Kuzma took him to vespers and on Sundays to matins and mass. 'On big holidays,' says Georgi, 'our master took us to mass at the Kremlin Assumption Cathedral or, sometimes, to the big Cathedral of the Saviour. We did not like going to church, always looking for a chance to escape. However, he Assumption Cathedral was an exception, for there we enjoyed the glorious choir, and were especially eager to hear Deacon Rozov who had a voice like a trumpet.'

Zhukov made good progress in his trade. But there were chronic beatings. 'Our master beat us pitilessly for the slightest mistake. We were beaten by the craftsmen, the craftswomen and the mistress, too. Whenever the master was out of sorts, it was better to avoid him, as he would hit out at us so severely that one felt a ringing in the ears for the rest of the day.'

His master told his charges that 'no one could take him to task' for inhuman treatment of children. Indeed says Zhukov, 'no one ever took any interest in our working conditions, in what we ate, or how we lived. Our supreme judge was our master. So we slaved and sweated, though not every adult would have borne it.'

Time passed. He had turned thirteen. Although Georgi says that at his job 'I was run off my feet', he had a new-found interest: reading books. It was thanks to his schoolmaster Sergei Nikolayevich Remizov 'who infected me with a passion for reading'. The master's eldest son, Alexander, also helped further this habit in Georgi. He mentions reading 'the full Pinkerton and Sherlock Holmes series, and some other adventure stories'.

> We undertook further studies of Russian, maths and geography, and read popular books on science. We usually did this together, for the most part on Sundays and when the master was out. Though we took great pains to conceal our studies from him, he nevertheless found us out. I thought he would kick me out or give me a good hiding. For some reason, however – I do not know why – he commended us for doing a sensible thing.

Georgi applied himself to these studies for more than a year on his own and then entered a night school which provided a course of instruction equivalent to that of a city high school.

It was now 1911. He had already done three years of his apprenticeship. He wanted to continue his studies but had not even the slightest opportunity. Still he managed to keep up his reading.

'I read the papers ... I got some magazines from Alexander and bought my own books with my savings.' (Zhukov's two eldest daughters, Era and Ella, told the author when he visited them in Moscow in 2002 that in the postwar years their father had a library in his dacha of 20,000 volumes.)

Georgi also saved money on tram fares. 'Now and again my master would send me with a parcel somewhere further out and gave me a couple of coppers for the tram. I would walk the distance and save the money.'

A year later there was a fair in the city of Nizhny Novgorod, on the

Volga river. His master rented a stall there for wholesale trading in furs. 'My duties at the fair were mostly to crate the lots sold and to dispatch them to consignees via the wharves on the Volga or the railway goods depot.'

This was Zhukov's first encounter with the mighty waters of the Volga. 'It was the first time I glimpsed the Volga. The river sparkled in the rays of the rising sun. I stood staring, unable to tear my eyes away. Now I understand, I thought to myself, why so many songs are sung about it, why it is called the mother of rivers.'

It was now 1912. He was nearly 16. He was lucky, he says, to get ten days' leave to visit his family. It was the time of haymaking, which he calls 'the most interesting type of farm job'. Menfolk and the young chaps came home from the city to help the women cope more quickly with the job and stock up enough fodder for the winter.

> I had left the village a child and returned a young man getting on for sixteen, about to finish my apprenticeship. Many faces were missing: some had died, others had been apprenticed out, or had gone to town in search of work. Some I failed to recognize; some failed to recognize me. Some were twisted by their hard life, by premature old age, others had grown to adulthood.

> He was met at the railway station by his mother. She had changed greatly, and had aged in these four years. I could hardly speak and was barely able to restrain my tears.

> Mother cried and cried, hugging me close with her work-hardened horny hands and kept saying: 'Sonny darling, I never thought I'd see you again.'

> 'Now, now, Mother,' I comforted her. 'See what a grown-up boy I am. Now life will be easier for you.'

> 'May God grant it,' she said.

By the time they got home it was dark.

> Father and sister were waiting for us on the porch. My sister had grown up into a pretty girl, but father was bent and aged. He was nearing 70. We kissed, then apparently thinking of something of his own, he said: 'It's good I've lived to see you. I see you're grown up and strong.'

> ... To sooner relish the delight I was sure my parents and sister would show, I unpacked my basket. I had presents for everyone. [Georgi also gave his mother three roubles in cash, a couple of pounds of sugar, a pound of sweets and half a pound of tea.]

> 'Thanks ever so much,' said his mother who was overjoyed. 'It's a long time since we had real tea with sugar.'

Next, Georgi gave his father a rouble to spend at the tavern.

'Twenty kopecks would be quite enough for him,' mother grumbled.

'I've waited for the boy for four year, so don't spoil it with talk of our poverty,' said his father.

A day later, Georgi's mother, sister and himself went out hay-making. 'I was glad to see my old friends and bosom pal Alexei.'

Georgi says he kept up with the rest although his throat and mouth ran dry and he was more than thankful when they knocked off.

'Well Georgi surely it's no picnic to be a farmer?' his uncle Nazar observed, throwing an arm around his sweating shoulders.

'That's certainly so,' Georgi said.

'The English use machines to mow,' a young chap he did not know said.

'Very true,' said Nazar. "But here we stick to our wooden plough and scythes.'

Georgi asked who the chap was who spoke of machines.

'Why that's Nikolai, the village elder's son He was expelled from Moscow for his part in the 1905 demonstrations. He's got a razor-edged tongue and even curses the Tsar.'

'That's all right,' Alexei remarked, 'as long as the cops and inform-ers don't hear you.'

Georgi mentions the evenings when, fatigue forgotten, the young people gathered around the barn to make merry.

> We sang songs that gripped your heartstrings. The village girls led in rich ripe voices, the young men catching up the melody in unsteady basses and baritones. Then we danced till ready to drop. We broke up towards dawn, barely managing to catch a few winks of sleep before we were roused and went out mowing again. As soon as evening came the fun started anew. It was indeed hard to say when we slept. In one's salad days one can even go without sleep. It's good to be young!

His leave flashed by and Georgi had to return to Moscow. The night before he left a fire broke out in the nearby village of Kostinka. The flames spread to neighbouring houses, sheds and bars. 'We were still up and awake,' says Georgi, 'and all of us ran to roll out the fire barrel, reaching Kostinka even before the local fire brigade did. Running with a pail of water past a house, I heard shouts for help, rushed in and dragged out several very frightened children and a sick old crone.'

At last the blaze was put out. Georgi saw that many villagers were left homeless and had lost all their possessions. Some of them, he says, had not even a crust of bread left.

Back in Moscow Georgi found his own lodgings which would give him more time to do some reading in the evenings. He was now an independent craftsman earning above the average wage.

Between 1910 and 1914, when the First World War broke out, revolutionary ferment increased, and strikes flared up more and more often in Moscow, St Petersburg and other industrial cities. Student rallies and strikes were also more frequent. In the countryside, the peasants were desperate owing to the effects of the famine of 1911. Georgi says that in the fur trade, although the workers were not 'politically mature', they'd heard for example of the shooting of workers at the Lena goldfields in Siberia, and mostly identified with the workers and peasants.

Georgi records in his memoirs the outbreak of the First World War, saying he first knew about it because of the raids on foreign-owned shops in Moscow. He also remembers secret police agents and members of the Black Hundreds looting German and Austrian firms. But since ordinary citizens knew no foreign languages, they also raided French and British firms, too.[2]

With patriotic sentiment spurred on by the government, many young men, especially from those families who were better off, volunteered for the front. Georgi's cousin Alexander made up his mind to enlist and tried to persuade Georgi, who was now 19 years of age, to follow suit.

'I liked the idea,' he says. But he decided to ask a friend, Fyodor Ivanovich, whom he respected, for advice. His friend ridiculed the idea, saying:

'You silly boy! I can understand why Alexander wants to go. He's got a rich father and so has got something to fight for. But you – what have you got to fight for? For your father having been chased out of Moscow? For your mother all swelling up with hunger? You'll come back a cripple and no one will want you.'

This advice convinced Georgi, but his cousin, after giving him a tongue-lashing, ran away to join the army only to be brought back gravely wounded a couple of months later.

A love interest now briefly occupied the life of the young Zhukov. He had become attracted to the daughter of a widow from whom he was renting a room and they planned to marry. But the war upset their plans as young men of his age were now being conscripted. He was far from enthusiastic about going to war, especially since he saw many unfortunate cripples coming back from the front.

Still, Zhukov felt Russia was in danger and he made up his mind: 'When my turn came I would fight honestly for my country.'

Notes

1. Police bullets in St Petersburg killed hundreds of the demonstrators and the incident entered the history books as Bloody Sunday. Sympathetic workers joined a mass protest which reached an estimated 400,000 workers by the end of January 1905.
2. The Black Hundreds were notorious ultra-patriotic, pro-monarchist and anti-Semitic gangs responsible for crimes of violence including pogroms in the early twentieth century.

2

A TSARIST CAVALRYMAN

The son of peasants ... he was conscripted into a cavalry squadron of the Tsar's dragoons in 1915.

New York Times, 20 June 1974

All around me were strangers, as green and callow as myself. Towards dusk we entrained and headed for the seat of the military district in Kaluga, south of Moscow, to the induction office. It was 7 August 1915 and the First World War was now in full swing. Already I felt a gnawing loneliness. My youth was over. Was I really prepared to perform a soldier's onerous duties, and go into battle if need be? Being used to previous hardships, I hoped I would do my duty honourably.

So begins Zhukov's account of his entry into the Tsarist military service.

At that time politically motivated veterans in the army were blaming Tsar Nicholas II for recklessly pushing Russia into the First World War, saying the country was going to ruin and was now engaged in a senseless war. There was more than a grain of truth to this complaint. At the end of July 1914 war seemed just around the corner. An Austrian archduke was murdered and Austria declared war on Serbia, a close ally of Russia. The Tsar, wishing to help Serbia, ordered general mobilization of his army, a blatant provocation. Kaiser Wilhelm II of Germany, meanwhile, sent a telegram to his cousin the Tsar (whom he called 'Nicky') saying he wanted Austria and Russia to be good chums. But 'Willy' (the Tsar's nickname for the Kaiser – they had been in the habit of exchanging Willy–Nicky letters) couldn't resist a veiled threat of war with his 'dear cousin'. In this situation, the Tsar, possibly sensing the perils of general European war, changed the orders from 'full mobilization' to 'partial mobilization'. But this didn't sit well with his hawkish ministers who pleaded with him on behalf of the military to issue a new order, which he eventually did.

At the outset Zhukov was assigned to the cavalry which raised his spirits because he had always harboured romantic ideas about that branch of service. As most of his chums were sent to the infantry, they looked upon Georgi with envy.

The goods wagons into which the young men were crammed, forty to each wagon, were not adapted to carrying people. So each recruit had the choice of either standing all the way or sitting on the filthy floor. Some of the men sang, some played cards, some sobbed on their neighbours' shoulders, some sat gritting their teeth, staring vacuously, and reflecting on their soldier's future.

> We arrived at Kaluga at night, and were told to line up on the goods siding. We then marched away from town. Someone asked the corporal where we were going. He must have been a nice fellow, for he gave us the following advice: 'Look here, men, never ask your superiors such questions.The soldier's got to do evertything he's told and ask no questions. Where he goes is for his superiors to know.'
>
> As if to confirm this there rang out from the head of the column a loud voice: 'Quit talking in the ranks!'
>
> Nikolai Sivtsov [Zhukov's new chum] poked him in the ribs and whispered 'Well, there you are, we're in the army now.'

The boys had been slogging along for some three hours when a brief halt was called. It was near daybreak and the boys flung themselves down on the ground and almost at once snores were heard. But soon they were ordered to fall in again and after another hour reached camp. Here they were put up on bare boards in a hut holding already about a hundred men. Zhukov remembers that the wind whistled freely through the many cracks and shattered windowpanes and the odour was terrible.

> We were told we could rest till 7 o'clock. After breakfast we were lined up and told that we were with the 189th Reserve Infantry Battalion, where a detachment for the 5th Reserve Cavalry Regiment would be activated. Prior to being sent to our assignment, we would be taught ordinary drill. We were then issued training rifles and Corporal Shakhvorostov, our squad commander, announced the rules, regulations and duties. He warned us that we could not fall out except to attend to the call of nature, if we didn't want to be sent to the stockade. Each word that he snapped out he stressed with a sweep of his fist. His tiny eyes glittered menacingly as if we were his sworn enemies.

Zhukov overheard someone say: 'Can't expect anything good from him.'

The senior NCO came up and our corporal rapped out: 'Shun!'

'I'm your platoon commander Malyavko,' said the senior NCO. 'I hope you've all understood what your squad commander has told you and will loyally serve Tsar and country. I will tolerate no insubordination!'

The first day of infantry drill began. Everyone had to perform well, but it was not easy to please the superiors. Picking on a man who had fallen out of step, the platoon commander kept all of the recruits at extra drill. As a result, says Georgi, their dinner (he calls it 'slops') was cold when they sat down to eat.

> I was depressed [says Zhukov]. All I wanted was to turn in for the night. However, as if reading our minds, the platoon commander ordered us to fall in again and announced that tomorrow night we would have evening roll-call, and that therefore tonight we had to learn the national anthem, 'God Save the Tsar'. This choir [practice] continued till late at night. And at 6 a.m. we were roused for morning exercises.
>
> The days rolled by in dreary monotony. Then came our first Sunday. We thought we would have a respite and have time to take a bath, but we were marched out for fatigue detail. This continued till the mid-day meal. After the siesta we cleaned our weapons, patched and darned our clothes, and wrote letters home. Our corporal warned us not to complain in letters because that sort of thing would be cut out by the censors anyway.

It was hard for Zhukov to accustom himself to army routine but he had had it none too easy before, and after about a fortnight almost everyone felt broken in.

> After a couple of weeks of training our platoon was lined up for inspection by Captain Volodin, the company commander. He was said to be a heavy drinker, whom it was best to avoid when he was in his cups. Outwardly, though, he seemed no different from the other officers. The recruits could see, however, that for him the inspection parade held no interest. After a short speech he wound up by urging the men to display zeal: 'God repays you for your prayer and the Tsar for your service.'

Before the men were transferred to the 5th Reserve Calvalry Regiment they saw the company commander a few more times, and invariably he seemed to be drunk. As for the commanding officer of the 189th Reserve Battalion, they never saw him once during the training period.

In September 1915, Zhukov was sent to a new regiment which was quartered in the town of Balakleya in Kharkov province in the Ukraine.

They bypassed the town and came to the railway station of Savintsy where replacements were being marshalled for the 10th Cavalry Division. On the platform they were met by smartly dressed cavalry NCOs. Their different uniforms denoted whether they were from the Hussars, the Uhlans, or the Dragoons.

> Our group, mainly from Moscow, and a few young chaps from Voronezh province, south of the capital, were assigned to a squadron of Dragoons. We were disappointed that it was not the Hussars, and not only because they had nattier uniforms. We had been told that the NCOs there were more decent. And in the Tsarist army the soldier's entire life depended on his NCOs.

A day later they were issued with cavalry uniforms and all the other accoutrements of the cavalry and assigned horses. Zhukov drew 'a shrewish dark-grey mare' by the name of Chashechnaya.

Though service in the cavalry was much more interesting than in the infantry, they had a much harder time. Besides general drill they had to learn horsemanship and the use of side-arms and to curry the horses three times a day. Reveille was at 5 a.m., not at 6 as in the infantry, and taps (lights out) also came an hour later.

Hardest of all was the horsemanship and the use of sabre and lance, says Zhukov. Many of the men had blisters which drew blood, but complaints were forbidden.

> We were told to grin and bear it, and we did as best we could until we were finally able to sit straight in the saddle. Our platoon commander, senior NCO Durakov, was, despite his name [which meant 'fool'], quite a clever person. Though most exacting, he was fair and reserved. Our other commander, however, Junior NCO Borodavko, was his complete opposite – a blustering bully who would lash out for no reaon at all. Veterans said that he had knocked out soldiers' teeth more than once. He was especially ruthless when in charge of our riding drill.
>
> When Durakov went on a brief furlough for family reasons, he [Borodavko] did all he could to break us. In the daytime he rode us until we were half dead, picking especially on those who had lived and worked in Moscow, as he considered them 'bookworms' and too big for their boots. And at night he inspected the posted sentinels, mercilessly pummelling those whom he caught napping. The men were driven to despair. One day we trapped him in a dark corner and, throwing a horse-cloth over his head, beat him up till he was unconscious. We would certainly have

been court-martialled if not for the return of our decent platoon commander who hushed the matter up and then had Borodavko transferred to
another squadron.

By the spring of 1916 the platoon was essentially a well-trained
cavalry unit. The men were told they would soon receive marching
orders, but would continue field training pending departure for the
front line. New recruits took their places as they prepared to move to
other quarters in another village.

Some thirty of the best men were picked for the NCO training
courses and Zhukov was one of them. He says he did not particularly
relish the idea, but that his platoon commander, whom he respected
for his cleverness and friendly disposition to the men, persuaded him
to file an application.

'You'll still have time to get to the front,' he said. 'First learn sol-
diering a bit more. I'm sure you'll make a pretty good NCO.'

Then, after some reflection, he added: 'I for one am in no hurry to
go back to the front. I had a year there and it taught me a lot. It's a
pity our men die so senselessly. What for, I ask you?' He said nothing
more, but Zhukov realized that deep down he could not reconcile his
army service and the fact that he could no longer brook Tsarist des-
potism. 'I thanked him for his advice and agreed to join the training
course in the town of Isyum in Kharkov province. There were about
240 of us there, from different units.'

They were now billeted in private quarters, and soon their training
began.

> Unfortunately, we had a savage senior NCO, worse than Borodavko. I
> don't remember his name, only that he was nicknamed 'Four-and-a-half' –
> because a phalange was missing on the index finger of his right hand. This
> did not prevent his knocking a soldier down with one swipe of his fist.
> Somehow he disliked me more than the others, but for some reason he
> never struck me. But he picked on me on the slightest pretext, and sub-
> jected me to all sorts of punishments.

Apparently, Zhukov's self-confidence, physical strength and absence
of shyness provoked the churlish non-commissioned officer. Zhukov
was given lots of extra duties.

> I guess I must have done more pack drill, KP [kitchen duty] and extra
> Sunday detail than anyone else. I knew that it was all due to the frustrations
> of an exceedingly doltish and unkind man. On the other hand, I was glad
> that he could never find fault with me during classes. Seeing that he could

not get me down, he decided to change his tactics, maybe simply to divert me from my training in which I was making better progress than the rest.

One day he summoned Zhukov to his tent and said:

'Look here, I see you're strong-minded, educated and learn easily. You're a Muscovite, a worker. Why sweat every day at drill? You be my clerk and do all the paper work and other tasks.'

Zhukov told him he had joined the course not to be somebody's errand boy but to learn the job properly. The NCO grew red in the face and threatened: 'All right! You'll never be an NCO! I'll see to that!'

The course was to end in June and the students were then to pass their exams. According to the regulations, the top man would achieve the rank of a junior NCO, the others getting only candidate rank. Zhukov's mates had not the slightst doubt that he would get first place and be made an NCO, and later a squad commander as soon as there was a vacancy.

But it came as a surprise to everyone when a fortnight before the exams it was announced at roll-call that Zhukov was being discharged for insubordination and disloyalty to his immediate superior. All realized that 'Four-and-a-half' was settling scores. There seemed that nothing was to be done.

Help came, though, from quite an unexpected quarter.

One of the trainees, Skorino by name, who was a volunteer and not a drafted man like the rest of us, happened to be the brother of a commanding offcer in my former squadron. Though he made poor progress and had no fancy for the army, he was a pleasant and sociable fellow whom our Four-and-a-half feared. He at once informed the chief of the course of the injustice that was being done to me.

Summoned to appear before the commander Zhukov fell into a funk as he had never spoken to an officer before.

I thought it was curtains for me, that I would be packed off to the stockade. We knew very little about the training course chief, only that he had been promoted for gallantry, had been decorated with St George crosses of almost every class, and that before the war he had served in the Uhlans as extended-service NCO. We had seen him only a few times at evening roll-call. It was said he was unwell after being wounded.

To Zhukov's astonishment, he saw before him a man with gentle, even, says Zhukov, 'warm eyes in a kind, open face'.

'Well, it looks as if you're not too lucky,' he said motioning Zhukov to sit down. But he kept standing as he was too scared to sit down.

'Take a seat. I won't eat you. I hear you're from Moscow?'

'Yes, sir,' I replied loudly.

'I'm a Muscovite too. Before the army I was a cabinet-maker, but I seem stuck here in the army,' he said quietly. After a pause, he continued. 'You seem to have a bad name. They say that in four months of training you've chalked up a dozen demerits, and that you cuss your platoon commander behind his back. Is that true?'

'Yes, sir,' Zhukov replied. 'But, sir, I can say that in my place any other man would do the same.'

Zhukov described all that had happened. The officer listened and said: 'Go back to your platoon and prepare for your exams.'

Zhukov was thrilled. Although he did not achieve first place, he got 'candidate rank' like all the rest.

Looking back, Zhukov says that the NCO course in the old army gave good training, especially in marching drill. The graduate became a good horseman, adept in the use of weapons and a good drill master. He says that it was no wonder that after the Revolution many NCOs of the Tsarist army rose to prominence as commanders in the new army. As for the general training, drill was all-important. But he notes that the future NCO was not taught 'the human approach'. He was expected to mould the soldier into 'a pliant robot'. Discipline was maintained by harshness. Though regulations did not stipulate corporal punishment, it was all too common.

Zhukov says that the salient feature of the old Tsarist army was the total absence of any rapport between the ranks and the officers.

However, in the course of the war, especially in 1916 and early 1917, when the heavily depleted officer corps had to draw for replenishments on working intellectuals, factory workers and peasants with some amount of schooling, in army units up to battalion strength this deep divide was to some extent overcome. But generals and other high-ranking officers had no affinity with the rank and file and had no idea of what went on in the minds of the men. Because of this and also because of their poor knowledge of tactics, most generals and lower-ranking officers – with few exceptions – enjoyed no prestige among the soldiers. On the other hand, especially towards the close of the war, there were among the lower-ranking officers many who were close in sentiment and spirit to their subordinates. 'Such men,' says Zhukov, 'were liked, trusted and followed through thick and thin.'

The backbone of the old army, he says, were the NCOs who instructed and knit together the mass of the soldiers. 'My many years in the army have demonstrated that whenever confidence in NCOs is lacking and whenever they are continuously bossed by the officers, you have no real NCOs and no really combatworthy units.'

In early August orders came from the regiment to assign the graduates to combat squadrons. Fifteen men were to report to the 10th Cavalry Division at the front. Zhukov was second on the list and was not surprised for he knew who was behind it.

When the list was read out, Four-and-a-half grinned hugely, as if to intimate that the mens' fate depended on him. The men were treated to a special celebration dinner and then ordered to pack. After they shouldered their kitbags, they lined up and a couple of hours later were entrained for Kharkov.

It was a slow journey, with hours spent idling at small junctions, for at that time an infantry division was being rushed to the front. Hospital trains from the front were also shunted to let troop trains through. 'The wounded gave us plenty of information. We learned that our armies were very poorly equipped, that the generals were held in bad repute, and that the opinion was widely current amidst the rank and file that the Supreme Command was a nest of traitors bought by the Germans. We were also told that rations were terrible. Oppressed, we lapsed into a moody silence.'

The men detrained some hours later along with replacements for the 10th Hussars Regiment and about a hundred horses for the 10th Dragoons, with all the appropriate accoutrements. This had just been accomplished when an air alert was sounded. Everyone dived for cover as an enemy reconnaissance aircraft circled a couple of times above us, dropped some small bombs, and headed westward. One soldier was killed and five horses injured.

This was Zhukov's baptism of fire. The men were soon marched to the bank of the Dniester river, where their division was stationed at the time as part of the reserve of the South-Western Front. They learned on arrival that Romania had declared war on Germany and would fight on the side of the Russians against the Germans. Rumours were also afloat that their division would soon be sent directly to the front line.

In early September, Zhukov's division marched to the hilly and wooded Bystritsa area, where they engaged the enemy, but mostly on foot, for because of the terrain they could not mount cavalry attacks. The news received grew more and more alarming. Russian armies were suffering huge casualties. The offensive had, in effect, petered out, and the armies were checked all along the line. Romanian troops were also having a hard time of it. They had been poorly prepared and badly equipped when they entered the war, and had sustained heavy losses in the very first engagements with the Germans and Austrians.

Resentment in the ranks continued to mount, especially after news reached them from home of starvation and widespread unrest. What they saw for themselves in front-line villages in the Ukraine, Bukovina and Moldavia spoke volumes. Under the Tsar, whose recklessness had plunged them into a bloody war, the peasants had truly reached the end of their tether. Hordes of soldiers felt they were being sacrificed for no good reason.

In October 1916, Zhukov had a stroke of bad luck. While on a reconnaissance patrol, two of his comrades were heavily injured by an exploding mine while he was unhorsed by the blast and knocked unconscious. He came to in a hospital some 24 hours later but because of shell-shock was evacuated to Kharkov, where he was sent to a hospital. He was discharged still feeling weak and with impaired hearing, something which continued to bother him a quarter of a century later when he was fighting the Wehrmacht. When he left the hospital the medics assigned him to a combat squadron where he met some of his friends. He was delighted.

Zhukov had left his squadron as a young soldier. He was now returning to it with the stripes of a non-commissioned officer, with combat experience, and two St George crosses received for having been wounded in action and capturing a German officer.

Note: The events in Zhukov's early life and prewar military service in the cavalry are based largely on the marshal's memoirs and on the introduction to them written in 1977 by Zhukov's wartime colleague, Marshal A.M. Vasilevsky, and on interviews with Zhukov's daughters.

3

A NEW REGIME

After the Russian Revolution, Zhukov joined the Red Army (1918) and served throughout the civil war as an officer of cavalry. He was wounded in 1919 and was later awarded the Order of the Red Banner.

Annual Register

Towards the close of 1916, periodic rumours of factory strikes in St Petersburg, Moscow and elsewhere filtered into the front lines. Chatting with his men, Georgi could see that their taste for fighting had almost evaporated. Uppermost in their minds were thoughts of home, farming the land and thus returning to the tranquillity of a peaceful life. By now Bolshevik propaganda had widely circulated among the troops who more and more agreed with its tirades against the Tsarist regime, against war, and for distributing land to the peasants. But soldiers risked arrest, or worse, if they entertained such seditious ideas.

Zhukov was now a non-commissioned officer but the lower ranks trusted him and together they often talked privately about politics, although Zhukov admits he was 'still politically naive'. But increasingly he felt that a change of regime as advocated by the new revolutionary party would give ordinary Russians the peace and stability the country needed. 'I tried to impress this on my subordinates as best I could,' he says, adding, 'And I was rewarded for it.'

Here is what happened:

At daybreak on 27 February 1917, Zhukov's squadron was alerted. Everybody lined up near the lodgings of the squadron commander, Captain Baron von der Goltz. No one knew what was up. Zhukov asked the platoon commander, Lieutenant Kievsky:

'Sir, where are we going?'

Kievsky countered with his own question: 'And where do you think we're going?'

Zhukov said the men should be told where they were going, all the more since they had been issued live ammunition.

'Well, the ammo may come in handy.'

At that moment von der Goltz himself appeared. Though a gallant soldier who had been awarded a gold sword, the soldier's Order of St George and many other military decorations, he was in the eyes of Zhukov and others a repulsive person, savage towards the soldiers who disliked and feared him. He greeted the squadron, lined up the column of horses three abreast, and set a fast pace as they headed for the headquarters of the 5th Reserve Cavalry Regiment in Balakleya. Here the men saw that the Dragoons and Hussars were lined up on the parade ground. Everyone fell into formation. More squadrons were trotting up. All were still in the dark as to what was happening.

Soon everything became clear. From around a street corner appeared a demonstration carrying red banners. Spurring on his horse, the squadron commander, followed by other squadron commanders galloped towards regimental headquarters, from which a group of officers and factory workers had emerged.

In stentorian tones, a tall cavalryman addressed the soldiers, saying that the working class, the peasants and the soldiers no longer recognized Tsar Nicholas II and the exploiting classes and rich landowners. The Russian people, he said, wanted an end to the slaughter of the world war; they wanted peace, land and liberty. He wound up his brief speech shouting, 'Down with Tsarism and the war! Long live peace among the peoples, long live the Soviets of Workers' and Soldiers' Deputies! Hurrah!'

Though there had been no command, the soldiers shouted and cheered, mingling with the demonstration.

Later Zhukov learned that von der Goltz and several other officers had been arrested by the soldiers' committee. The troops were at once ordered to return to their quarters and await further instructions from the committee. It was headed by a Bolshevik named Yakovlev. Next morning an officer came telling the men to delegate representatives to the regimental Soviet and to elect their own squadron soldiers' committee. Zhukov was unanimously elected its chairman. Lieutenant Kievsky, Zhukov and a soldier from the first squad were chosen as delegates to the regimental Soviet.

In May, after Yakovlev had departed, the Socialist-Revolutionaries and Mensheviks largely replaced the Soviets and gave their support to the Provisional Government which wanted to continue the war. As a result, says Zhukov, in early autumn 1917 some of the cavalry units sided with the Ukrainian counter-revolutionary Petlyura.

Meanwhile, the squadron committee disbanded Zhukov's cavalry unit – made up mostly of people from Moscow and Kaluga. Papers were issued to certify that the men had been demobilized, but they were advised to keep their carbines and ammunition. Later they learned that near Kharkov a road block had disarmed most of the men. Zhukov says he had to spend several weeks in hiding in several villages because officers now serving with the Ukrainian nationalists were looking for him.

On 30 November 1917, Zhukov got back to Moscow where in October power had passed into the hands of the Bolsheviks. Zhukov spent December and January at home with his relatives. He decided that after a little rest he would join the Red Guards but in early February he came down with typhus and in April was stricken with relapsing fever. He was therefore unable to join the Red Army until six months later, enlisting in the 4th Regiment of the 1st Moscow Cavalry Division.[1]

At that time the new Soviet Government attempted a difficult task: demobilizing the old army and simultaneously creating a new one made up of workers and peasants. Control of the new army was being handed over to soldiers' committees. Servicemen were given equal rights, and all commanders, up to regimental level, were elected by general meetings. Many officers and men of the Tsarist army went over to the Soviet side and became prominent Red Army commanders.

The first units of the Red Army were activated in January 1918. To be accepted, each volunteer had to produce recommendations of army unit committees, party or other public organizations supporting Soviet power. When whole groups volunteered, a collective reference was required. Red Army men received 50 roubles a month and, later, from the middle of 1918, 150 roubles in the case of single men and 250 roubles in the case of married men. Zhukov says that in the spring of 1918 the Red Army numbered nearly 200,000 men, but later the influx of volunteers began slowing down. In view of this the All-Russia Executive Committee passed a decree establishing universal military training in the country. Every working man aged 18 to 40 was obliged to complete a 96-hour course of military training without leaving his main occupation, to register himself as a reservist, and join the Red Army at the first call of the government.

Meanwhile the Party obliged its members to begin military training immediately. Election of commanders was abolished. Commanders were now to be chosen and approved by military authorities from among candidates who had had military schooling or had distinguished themselves in battle. The Fifth All-Russia Congess of Soviets passed a resolution on building up the Red Army and stressing the need for centralized control of the military and the importance of 'iron revolutionary discipline' of the troops.

As a result, by the time Zhukov joined the Red Army it was already over half a million strong.

Shortly after the revolution, Zhukov, now a part of the new army, received a letter from a childhood friend with the same surname, Pavel Zhukov. It is given here in its entirety as it portrays the chaos and cruelty of those times.

Dear friend Georgi,

Since you left for the Red Army nearly all our friends and acquaintances have been called up. Again I have had no luck. Instead of sending me to the army on active service, they sent me to Voronezh province to serve on a food surplus-appropriation detachment – squeezing grain out of kulaks [well-to-do peasants]. Of course, that is also necessary, but I am a soldier; I know how to fight and consider that my work here could be done by anybody who has not gone through the war. But that is not what I want to write you about.

You remember our arguments and disagreements concerning the Socialist-Revolutionaries? At that time I considered them to be friends of the people who were fighting against Tsarism in the interests of the people, and of the peasants, too. Now I agree with you. They are scoundrels. They are not friends of the people, but of the kulaks, they are the organizers of many anti-Soviet and bandit outrages.

The other day the local kulaks led by a Socialist-Revolutionary in hiding fell on the guards accompanying a horsedrawn caravan of grain and dealt with them in a bestial way. They killed my best friend, Kolya Gavrilov. He comes from somewhere near Maloyaroslavets. They gouged out the eyes of another of my friends, Semyon Ivanishin. They chopped off his right hand and left him on the road. He's in a bad way. Gangrene. Most likely he'll die. It's a shame. He was a good-looking lad and a great dancer. Our unit vowed to take vengeance on that scum and to give them what they deserve, so they won't forget it till their dying day.

Your friend,
Pavel

Zhukov says that for a long time after receiving this letter he heard nothing about his friend Pavel. Then In 1922, he learned that he had been murdered by kulaks 'somewhere in Tambov province'.

A word on the kulaks: there was latent bad blood between the masses of poor Russian peasants and the kulaks, and as might be expected Soviet propaganda pressed the issue. For instance, a well-known painting of 1930 by artist Sergei Ivanov depicts a fist hurled against a fat, surly kulak with these fiery words of Lenin emblazoned at the bottom: 'The Kulaks are the most beastly, rude and wild exploiters. More than once in the history of other countries they have restored the power of the landowners, Tsars and corrupt priests.'

Between 1918 and 1922 Zhukov saw plenty of action in Russia's bloody Civil War. As he writes, the country was not only in utter ruin but the situation was further aggravated by the occupation of vital economic regions by foreign interventionist troops as well as counter-revolutionary White Guards.

In the spring of 1918 the Entente forces landed in the North and Far East. The Japanese and then also American and British troops seized Vladivostok. In May the organizers of the intervention pro-voked the Czechoslovak Corps to rise up against the Soviets. It mounted armed actions against the Red Army in the Urals, Siberia and the Volga region. At the same time, the Russian White Guards went on the offensive. Both sides fought without quarter. There was a 'White terror' and a 'Red terror'. The shooting and attempted assassin-ation of leading Soviet personalities, including Lenin, unleashed a Red terror. William Henry Chamberlain (*The Russian Revolution, 1917–1921,* New York, 1935) estimates that 50,000 persons were killed by the Red Terror during the three years of Civil War.[2]

The Germans also joined the fight against the new revolutionary Soviet republic, overrunning the Baltic provinces, Belorussia and the Ukraine, even occupying Rostov-on-Don, southwest of Stalingrad (now Volgograd). But the German defeat in the First World War and a short-lived revolution that broke out soon afterwards, spelled an end to German inroads into Russia. Clearly, the new revolutionary regime was in deadly peril. In 1919 the number of war theatres rose to six, and the total length of the front lines was nearly 8,000 kilometres. The Civil War, says Zhukov, had reached its apogee.

By the beginning of the year the new Red Army comprised 42 infantry divisions equipped with rifles, Maxim machine-guns, revolvers and hand grenades. The cavalry had 40,000 sabres, and there were

1,700 field guns. Red Army forces included armoured trains, each consisting of an armoured locomotive, two protected firing platforms and detachments of armoured cars. The fledgling air force had 450 planes while the navy had 2 battleships, 2 cruisers, 24 destroyers, 6 submarines and several dozen other types of vessels. By the spring of 1919 White Admiral Kolchak, who had the title of 'Supreme Ruler of Russia,' had 300,000 well-armed men

After Mikhail Frunze took over the command of the Southern Group of Soviet armies, the state of affairs changed for the better. Here is what Frunze, a hero of the Civil War, writes in his memoirs about the year 1919:

> The Kolchak forces were already close to the Volga. We had great difficulty in holding Orenburg which was surrounded on three sides. The army defending the town was ready to withdraw. To the south of Samara the Ural Cossacks had broken through and were moving north, threatening Samara and the Samara–Orenburg railway line. We were retreating almost everywhere, but I cannot say that we felt ourselves to be the weaker side. But since the initiative was in the hands of the Whites and their blows followed one after the other, binding our will, we did not feel particularly comfortable. To launch an offensive required tremendous will power and also the deep conviction that only such an offensive could change the situation. At that time we had to take into account not only the morale of the units that wanted to retreat, but also pressure from above, from the High Command [which favoured withdrawal] . . . Despite all this we went over to the offensive.

This was the beginning of a brilliant operation which led to the complete defeat of Kolchak.

Zhukov speaks highly of Frunze and lauds his intimacy with the troops, something which Zhukov himself practised in the Nazi–Soviet war. Says Zhukov: 'Frunze stopped in the field and talked with the soldiers of our regiment. He showed an interest in their sentiments, food supplies and arms. He asked them what their relatives back home in the villages were writing. He wanted to know whether the army men had any requests. His straightforward manner, charm and pleasing appearance won the soldiers' hearts.'

Frunze's optimism is also noted by Zhukov: 'Things are going not badly now,' Frunze told the regiment, adding, 'The White Ural Cossacks have been smashed and very soon we shall definitely finish off the rest of the counter-revolutionaries. We'll finish off Kolchak and free the Urals, Siberia and other regions from the interventionists and Whites. Then we shall rebuild our country!'

After the defeat of Kolchak and the retreat into Siberia of what was left of his armies, the Entente pinned their hopes on General Denikin whose troops were regularly supplied with arms, ammunition and food from the West. In the summer of 1919, says Zhukov, the White armies were still a large and dangerous force. He says that Entente ships that brought supplies to the White armies sailed back home loaded with furs, fish, timber and other valuable Russian goods.

1919 was a key year for Zhukov politically, it being the year he joined the Leninist party. At that time, he notes, there was no such thing as probationary membership. It appears that his membership was not perfunctory, that he was quite serious about it. Here is how he describes it: 'I have forgotten many things, but I will remember the day I joined the Party as long as I live. Since then I have tried to suit all my thoughts, aspirations and actions to the demands made of a Party member. And when it came to fighting our country's enemies, I bore in mind the Party demand that a member must be a model of selfless service to the people.'

In hand-to-hand fighting towards the end of 1919 Zhukov was wounded when a hand grenade exploded, sending splinters deep into his left side and thigh. Sent to hospital, he again succumbed to a bout of typhus. 'I left the hospital in bad shape, and was granted a month's leave to recuperate.'

Zhukov spent his leave with his parents in his native village.

The village folk, he notes, were very badly off but had not lost heart. The poorer villagers had organized committees of poor peasants, which took part in confiscating grain from the kulaks. The middle peasants, despite hardships and the grave situation at the front, were leaning more and more towards the new regime.

'Before I knew it, my furlough was over and I reported to the local military commissariat, asking them to assign me to the active forces,' says Zhukov. But he was not quite fit, however, and they sent him to the Tver Reserve Battalion and later to the Red Commanders' Courses. The 1st Ryazan Cavalry Courses, where he found himself in January 1920, were located on a former landowner's estate. The enrolment was chiefly made up of cavalrymen who had distinguished themselves in combat. Zhukov was given the post of trainee sergeant-major, 1st Squadron. He had the job of instructing trainees in the handling of side arms (lance and sabre), bayonet fighting, drill and physical training.

Zhukov notes that most of the trainees were weak in general education, that many could barely read and write. But he says 'they should
be given credit for trying hard; they realized they had to learn a lot in
a short time to become worthy commanders'.

In mid-July Zhukov and his men were ordered to board a train, destination unknown. They headed in the direction of Moscow and were
billeted in the city's Lefortovo barracks. 'We were issued combat
equipment and arms. Our outfits and the horses' harnesses were all
new, and we looked very smart.'

There was also an opportunity for romance.

Zhukov says:

> I had many friends in Moscow, and wanted to look them up before going
> to the front – especially one girl, an old flame. Unfortunately, I could not
> manage to see anyone. As sergeant-major I was usually left in charge by the
> squadron commanders who often had to be away for various assignments.
> So I had to be content with writing to the people I knew. Perhaps that was
> why Maria and I parted ways, and she soon married. I never saw her again.

By the summer of that year, the Red Army was more than 3 million
strong. The Entente powers decided to organize one more offensive
against Soviet Russia with Baron Wrangel's troops that had been
recruited in the Crimea. Zhukov's regiment meanwhile was
bivouacked in Krasnodar, east of the Crimea, near the Black Sea. At
that time Wrangel had an army of about 130,000 men, including
4,500 cavalry. Wrangel counted on help from large numbers of kulaks
among the Cossacks in the Kuban area in Russia's south.

By that time, however, a considerable part of the Kuban Cossacks
had realized, says Zhukov, what the White Guards and the 'supreme
government' financed by the Entente held in store for them. He says
that the Red commissars and soldiers 'did their best' to convince the
Cossacks of the necessity of eliminating the anti-revolutionary bands
as speedily as possible.

At the same time, says Zhukov, 'we helped the poorer Cossacks and
families of Red Army men in every possible way. This was important
since before the Red Army came, the Whites often robbed them of
their last loaf of bread and humiliated them in many other ways'.

He recalls the regimental commissar coming to his squadron one
evening and suggesting that everyone should devote a few days to
repairing houses, barns and farm implements for the families of Red
Army men and poor families in general. 'We agreed enthusiastically.'

Our commissar, V.A. Krylov, picked the hardest job – cleaning the public well which the White soldiers had filled with garbage. The well was a rather deep one, and when he reached the bottom he nearly suffocated. He was pulled out of the well half-dead, but as soon as he got his breath back he ordered us to lower him into the well again. In a short while we had to pull him up once more, and so it went until all the dirt was cleared out of the well. By nightfall the commissar's bravery was the talk of the village.

When all the work was done, the Cossacks invited Zhukov and his men to a dinner. The future marshal remembers a funny episode. A group of trainees was given the job of repairing a barn and a horse's harness for a Cossack widow. They did it, but for a kulak family who had the same name. Everybody laughed, but the 'culprits' were clearly upset.

Zhukov took part in seeking out bands of White troops in southern Russia and the Ukraine. At this time he and three of his friends were assigned to the 1st Cavalry Regiment under a battlewise Don Cossack named Andreyev who had the reputation of being a fearless fighter.

The four reported to headquarters, handed in their papers, and were received by the regimental commander who looked disapprovingly at their breeches and said: 'My men don't like commanders in red breeches.'

But, says Zhukov, there was little they could do about it. Military trainees were issued only that style of breeches, and they had no others. Still a bit distrustful, the commander continued:

'My soldiers are mostly old hands and we don't care much for greenhorns.'

After this anything but encouraging introduction, he began questioning Zhukov and his friends: who they were, where from, if they were Party members, had a fighting record, when and where they had seen action, and so on. He seemed relieved when he learned that the four were not green, and that two of them had fought in the First World War.

Zhukov describes his first meeting with his men. His lifelong habit of simplicity and straightforwardness in dealing with others is clearly evident.

First Zhukov gave orders for the men to line up mounted so he could get acquainted with them. After he greeted the men, he said:

'See here, comrades, I have been appointed your commander. How good a commander I am and how good you are as soldiers remains to be seen. Right now I want to inspect your horses and equipment, and get acquainted with each of you personally.'

Zhukov says that while inspecting the men he noticed that some of them were casting critical glances at his red breeches. So he explained:

'Regimental commander Andreyev has already warned me that you don't like red breeches. But I don't have any others. I wear what the government gave me, and I'm grateful for it. As for red, as you know, it is the revolutionary colour symbolizing the working people's struggle for freedom and independence.'

The next day he invited the platoon to his hut and asked the men to tell him about themselves. His idea did not come off very well, he says.

> 'What is there to tell?' machine-gunner Kasyanov said. 'The platoon roll contains all the information – what kind of people we are and where we come from.'
>
> So I told them all I knew about the fighting against the White Poles and Wrangel in Northern Taurida. The men listened attentively, and were anxious to know if the Entente would land its troops again. I said the Entente governments would certainly like to bring in their troops but that the people and the soldiers in the Entente did not want to fight against us.

A few days later Zhukov led his platoon into battle mopping up the remnants of White Guard bands along the Black Sea coast. The enemy were killed or captured, while his platoon had no casualties. 'That was important: no one mentioned my red breeches after that.'

During his fighting against counter-revolutionary bands, Zhukov encountered a number of glittering Soviet army leaders like M.N. Tukhachevsky and I.P. Uborevich both of whom he praises highly in his reminiscences. (The two, among others, were accused of treason in Stalin's Great Terror of the late 1930s and shot.)

Zhukov was in the thick of a number of life-and-death skirmishes in 1921, largely in fighting against large bands of anti-Soviet 'Antonovites' who had a striking force of cavalry regiments, with a total strength of from 1,500 to 3,000 men.

> There were many fierce engagements with the Antonovites. One that took place in the spring of 1921 near the village of Vyazovaya Pochta, not far from the Zherdevka railway station, has stuck in my memory. Early in the morning our regiment, which was part of a brigade, was alerted. Scouts had reported a concentration of up to 3,000 of Antonov's horsemen some 10 or 15 kilometres from the village. Our 1st Cavalry Regiment proceeded

from the village in a column to the left while the 2nd Regiment advanced to the right. My squadron with four machine-guns and one artillery piece was ordered to move along the highway, taking up a leading position. We had covered some 5 km when the squadron came upon an Antonov detachment of about 250 sabres. We deployed fast, turned the gun around and, despite the enemy's numerical superiority, launched an attack. Our swift blow broke the Antonovites and they retreated with considerable losses.

In hand-to-hand fighting, one enemy horseman fired his sawed-off rifle at Zhukov and killed his horse. 'We fell,' says Zhukov, 'the horse pinning me down, and the next moment I would have been slashed to death but for Nochevka, the political instructor, who came to my rescue. With a swing of his sabre he killed the bandit, caught the reins of his horse and helped me into the saddle.'

Soon they noticed a column of enemy cavalry trying to outflank them. They immediately concentrated their fire on this column, and sent a messenger to report the situation to the regimental commander. In 20 to 30 minutes the regiment drew up and engaged the enemy. The 2nd Regiment, running into superior enemy forces, had to retreat. Taking advantage of the situation, an enemy unit attacked the flank. Meanwhile the enemy charged into Zhukov's squadron which acted as the rearguard for the regiment.

The engagement was extremely fierce. The enemy was aware of its superiority and felt certain they would crush Zhukov's squadron. 'But that was easier said than done,' says Zhukov.

What saved us was that the squadron had four machine-guns with plenty of ammunition and a 76-mm field gun. By moving these weapons from place to place we fired at the attackers almost point-blank. Moving slowly backwards, we saw the battlefield become covered with dead enemy soldiers and horses. But we, too, were suffering great losses. I saw my good friend, platoon commander Ukhach-Ogorovich fall out of he saddle, badly wounded. He was a competent commander and well brought up. His father, a colonel in the old Russian army, who sided with the Soviets from the very first, was a leading instructor at our Ryazan commanders' courses. Before he lost consciousness, Ukhach-Ogorovich whispered:

'Write my mother. Don't leave me to the bandits.'

Zhukov says he put the wounded beside the dead on the gun carriage and machine-gun sleds and took them along so the Whites would not mutilate them.

The counter-attack planned by the regiment did not materialize –

the thin ice on the river they were to cross gave way and they had to continue their retreat by a much longer route.

They were already in the village when Zhukov rushed to a group of White Guards who were trying to get one of his machine-guns. For the second time that day his horse was killed. 'Revolver in hand, I fought the bandits who were trying to capture me alive. Political instructor Nochevka again came to my rescue, assisted by soldiers Bryksin, Gorshkov and Kovalev.'

Casualties in Zhukov's squadron that day were 10 men killed and 15 wounded. Three of the wounded died the next day; Ukhach-Ogorovich, his friend and mate, was one of them.

'That had been a hard day for us. We grieved over the loss of our comrades. The only thing that took the edge off our pain was the knowledge that we had eliminated such a large bandit force.'

Zhukov later received one of his first Soviet decorations.

He writes: 'For this operation most of the commanders and political officers, and many of the soldiers, were decorated. I was among them. Here is what is said in the order of the top command of 31 August 1921:

> Decorated with the Order of the Red Banner is the commander of 2nd Squadron, 1st Cavalry Regiment, Detached Cavalry Brigade, for having held off an onslaught of the enemy numbering from 1,500 to 2,000 sabres for seven hours with his squadron in a battle at the village of Vyazovaya Pochta, Tambov province, on 5 March 1921, and then, counter-attacking, smashed the bandits after six hand-to-hand clashes.

Zhukov recalls a curious incident during a final mopping up operation at the end of the summer of 1921:

> As we pursued an Antonov band we suddenly came upon two armoured cars that came rolling from a nearby village. Since we knew the band had no armoured cars, we did not fire on them. The cars, however, took up an advantageous position and trained their machine-gun on us. Why on earth? We sent out messengers. It turned out they were our armoured cars with the famed Commander Uborevich himself in the leading one. On learning of the band's retreat in the direction of the forest he had decided to intercept it. Good thing we cleared up matters, or the consequences might have been disastrous.

That is how Zhukov first met Uborevich. They saw much of each other later, between 1932 and 1937 when Uborevich was in command of the Belorussian Military District, where Zhukov was a cavalry division commander.

In his memoirs Zhukov quotes British General Knox who wrote to his government at the time of the Revolution that it was possible to crush a million-strong Red army, but when 150 million Russians were opposed to the White Guards and favoured the Reds, it was futile to help the former.

Zhukov provides a few statistics on the Party's influence in the military. In October 1918, he says, there were 35,000 party members in the army. A year later the number was about 120,000, and in August 1920, as high as 300,000, or 50 per cent of the total Party membership at that time. By the end of 1920 the Red Army numbered 5,500,000 men, though it had suffered huge losses between 1918 and 1920. During those years as many as 800,000 were killed, wounded or missing and nearly 1,400,000 perished from serious diseases caused by malnutrition and lack of clothing, footwear, medicines and medical services.

Zhukov speaks of the 'incredible sacrifices' made by the people during the Civil War and says that 'the strictest centralization' of the army and 'iron discipline' made victory possible.

Zhukov's zeal as an army commander was equalled by his efforts to fill in the gaps in his education. When opportunities arose to take advanced training courses he promptly took them. In 1924, for example, he attended a one-year course at the Higher Cavalry School in Leningrad. After finishing the course, he was granted a short leave and visited his native village. He found that his mother had aged greatly but still worked very hard; his sister had two children 'but also looked old'. The harsh postwar years and the famine of 1921–22 had affected all the villagers. Many families had lost all their livestock during the crop failure of 1921. Zhukov felt sad to see his birthplace so impoverished.

Zhukov says he became instant friends with his little nephews. 'They loved to rummage in my suitcase, extracting from it whatever they liked.'

Again in 1929–30 Zhukov enrolled in a course in Moscow preparing officers for command of larger units. Returning to his regiment he was promoted to command a brigade under the 7th Samara Cavalry Division. To his credit, in the eyes of his superiors, was his long-time party membership. (Many officers of that time had served under the Tsarist regime, were not of peasant stock, were not party members and, therefore, were continually suspect.)

In 1931 Zhukov was, at 34, ordered to take up duties as assistant to the Inspector of Cavalry of the Red Army. Some of Zhukov's subordinates were glad to see him go because of his alleged 'unfounded strictness and crudeness'. But some contemporary historians like William J. Spahr observe that Zhukov's reputation for strictness may have been a plus in the expanding army of that era. Zhukov himself often returns to this subject, sometimes admitting his faults but also providing an explanation. Thus he says in his memoirs:

> Careless work by a serviceman [always] upset me. Some didn't understand that and I, in my turn, evidently was not sufficiently indulgent toward human weakness. Of course, now these errors have become more obvious; having experience teaches much. However, even now [1968] I consider that no one is given the right to enjoy life because of the labour of another. And this is especially important for military people to realize, who must on the battlefield, without regard for their lives, be the first to defend the Motherland.

In 1933 a new man was needed to take command of the 4th Cavalry Division whose combat readiness was said to be very low. The legendary Civil War leader S.M. Budenny chose Georgi Zhukov as the new commander. In just two years' time, the 4th Cavalry was awarded a high decoration. Under Zhukov it had now become one of the best divisions in the entire army.

Summing up the prewar years, Zhukov says that the experience gained in the Civil War and the basic principles formulated at that time were elaborated upon in the 1930s and early 1940s.

Throughout the thirties the country took steps in preparation for an outbreak of war with Nazi Germany. But before that calamity, Russia would be rocked by the Great Purge Trials of the late 1930s, otherwise known as The Great Madness.

Notes

1. In 1917, units of armed workers devoted to the revolution were known as Red Guards. The Bolsheviks had begun training Red Guards shortly before the armed uprising in October 1917 (Old Style). Party influence spread rapidly in the front lines, the bigger rear garrisons, and the Baltic Fleet. During and after the revoution, the Red Guards were unified and supervised by the military branch of the Party's Central Committee.

2. A description of the White Terror is to be found in George Stewart, *The White Armies of Russia*, New York, 1933. Stewart's account, based mainly on Russian language sources, says that White brutality 'made Bolsheviks where none had been before'. He adds: 'The Whites throughout the Civil War suffered from a political short-sightedness which made no provision for a middle view, considering all who were not avowedly White as Bolsheviks and as such deserving of death.'

4

THE GREAT MADNESS

Zhukov spoke bitterly about the damage Stalin had inflicted on the country by his massacre of the top echelons of the army command. 'Of course, I regard them as innocent victims,' he said.

ANDREI GROMYKO, *Memories*, London, 1989

In June 1937 much of the Western world was alarmed by events in Red Russia. And like most people East and West nowadays talk about facing up to acts of terrorism, back then there was no end to talk about the evils of totalitarianism. Out of the blue an announcement from Moscow said a group of high-ranking army officers had been arrested and charged with treason, espionage and plotting to overthrow the government. There was ominous mention of a 'military-Fascist conspiracy' against Josef Stalin's regime. Members of this cabal included not only the firebrand Leon Trotsky (although then in exile in Mexico he was soon to be felled by an assassin with a pickaxe) but also alleged Trotsky confederates in the Red Army. The world was told of a plot to murder the Kremlin leaders. Piecing together the available information, it appeared that Hitler's Gestapo had accomplished the biggest hoax of the decade. Exploiting Stalin's well-known paranoia, it arranged for bogus documents to fall into the hands of high Czechoslovak officials, 'proving' that one of Stalin's famed marshals – Mikhail Tukhachevsky – was planning to eliminate the Soviet dictator with the support of Germany. The Czechs dutifully gave the 'intelligence' to the Kremlin; the infamy of a blood purge against the Red Army followed.

Stalin railed against 'enemies of the people' hiding in the army who must be uprooted. In the Dictator's words these marked men were used as puppets in the hands of the German Reichswehr. Hitler and his generals, he alleged, were out to throttle the Red Army so that it could not defend the country; they hoped to make of Russia a 'second

Spain'. Although the military trials were held in secret the Government and Party-controlled press claimed that the arrested officers had received German and Japanese gold. The officers were tried, sentenced to death or imprisoned. The military trials followed several momentous 'show trials' that were open to the public and foreign guests, including diplomats. The open trials were open to Party leaders, apparatchiks, diplomats and others.

At one of the Moscow show trials evidence was given that Stalin twice narrowly escaped assassination – in 1933 and 1935. Were Stalin's (or Hitler's) secret services behind these real or mythic assassination plots? According to the British Annual Register, a chief of the local OGPU (the secret police) in Georgia and two border guards had fired at Stalin's cutter on the Black Sea when he was cruising off the coast in the summer of 1933. The attempt failed because of the cutter's speed and distance from shore. A second attempt with a German automatic rifle in 1935 was frustrated by the late arrival of the 'conspirators' at the place where Stalin was spending his holiday. The instructions for the planned murders had, it was claimed, come from Yuri Pyatakov, the Deputy Commissar for Heavy Industry, who was alleged to take his orders from the exiled Trotsky. Pyatakov was later accused of treason and shot.

Historian and biographer Dmitri Volkogonov says he is certain the plots against Stalin were fabricated. 'I'm absolutely sure there were no plots, no attempts on Stalin's life during this time.' He added: 'There was not a single person who would dare make an attempt on his life.' (But he said that, if it were the United States, then Stalin would surely be 'bumped off' because Americans wouldn't tolerate a tyrant like Stalin. 'But it was easy for Stalin to govern the Russians; they were treating him as a god while at the same time he was annihilating millions of them.') However it can not be said that Stalin had no enemies; with the purges of the 1930s he clearly gave rise to disaffected elements within the population, not to mention those who were ardent supporters of Leon Trotsky.[1]

But the purge of the military was most harmful to the security of the country. Among those arrested in addition to Marshal Tukhachevsky, who was a pioneer in the reorganization of the Red Army, were Marshal Vasily Blyukher, a hero of the Civil War who had joined the Bolshevik Party in 1918 and volunteered for the new Red Army; and I.P. Uborevich, who was much admired by Zhukov. ('One could always learn a great deal from this brave and courageous man,' he writes.) Also court-martialled at the same time were other top officers, all accused of treason. (The Czech President Edvard Benes says in his memoirs that he learned of an 'anti-Stalin clique' involving Tukhachevsky and sent the incriminating documents, believing them to be genuine, to Moscow.)

Another Soviet marshal charged with treason, Jan Gamarnik, was found dead, apparently by his own hand. (Military historian Dmitri Volkogonov told the author in 1989 that Gamarnik was asked to be a member of the court to judge Tukhachevsky, but he couldn't because they were friends. But he knew that if he refused to join the 'jurors' he would be shot. 'So Gamarnik chose the only possible way of protesting: he shot himself.' Volkogonov added: 'There were quite a number of cases like that – officers who committed suicide as their way of expressing disagreement with Stalin.')

One bizarre case (among many) involved Lieutenant General A.Y. Lapin, Commander of the Far Eastern Air Force, who was reported to have killed himself in prison after being arrested in the military purge. According to *The Times* of London, Lapin had written a letter 'in blood' that was, apparently smuggled out of prison. The letter said: 'I falsely testified to matters of which I knew nothing and under the constant menace of new tortures I affirmed everything imputed to me. I am not a counter-revolutionary and have no connection with such elements whatsoever.'

The trial of these distinguished military leaders was unquestionably painful for Georgi Zhukov who had personally known some of these so-called 'enemies of the people'. Although he said little about the trial in the first editions of his memoirs he said much more later on, mentioning those who were liquidated, especially Tukhachevsky and Uborevich. He has some two dozen references to the former. Some of the very principles of warfare that Zhukov had learned and which he showed off to good advantage in the big-scale operation at Khalkin Gol in Mongolia had been elaborated by Tukhachevsky and the other alleged conspirators. (For example, armour must strike out independently, operations must be conducted in depth, good intelligence must always be maintained, deception and pre-emption must be given high priority, etc. All this helped to form the core of the 'Zhukov method of warfare.')

But in the spy mania of that time, Zhukov and thousands like him were being questioned about their relationships with those who had been accused of various crimes and imprisoned. In fact, dozens of high-ranking officers whom Zhukov knew personally were not immune from arrest.

It is estimated that 45 per cent of senior officers and political officers of the army and navy were shot or discharged. Of some 850 commanders, from colonel to marshal, about 85 per cent were eliminated. Many were later reinstated, including K.K. Rokossovsky, who served a two-year prison term before the war. (General Gorbatov, in his book, *Years Off My Life,* records his own arrest and pathetic existence in a Siberian gulag before being summoned back for front-line duty against the German invaders.)

Specifically, from 1936 to 1938 a total of 41,200 were purged.

The purges had the effect abroad of downgrading the strength of the Red Army. In Germany especially there was a judgement among generals that the Red Army was no match for the Wehrmacht. Historian Richard Overy makes an interesting point. He says the argument that the purges weakened the Red Army and Navy rests on the assumption that the pre-purge army was hugely more effective. But this wasn't so, he explains, as there was a big gap between theory and practice. Efficiency in command and control was not high. Also there was a relatively low level of military education among officers and non-commissioned officers, not to mention a pervading fear of responsibility or initiative throughout the Red Army.[2]

Zhukov was questioned in Minsk by a member of the Military Council of the Belorussian Military District, Filipp Golikov. Zhukov had known some of the arrested officers, including Rokossovsky and Serdich, but he frankly called both of them patriots and honest party members. Zhukov could see that his answer did not please Golikov.

Two other points were brought up by Golikov. There were reports that Zhukov was harsh with his men and even crude and did not appreciate fully the importance of political workers. In reply Zhukov said he was sharp only with those who were slack in their duty. Golikov also said he had heard that Zhukov's wife had baptized their second daughter, Ella. Zhukov denied it.

Obviously it was not a pleasant interview and Zhukov wondered if it would hinder his chances of becoming the new commander of the 3rd Cavalry Corps. But it did not. When he finally took over his new command Zhukov found that the units were wanting in their levels of military and political education. This he blamed on the effect of the purges on the morale and discipline of the men. Too often the most demanding commanders were the targets of demagogues who tried to bring them down with accusations of being 'enemies of the people'. Zhukov, not one to sit back in the face of rank injustice, often intervened boldly. But he would admit to being wrong in a number of cases.

He tells how one of his subordinate officers asked for his help because he was worried about being called unworthy and expelled from the Party at an upcoming meeting, perhaps even arrested by the NKVD, the forerunner of the KGB. The officer was being accused of having a close friendship with one of the higher ups arrested and shot in the purge. Zhukov ageed to attend the meeting. This officer was also accused of being too insensitive and demanding in the performance of his men. It appeared that they were going to expel the officer from the Army and the Party. Zhukov took the floor and defended the man, praising his honesty and high ability as a commander. He said that before 'enemies of the people' were arrested, how did anyone know if and why they would be arrested? The other criticisms, he said, were minor in importance. When the meeting ended, Zhukov's viewpoint won out. The accused officer, says Zhukov, thanked him with tears in his eyes.

However, another case ended in tragedy. Zhukov had accepted command of the 6th Cavalry Corps when there was a vacancy caused by the transfer of its commander to the Kiev Military District. But due to the climate of repressions, when the man was faced with the ordeal of being accused of severe shortcomings during a Party meeting – he admitted having close ties with one of the executed marshals and feared torture by the organs of the secret police – he took his own life. Zhukov did not mention this in the first editions of his war memoirs.

Zhukov had another confrontation with various Party organizations within the cavalry corps. This time no fewer than 80 party men attended. Again, they brought up Zhukov's crude behaviour, the way he exercised his command, his relationship with the recently executed Uborevich (apparently they had at least once dined alone) and other 'enemies of the people'.

Unfortunately for Zhukov his main accuser was chief of the political section of the 4th Cavalry Division, S.P. Tikhomirov, who had served with Zhukov for a number of years, although the two men were never close friends. Zhukov says that at the meeting his accuser was evasive and sly, avoiding straight answers to Zhukov's direct questions. He did not give Zhukov a clean bill of health. Zhukov spoke in his own behalf, admitting his lack of restraint at times in dealing with those who were poorly performing their duty. As to his dining with Uborevich he said that friendly relations between officers should be the goal of all party men but only if they were totally unaware of any signs of disloyalty. He felt strongly about unit discipline and performance, he said, and that this must come first before 'kind words and comradeship'.

Zhukov's explanation was accepted. But for good measure he sent a telegram to Stalin and Voroshilov in the Kremlin. (He never received an answer.) However, he was allowed to get on with his work. He says that he never forgave the political officer Tikhomirov and cut off all communication with him.

Note

1. The historian Dmitri Volkogonov was interviewed by the author in 1991.
2. The British historian Jonathan Haslem has written that Stalin's repressions served as a convenient alibi for Western governments who before the war 'through ideological hostility born of Russian *revolutionary proselytism*' had no intention of entering into an alliance with Moscow. (J. Haslem, *The Soviet Union and the Struggle for Collective Security in Europe, 1933–1939*, New York 1984.)

5

ZHUKOV IN MONGOLIA

I witnessed feats of great courage by Red Army and Mongolian Army men and their commanders.

G.K. ZHUKOV, *Reminiscences and Reflections*

Almost unknown in the West, the Battle of Khalkin Gol seems at first glance only of minor importance. But the heavy fighting between Japanese and Soviet forces in Mongolia in 1939 had consequences far beyond the borders of the countries involved. The victory won by Georgi Zhukov helped stabilize the incendiary situation in the Far East. Second, the defeat administered to Japanese forces in Mongolia quite possibly prompted Japan not to join Hitler in his invasion of the Soviet Union. Instead, Japan moved south towards Hong Kong and Singapore after hitting Pearl Harbor. And for Zhukov, personally, it was the start of a career in which he would be called by some experts the premier warrior of the century.

It began with a phone call on 1 June 1939 from Moscow. Zhukov was then the Deputy Commander of the Belorussian Military District, and was busy conducting field exercises. The caller said Zhukov must be in Moscow the next day.

'Do you happen to know why I'm being called there?' Zhukov asked the officer at the other end of the line.

'I don't know,' replied the officer. 'All I know is that in the morning you have to be at Marshal Voroshilov's office.'

The next day Zhukov reported to Marshal Voroshilov, the head of the Soviet defence establishment, who told him to get ready to fly to Mongolia where fighting was going on, that Japanese units in division strength had invaded Mongolia from the east. In Moscow earlier that morning (2 June) Zhukov was given a briefing and shown maps of the fighting area.

'Here,' said Voroshilov, pointing on the map, 'the Japanese have for a long time carried out provocative attacks on Mongolian frontier guards, and now the Japanese Hailar garrison has invaded Mongolian territory and attacked frontier units which were covering the area east of the Khalkhin River. I think they've embarked on a big military gamble. At any rate, it's only the beginning ... Could you fly there right away and if need be assume command of the troops?'

'I am ready this minute,' said Zhukov.

'Good,' said Voroshilov, an old warhorse of the Civil War and one of Stalin's cronies. 'Your plane will be waiting at the Central airfield at 16:00 hours. Get in touch with Smoridonov who will give you the requisite information and arrange for liaison with the General Staff. A small group of military experts will be flying with you. Goodbye now, and all the best.'

Before Zhukov left, Voroshilov informed him about the Soviet Government's commitment to defend Mongolia from external aggression by the Treaty of 12 March 1936.

Zhukov visited Ivan Smorodinov, the acting Chief of the General staff.

'The moment you arrive,' he said, 'see what's going on and report to us. But pull no punches.'

Zhukov's plane landed first at the Siberian city of Chita, north of Mongolia, where he met members of the army's District Headquarters who briefed him on the latest developments. In addition to fighting on the ground, the Japanese Air Force was penetrating deep into Mongolia's air space, chasing Red Army and Mongolian vehicles and shooting them up.

Three days after he left Moscow, Zhukov arrived at Tamtsak-Bulak where the Headquarters of the 57th Special Corps was stationed, and he met the Corps Commander, N.F. Feklenko, and his aides.

It is noteworthy that Japanese military intelligence quickly learned about Zhukov's assignment in Mongolia, the news apparently coming from a future 'Kamikaze' general named Kyoji Tominaga who was fluent in Russian. He had once served as a military attaché at the Japanese Embassy in Moscow where he had met Zhukov. Now working at the Imperial High Command in Tokyo, Tominaga, remembering Zhukov's 'style', correctly predicted that a major Russian offensive would soon start because Georgi Zhukov had arrived at the scene. (During the Pacific War he would command a Kamikaze base in the Philippines.)

Clearly, this was the moment Zhukov had been waiting and preparing for since his Civil War days as a cavalryman. Now he would command a large body of troops facing a modern military force. Not wasting a minute, Zhukov quickly sized up the situation and concluded that the Japanese military had not given up their plans against the Soviet Far East and that they would shortly escalate the conflict.

At this time, the Western press began to take an interest in the fighting in Mongolia. On the hostilities in that faraway land, *The Times* correspondent in Moscow wrote: 'The Japanese may be anxious, not only to show the Russians that they have adequate forces in Manchuria, but to demonstrate to the Western democracies the risks involved in becoming the allies of Russia.'

When victory was won, Zhukov said in newspaper interviews that if the Japanese had been successful at Khalkin Gol, they would have launched further offensives; that their long-term goals were to reach Siberia's Lake Baikal and the city of Chita, in order to close off the strategic Trans-Siberian Railway. He said the Japanese assault on Mongolia was a serious reconnaissance in force, a 'serious test. It was important for them to determine whether the Red Army was in condition to fight with them.' He added solemnly: 'The outcome of the battle at Khalkin Gol was the reason why their conduct was more or less restrained at the beginning of our war with the Germans.'

In Mongolia it was soon obvious to Zhukov that the Red Army corps commander there did not know the real state of affairs. For one thing, the command post was much too far from the front line. Zhukov asked Feklenko whether he believed it was possible to control troops 120 kilometres from the battlefield.

'It's hard to deny that we are a bit far away,' Feklenko said. 'But the fighting area is operatively unprepared. There is not one kilometre of telephone or telegraph wires in that direction, no effective command post and no landing strips.'

'And what is being done about all that?'

'We are about to send for timber and start building a command post.'

It turned out that only one of the commanding officers had actually visited the battle zone. Zhukov, intolerant of slackers, suggested that the corps commander accompany him to the front line immediately so that they could both study the situation. But Feklenko said he expected an urgent phone call from Moscow and suggested that his deputy go instead.

On the way to the front Zhukov learned in minute detail about the corps, its combat readiness, its headquarters, its commanding officers and political instructors. The deputy, M.S. Nikishev, made a good impression on Zhukov who noted afterwards: 'He obviously knew his job, his people, and all their weaknesses and merits.'

Zhukov was now completely in charge of operations. An order had been received from Moscow relieving Feklenko of the command of the 57th Special Corps and assigning it to Zhukov.

After making a detailed survey of the terrain in the area of the fighting and talking with the commanding officers and commissars (political officers) of both the Soviet units and those of the Mongolian Army, including the staff officers, Zhukov came away with a more or less clear picture of the nature and scope of the hostilities and of the capacity of the Japanese troops. He also noted the errors made by the Soviet and Mongolian troops. One of the most serious was the lack of thorough reconnaissance.

From his observations, Zhukov was certain that this was no mere border incident; that the Japanese had ambitions to invade Siberia and therefore would soon escalate the fighting. Consequently Zhukov was convinced that the forces of the 57th Special Corps as now deployed in Mongolia would not be able to stop the Japanese, particularly if they took action in other areas and from other directions. He immediately asked Moscow to send help, giving Voroshilov a big shopping list: more air units, three additional rifle divisions, one tank brigade and substantial artillery reinforcements. Without this, he made it clear, victory was out of the question.

The following day all of Zhukov's requests were approved by the General Staff in Moscow. Hundreds of additional aircraft were flown to Mongolia and, with them, arrived experienced pilots including almost two dozen decorated Heroes of the Soviet Union. One of them was Y.V. Smushkevich, Deputy Commander of the Air Force of the Red Army, who had seen combat over Spanish skies against the famed German Condor squadron which took part in Spain's Civil War. Zhukov refers to Smushkevich as an excellent organizer, an expert in airplanes, and an ace flyer. Also: 'He was a very modest man, a splendid commander ... loved by all the pilots.' Yet that didn't save him from Stalin's purge of the military and he was arrested and shot, reportedly in late 1939.

Good results, following the arrival of the new pilots, were soon felt. Zhukov records: 'On 22 June 1939, 95 of our fighters engaged in a fierce dogfight with 120 Japanese planes over the territory of the MPR [the Mongolian Peoples Republic]. Many of our Hero-pilots participated and gave the Japanese a lesson to remember. On the next day the Japanese Air Force repeated its massive raid and was again thrashed.' Zhukov says that on 26 June the Japanese brought into action the aces of their air force operating in China but even then could not come out on top. In four days, he says, the Japanese lost 64 planes.

Dogfights occurred regularly, almost every day, up to the beginning of July, though not with the same intensity. But, notes Zhukov, 'in these battles our pilots improved their skill and tempered their will power'.

Konstantin Simonov, the popular novelist–journalist, paid a visit to Zhukov's command post during the Khalkin Gol battle. The command post was made of freshly cut logs and had a curtain to keep out the masses of mosquitoes. Access was by a deep trench lined with artillery telescopes for observing the battlefield. Simonov relates a telling incident that occurred while Zhukov was talking to visiting journalists. Suddenly one of his intelligence officers arrived with a report. Zhukov read it disapprovingly.

Looking at the officer, he said:

'You say six divisions – that's a triple exaggeration. We've confirmed only two. The rest are fictitious. An exaggeration about the enemy is just as dangerous as underestimation.' Before he dismissed the officer, he added: 'Tell your people to stop imagining things. If we have blank spots, let them be blank spots honestly, and don't put nonexistent Japanese divisions in their place.'

There are a number of good stories dealing with the fighting at Khalkin Gol that provide insights into Zhukov the man and soldier. The following story is told by Zhukov himself.

He asked Simonov if he knew Remizov, an army major. No, he didn't. Zhukov called him 'a good person and a good commander'.

I liked him a lot, and I also liked visiting him [Zhukov continued]. Sometimes I would stop by for a cup of tea. Once when we were fighting the Japanese, Remizov charged ahead with his regiment, breaking through so far that he crossed the border without realizing it. The Japanese immediately sent major forces against him. We moved our armoured brigade there at once, which headed toward Remizov from both sides, and bust open a gap ... This enabled him to withdraw. Then, someone sent a bad report about him to Moscow, suggesting that he be court-martialled for wilfully crossing the border. But I didn't think he should be court-martialled at all. I liked him; he had an urge to thrust forward. What kind of a commander is it that during a battle can't go forward or back, to the right or the left, and can't decide anything for himself? Who needs that kind! We need impulsive people. So I made a counter proposal to Moscow – that Remizov be given a citation. He wasn't court-martialled, nor was he given a citation. Later, posthumously, he was given the title of Hero of the Soviet Union.[1]

Zhukov describes how the officer met his death.

'Remizov was a heroic person, but he died senselessly, while he was on the telephone. He had his observation post in a bad place – it was wide open. When he was talking on the telephone a bullet struck him right in the ear.'

Another senseless death is mentioned by Zhukov, one that could have been avoided.

Yakovlev, the commander of the tank brigade, was a very brave person and a good commander. He died senselessly. A group of Japanese broke through in the vicinity of our central crossing, about 300 men. That wasn't very many, but the crossing was in danger. I ordered Yakovlev, taking personal responsibility, to crush this group. He began gathering his infantry and organizing an attack. Yakovlev got on top of a tank and commanded from there. A Japanese sniper hit him and killed him on the spot. It's a shame, because he was a very good military commander.

Zhukov is one of those military leaders who is often criticized for disregarding the human cost of an operation. At Khalkin Gol, pending operations with the certainty of heavy losses were declared justified if they would result in victory.

Here is a case in point. In late June major Japanese forces of infantry and artillery crossed over to the western bank of the river at night and were planning to cut off Soviet–Mongolian units that were continuing to fight on the eastern bank. But Zhukov did not have nearby reserves of either infantry or artillery to prevent this. Only his advancing tank and mechanized armoured units could arrive in time. But an independent attack by tank and mechanized armoured units without infantry support was dangerous and not in keeping with the military doctrine of those days.

Despite this, Zhukov sent against the Japanese his tank and mechanized brigades and a separate armoured battalion, taking full responsibility.

'I decided to attack the Japanese on the march with our tank brigade,' Zhukov says. 'I knew that without infantry support it would sustain heavy losses, but we took the chance deliberately.'

Major losses did occur, he reports. Although the brigade was strong, with about 200 tanks and it went into action boldly, Zhukov admits big losses from Japanese artillery fire. 'But we were prepared for that,' he says. He admits that 'around half the personnel in the brigade were killed or wounded, and half the tanks destroyed'. And again: 'But we had expected that to happen.' He also admits that the Soviet and Mongolian armoured units that supported the tank attack 'suffered even greater losses. Tanks burned up before my eyes.' He says that in one sector 24 tanks out of the original 36 were destroyed by fire.

Zhukov offers this justification for the big losses: 'But we managed to completely crush the advancing Japanese division.'

Another 'difficult situation' (Zhukov's words) developed when the Japanese threw into battle major forces and tried to crush Soviet units on the eastern bank of the Khalkin Gol. The Deputy People's Commissar for Defence, Marshal G.I. Kulik, who was present at Zhukov's command post, demanded the removal of Zhukov's artillery that was on the eastern side of the river for fear it would be captured. Zhukov refused point-blank. If the artillery were removed, he countered, then everything from the bridgehead, including the infantry, should be removed. 'I would not keep the infantry without artillery. Artillery is the backbone of defence. Why should the infantry be wiped out alone? Then let's withdraw everything.'

In short, says Zhukov, he refused to follow Kulik's order, and he explained his refusal to Moscow – that he thought it was not expedient to withdraw the artillery from the bridgehead.

'My opinion,' says Zhukov, 'won out and Kulik was called back to Moscow that very day.'

Zhukov says the Japanese made only one mass use of their tanks. Having learned the Japanese tanks were heading for the front, he set up his artillery in the only accessible area to tanks, and the Japanese deployed them precisely in that direction. Red Army artillerymen fired at them as Zhukov watched. Around 100 enemy tanks were hit and burned, only one returning undamaged, he says.

In retrospect, Zhukov praises Japanese dive-bombers ('although they usually did their bombing from rather high altitudes'), and the quality of their anti-aircraft guns. Zhukov says the Germans tested their own anti-aircraft guns with the Japanese in combat conditions.

When Zhukov entered the war against Nazi Germany he was already a military leader with a decisive victory, an operation that used mechanized troops and aviation. Simonov says that in his postwar conversations with Zhukov the marshal had fond memories of his experiences at Khalkin Gol.

Zhukov says the Japanese Command was so sure of winning at Khalkin Gol that it had invited military attachés and foreign correspondents from Germany and Italy to the combat area to view the anticipated victory.

But very soon a new danger emerged for Zhukov.

Before dawn on 3 July, Colonel I.M. Afonin, senior adviser to the Mongolian Army, went to the Bain-Tsagan mountain to check the defences of the Mongolian 6th Cavalry Division. There he discovered Japanese troops which had crossed the Khalkin Gol river under cover of darkness and attacked Mongolian units. Taking advantage of their superior strength, the Japanese seized the mountain and the adjacent territory while the cavalry division retreated to the northwest. It was clear that nothing could prevent the Japanese troops in this area from hitting the flank and rear of the main Soviet–Mongolian forces.

Zhukov at once alerted all reserves to move in the general direction of the Bain-Tsagan mountain and attack the enemy. He also prepared a concerted strike by a Soviet tank brigade, motorized regiment, an armoured brigade and an artillery battalion together with a Mongolian armoured battalion. All available aircraft were also alerted.

Says Zhukov: 'It was extremely important for us to hold the enemy in check with aircraft and artillery fire until the arrival of reserves for the counterblow.' To keep the Japanese from crossing the river and prevent them from massing forces in the mountain area, the heavy bombing and shelling of the crossing was to continue without let-up. Despite the Japanese strength (they had 10,000 men on the mountain, while the Soviet troops had only a little over 1,000 men, in Zhukov's ranks was the 11th Tank Brigade with 150 tanks plus 154 armoured vehicles of the 7th Armoured Brigade and a Mongolian armoured battalion equipped with 45-mm guns.

Thus, says Zhukov, his trump card was his armour. But there was no time to lose, he says, because the Japanese, seeing his tanks advance, rapidly began to take defensive measures and started bombing the tanks. The Tanks had no shelter, as for hundreds of kilometres around the terrain was completely open. There was 'not even a bush in sight', says Zhukov. At 3 o'clock in the morning of 5 July Japanese resistance was broken and a general retreat was ordered.

A Japanese soldier recorded in his diary for 3 July: 'Several dozen tanks attacked unexpectedly, causing chaos among our troops … Horses stampeded, neighing and dragging gun carriages with them. Cars scattered in all directions. Two of our planes were shot down. The morale of our troops fell.'

Japanese troops began to retreat to the river but the crossing had been blown up by their own sappers who feared a breakthrough by Soviet tanks. 'Japanese officers,' says Zhukov, 'dived headlong into the water in full uniform and drowned before the eyes of our tankmen.'

In the end thousands of dead bodies, carcasses of horses, a multitude of crashed and broken guns, mortars, machine guns and cars littered Bain-Tsagan mountain. Forty-five Japanese planes, including 20 dive-bombers were shot down.

The rout of a large Japanese force on the Bain-Tsagan mountain and successful resistance on the east bank of the Khalka river boosted the morale of Zhukov's troops as well as that of the Mongolian units. Officers and men congratulated their neighbours on the victory. But at the same time a general offensive was being prepared for not later than 20 August.

The concentration of forces and all movements of troops was covered up as much as possible by noise specially created by aircraft, artillery, mortar and machine-gun fire. To conceal the noise of his own tanks on the move – including experimental models of what became the famous T-34 – he stripped silencers and exhaust mufflers from trucks. Night movement was masked under the din of Russian bombing attacks against the Japanese rear – a useful lesson in deception for a student of warfare.

Officers conducting reconnaissance wore soldiers' uniforms. Deception was vital, says Zhukov. 'We knew that the Japanese tapped our telephone wires and intercepted radio messages.'

Intelligence was hard to come by because, as Zhukov says, there was no civilian population in the area and no Japanese deserters. Soviet planes, however, supplied good pictures of enemy defences. But as the Japanese also used deceptive means including mock-ups, Zhukov's men had to be very cautious in their conclusions and establish what was genuine and what was not by thorough rechecking.

At this juncture, Zhukov had a sharp difference of opinion with a major military figure, G.M. Shtern, who had been an adviser to the republican government in the Spanish Civil War, and was now commander of the Trans-Baikal Front, but had been sent to Khalkin Gol. (However, his role seems unclear; it may have been more diplomatic than military.)

On the third day of Zhukov's August offensive at the Khalkin Gol when action had slowed down, Zhukov had a conversation with G.M. Shtern. It seems his role was to cover Zhukov's rear, and assist the forces under his command with everything necessary. In case military operations were transferred to other sectors, turning into a war, Zhukov's army group would come directly under the Front (headed by Shtern). Until then the two commanders functioned independently, each dealing directly with Moscow.

Zhukov:

> Shtern came to me and said that he advised against overdoing things. He thought we should stop in order to build up forces in two or three days for subsequent strikes, and only after that, continue encircling the Japanese. He argued that the operation had slowed down and we were suffering major losses, especially in the north.
>
> In reply I said that war is war, and that losses are inevitable, that these losses could also be heavy especially when we are up against a serious and fierce enemy like the Japanese. But if we postponed our original plan for two or three days because of these losses and complications, one of two things could happen: either we would not carry out the plan at all, or would do it with great delay and, because of our indecisiveness, our losses would be ten times greater than we are suffering now when we are acting decisively. If we followed his advice we would multiply our losses ten times.

Then Zhukov asked if Shtern was ordering or advising him. If it was an order he wanted it in writing. But he had to warn him that he would protest at this written order to Moscow, because he didn't agree with it. Shern replied that he wasn't giving an order but advice, and would not put it in writing.

Zhukov: 'If that's the case, then I don't agree with your suggestion. I am responsible for the troops, and I am in command here. Your job is to keep me supplied and cover my rear. So please do not concern yourself with matters outside the bounds of your duty.'

Zhukov admits that it was a 'tough, agitated and rather unpleasant conversation'. Shtern left. Later, after about two or three hours, he returned after apparently consulting someone. He told Zhukov:

'Okay. I suppose you're right. I take back my suggestion.'

On 20 August 1939 Zhukov's forces began their general offensive aimed at surrounding and wiping out the enemy. The Japanese fought to the last man, says Zhukov. He says at least some soldiers began to 'see through official propaganda about the invincibility of the Imperial Army since it was suffering heavy casualties without winning a single battle in four months'.

Zhukov relates a story of a Japanese soldier (he calls him 'a real soldier') who suffered terribly from mosquito bites because he had no net. His company commander had ordered him to sit tight and not move his post so as not to be spotted. At night he was attacked by swarms of mosquitoes but he did not move until morning, bearing the mosquito bites stoically.

'When the Russians shouted something and raised their rifles,' the captive said, 'I put up my hands for I could no longer bear the agony.'

Zhukov says that he ordered a glass of vodka to be given the soldier because vital intelligence was needed in the very sector where the soldier was captured.

'To my surprise he looked at the glass and asked one of our men to please a take a drink from it first because he was afraid of poison. He said he was the only son and therefore his father's sole heir.' Zhukov says his interpreter observed that according to military rules given to Japanese soldiers by their officers, when captured they should die with the word Banzai on their lips. The soldier grinned and said: 'My father told me to return home alive and not dead.'

Looking at Japanese regular divisions in general, Zhukov says they fought stubbornly. 'I must admit that their infantry was staunch.'

On 31 August the last seats of Japanese resistance were wiped out. High Mongolian officials, including Marshal Khorlogin Choibalsan, visited the command post to congratulate those responsible for the victory.

Zhukov singles out for special praise a Soviet pilot who rescued his downed commander, landing his one-seater fighter plane on pockmarked terrain and then taking off with him (squeezing him into the cockpit) inside enemy territory. The pilot, says Zhukov, acted according to Suvorov's maxim: 'Save your comrade even if you die.'

A 'first' occurred in the little war in Mongolia: a Russian pilot rammed a Japanese fighter plane, destroying it. When he managed to return to his airfield there were fragments of the enemy aircraft embedded in the wing of his plane.

In recognition of the performance of its troops involved in the clash with Japanese forces, the Kremlin conferred a gold medal and the title of Hero of the Soviet Union on 70 soldiers.

The Japanese forces in Mongolia were encircled on 24 August. For three days the Soviet–Mongolian troops repelled fierce enemy attacks, with the Japanese finally withdrawing after sustaining heavy losses. By the close of August all major hostilities ended. On 15 September 1939 the USSR, Mongolia and Japan signed an agreement terminating the conflict.

Casualties for the Russian side were high given the short duration of the Khalkin Gol battle but they were much higher for the Japanese side. From May to September, the Japanese troops which invaded Mongolia lost about 61,000 in killed, wounded, missing and imprisoned. Nearly 10,000 Soviet servicemen were killed, died of wounds and diseases or were registered as missing in action for the same period. In addition, 16,000 were wounded.

The Japanese lost 660 planes while Soviet losses were 249 planes.

The architect of the Khalkin Gol victory, Georgi Zhukov, received a gold medal and the title of Hero of the Soviet Union (and, later, the title of Hero of the Mongolian Peoples Republic). In addition, Soviet orders and medals were bestowed on more than 17,000 Soviet and 99 Mongolian servicemen. Three pilots – Y.V. Smushkevich, S.I. Gritsevets and G.P. Kravchenko – became the USSR's first twice Heroes of the Soviet Union.

Almost a year after the truce agreement was signed, *The Times* in July 1940 published an article on the 'little war' saying:

> The Far Eastern Red Army last September inflicted a bloody defeat on Japan's finest troops. The Japanese War Office admitted 18,000 casualties. Recently the story was told to a gathering of retired officers in Tokyo. The Japanese forces, it was then disclosed, had been beaten by huge tanks throwing flames some thirty yards farther than the Japanese tanks opposing them could reach. The effect was irresistibly and horribly destructive.
>
> Hundreds of Japanese infantry were found dead on the battlefield burned beyond recognition. The Japanese were using their best troops from the Kwantung Army. This army is partly mechanized, and has Japan's best tanks as well as a strong air force. The air force, according to Japanese reports, quickly mastered the Far Eastern Army's aeroplanes, but was mastered by the latter's tanks of which 700 were employed along with 50,000 infantry according to the Information Department of the War Office in Tokyo.
>
> The discovery of the terrific powers of these new tanks, and the knowledge that the flat Manchurian plains offered opportunities for developing their maximum power, was the decisive factor in influencing the Japanese Army to accept the truce.

Meanwhile, the world had greeted with raised eyebrows and little credence the extraordinary communiques that had been issued by the

Japanese military. It was generally felt that such reports which came from Tokyo during the 'little war' in Mongolia of astronomical Russian losses in air battles (for instance that in two months' fighting almost 550 Russian and Mongolian planes were destroyed) from which the Japanese apparently emerged virtually unscathed, lacked the essential quality of propaganda – credibility. Later it was learned that the chief of the Press Bureau of Japan's vaunted Kwantung Army was dismissed for publishing false and boastful reports on imaginary successes of Japan's air force.

After the truce agreement the Mongolian–Manchurian frontier remained where it had always been: east of the Khalkin Gol river.

Zhukov's victory in Mongolia assumed political and strategic dimensions that went far beyond the confines of a remote Mongolian river valley. Having brought about a tactically superior concentration of forces, with tight centralized command and maximum flexibility, Zhukov attacked with a four-to-one superiority. Never did he deviate in future from this method save in a dire emergency.

The devastating counter-offensive of the Soviet and Mongolian troops, the unheard-of defeat of a crack Japanese army, made the Japanese high command reconsider their views of the power and combat readiness of the Red Army, and especially the morale of Russian soldiers.

A curiosity: Japan touched off the Khalkin Gol incident near the Russian border only a week after the Chamberlain government announced in the House of Commons on 6 May that Britain and France had exchanged views after the receipt of Russian proposals on mutual security.

Note

1. Zhukov's *Reminiscences and Reflections*, 1985. Also, K. Simonov, 'The Khalkin Gol' (in *Literaturnaya Gazeta*, 24 July 1974).

6

HITLER GOES TO WAR

September 3, 1939: Hitler's attack on Poland has on this Sabbath day become a world war!

WILLIAM L. SHIRER, *Berlin Diary*, 1941

Russia will collapse like a pack of cards.

DR JOSEF GOEBBELS, *Diaries, 1942–3*

I told Stalin we would need about 40 minutes to get our bearings.

G.K. ZHUKOV at war, 26 June 1941

31 August 1939. It is a warm summer evening in the German border town of Gleiwitz where a Nazi-inspired provocation is about to occur. Suddenly, a group of Hitler's agents wearing Polish military uniforms break into a local radio station. Some reports vary, saying members of the group are criminals recruited from a local jail to do the dirty work. Next, one of the 'Poles' turns on the microphone and makes a short speech to the effect that it is high time to start a war with Germany – and he shouts anti-German slogans. While he speaks, the rest of the group fake an exchange of gunfire with German border guards, the shots being picked up by the microphone. It is not clear if the criminals (or 'Poles') survived the incident. Some versions mention the firing of bullets and a number of corpses.

The broadcast lasted only seven minutes but it served its purpose. The Nazi secret service had carried out its propaganda task of creating a pretext for Hitler's Blitzkrieg attack on Poland. Two years later, when Hitler attacked Soviet Russia to obtain *Lebensraum* in the East he justified it by saying that Stalin was getting ready to attack him. Therefore, it was a 'preventive war'.[1]

The opening shots in the war on Poland were fired by the German navy the morning after the border incident.

At 4.40 a.m. on 1 September 1939, the German battleship *Schleswig-Holstein*, which only seven days earlier had paid a 'friendship visit' to the Free City of Danzig (Gdansk), suddenly opened fire with all her guns on the Polish coastal fort of Westerplatte, while her armoured hold disgorged a 4,000-strong landing party. At the same time, German armies rolled into Poland along the length of the border, while 2,000 planes were readied to drop thousands of tons of bombs on hundreds of sleepy towns and villages of that peaceful country. On the main roads clogged with fleeing humanity, the Luftwaffe had a field day. (One report says that in the towns an hour before noon even groups of boy scouts were machine-gunned as they stood on the steps of churches.)

The Second World War had begun.

Zhukov makes a political comment on Poland in his war memoirs. He sums up the period leading to the eruption of the Second World War as one 'characterized by pressures on the part of Hitler, and passivity on the part of Britain and France'. He goes on to say that 'Even after Germany had attacked Poland on 1 September 1939, her allies – Britain and France – having declared war on Germany, in fact did not lift a finger.'

Poland was quickly overrun. But several parallel developments triggered protests in the West. Less than two weeks before the invasion, Russia and Germany signed a non-aggression pact, on 23 August 1939. Then, in mid-September Stalin invaded the eastern half of Poland, in effect preventing Hitler's armies from getting closer to Russia's western border. (A British author, Flight-Lieutenant Hubert Griffith, makes the interesting point in his book, *This is Russia*, London 1943, that if Germany's armies had got 'a few hundred miles nearer the heart of Russia, then on all the laws of human chances, Moscow would have fallen – and more than Moscow'.)

Hitler's determination to settle accounts with Poland had been obvious to many people for months. For instance, when Italian Foreign Minister Count Ciano spoke to Hitler and his Foreign Minister Ribbentrop in mid-August he entered in his diary: 'The decision to fight is implacable ... There is nothing that can be done. Hitler has decided to strike and strike he will.' As D.F. Fleming says, the decision to strike at Poland was therefore fixed before the pact with Russia was signed, and according to documents produced at the International Military Tribunal at Nuremberg, Hitler's concrete plan for war with Poland – Operation White – was included in a German military Directive in April 1939.

Losing no time, Hitler set about conquering Europe, introducing a regime of terror and violence in the occupied countries, meanwhile declaring the 'right' to eliminate whole peoples. The misanthropy was specifically aimed at Slavs, not to mention Jews. But the quest for *Lebensraum* in the East remained; it was one of Hitler's oldest theses.

Telltale evidence of Hitler's agenda for conquest as well as his spurious racial theories are found in his raging testament, *Mein Kampf*. A little-known fact is that Hitler had censored some of the more lurid parts of this National Socialist bible almost up to the time of the Munich deal of 1938. (This deal, signed by Germany, Italy, France and Britain, allowed Hitler, in the words of US historian Herbert Feis, to tear Czechoslovakia apart, leaving Poland and Russia exposed to German attack.) Before the war, politicians who read *Mein Kampf* in English or French translation were unaware that they were reading an expurgated edition of Hitler's book, put out with sanitary cuts to disarm the British and French. In the early 1930s Hitler's lawyers filed suit against a French publisher who vainly attempted to put out an unabridged version of the book.[2]

On 21 June 1941, the day before Hitler attacked Russia, he sent a message to Mussolini telling him he had previously lived in fear that Stalin would attack him first and spoil a mighty future air blitz on Great Britain. He said he would now start a 'war in the East' about which there was certainty of 'great success'. Hitler said he 'waited until this moment, Duce, to send you this information because the final decision will not be made until 7 o'clock tonight'. Hitler doubtless hoped that a significant number of people in the Western democracies who feared the Bolshevik menace more than the Fascist would now feel they had a spiritual home in his National Socialist party.

German preparations for the coming Blitzkrieg in the East, known as Plan Barbarossa, involved various measures – military, economic, political and ideological – to defeat and eliminate the Soviet Union, and liquidate a large part of the Russian population. In Britain, which would soon become an ally of Russia, Winston Churchill was alert to the precarious position of his nation, saying: 'We are no longer safe in our island home.'

Up until 22 June 1941, Zhukov, although anxious like many of his colleagues about Moscow's potential enemies, spoke out little, being reluctant to engage in polemics at high-level discussions on Russia's preparations for war. But with the arrival of Hitler's armies, Zhukov found his voice (after, he admits, a short period of awkwardness in front of Stalin) and his depth of experience showed itself when he took on the role of trouble-shooter. Also, he was ready and willing, when he thought necessary, to argue with Stalin. Stalin, despite his flaws, quickly recognized Zhukov's consistent ability to solve difficult problems on the battlefield.

Although the Kremlin miscalculated the time of the invasion, and was late in taking steps to alert front-line troops, the Soviet General Staff did not underestimate Germany's military might. Before the invasion, Zhukov was himself aware of the real possibility that due to the strength of the Wehrmacht, the Red Army would be unable to hold the borders in case of an attack. During the second half of the thirties, Germany was depicted as the main potential enemy, and foreign military experts noted the year by year strengthening of the Red Army. In a speech to military cadets in May 1941 one month before the invasion – Stalin admitted that Germany 'has the best army both in weaponry and in organization'. But he added: 'The Germans are making a mistake if they think that their army is an ideal, invincible army. There are no invincible armies.'

At the time of the invasion, the military might of the Third Reich was based on a powerful war economy built up in the thirties. During the war Germany's strategic potential sharply increased as the manpower and raw material resources and industrial facilities of nearly the whole of Europe came under its control. The Nazi forces were supplied by munitions and engineering plants in Austria, Belgium, France and Czechoslovakia, while neutral countries – Spain, Portugal, Turkey and Sweden – delivered strategic raw materials such as tin, tungsten, nickel, chromium and iron ore. By the time of the invasion of Russia, Germany and the occupied countries had at least twice the metal, electric power and coal producing capacity of the Soviet Union. This disparity became acute when Hitler's armies occupied the more industrialized western regions of Russia.

Given German superiority at the beginning of the war, most British and American experts agreed that the Germans would slash through Russia like a knife through butter, that the war would be over in a few months if not weeks. Much of the Western press viewed Mother Russia as a huge colossus with feet of Communist clay.

As Hitler's armies were poised to strike, Georgi Zhukov was on duty at the office of the General Staff in Moscow. All personnel of the Soviet General Staff and the Defence Commissariat (Moscow's defense ministry), like Zhukov, had been on the job since the previous day under orders to remain on duty. The reason: earlier that day

Lieutenant General Maxim Purkayev had telephoned Zhukov and warned him that a German sergeant-major had crossed over to the Russian frontier guards with information that German troops were moving towards jumping-off areas and that an attack would begin on the morning of 22 June. Zhukov was then Chief of the General Staff; Purkayev was Chief of Staff of the Kiev Military District which had the grave responsibility of defending a large part of the frontier in the event of an attack.

Dozens of other warnings of imminent invasion were received in Moscow, including some from Russia's future allies. Churchill, who made no bones about his loathing of Communism and had struggled against the Soviet regime for two decades, warned Stalin on 3 April 1941 about the danger hanging over Russia. In his memoirs Zhukov says that Stalin received Churchill's message with suspicion.

Stalin's paranoia was well known. He had earlier told Zhukov that 'a man is sending us very important information about the intentions of the Hitler government but we have doubts'. Zhukov says that Stalin was speaking of his intelligence agent, Dr Richard Sorge, who was then on the staff of the German ambassador in Japan, but that he himself knew nothing of this until the end of the war.

A month before the invasion Sorge dispatched to Moscow almost precise data on the concentration of Nazi divisions on the Soviet western border. At great risk to his life, a week before the attack (15 June) Sorge relayed to Moscow one short but accurate message: 'The war will start on 22 June.' Shortly after radioing this message, Sorge and members of his spy ring were arrested by Japanese police. Sorge was executed for spying in 1944.

In an attempt to mislead the Russians before the invasion, the Goebbels Propaganda Ministry launched a large-scale misinformation campaign. Military historian Pavel Zhilin admits that 'extensive dissemination of false reports coupled with the secrecy with which it shifted and concentrated troops in the East' enabled the German Command to achieve positive results in its preparations for a surprise attack on Russia. Zhukov describes in his memoirs a directive issued by Hitler's High Command entitled 'Misinforming the Enemy' drawn up to conceal all work on Plan Barbarossa. He mentions a flood of false rumours and false information released by the intelligence department of the German General Staff. Adding to the uncertainties and intrigues that were afloat during the year before the invasion, rumours had circulated that the British and French armed forces were themselves preparing to invade the Caucasus; that bogus documents were printed 'confirming' these orders. (During Russia's border war with Finland in 1939–40 there were in Paris and London advocates of retaliatory action against Moscow.)

Up until 22 June the Kremlin also received imprecise, even contradictory intelligence reports. General F.I. Golikov, the head of the intelligence division of the Soviet General Staff, issued a report three months before the German invasion saying an attack against Russia would come 'after the victory over England or the conclusion with her of an honourable peace treaty'. The Golikov report added: 'Rumours and documents to the effect that war against the USSR is inevitable this spring should be regarded as misinformation coming from the English or perhaps even the German intelligence service.' (In his memoirs Zhukov highlights the last sentence in italics.)

As soon as he was informed of the arrival of the German defector, Zhukov relayed the news to Marshal Timoshenko, who was the Defence Commissar, and Stalin. Zhukov was summoned to Stalin's Kremlin office with Timoshenko.

Zhukov recounts: 'Taking with me a draft of a directive [to alert the troops], I went to the Kremlin with the Commissar and, also, Lieutenant General Nikolai Vatutin of the General Staff. On the way we agreed that at all costs we must get permission to alert the troops.'

Stalin was alone when he received the visitors and was plainly worried.

'The German generals may have sent this turncoat to provoke a conflict,' Stalin said.

'No,' Timoshenko replied. 'We think he is telling the truth.'

At that moment members of the Politburo (the Communist Party's chief policy-making body) came in.

'What are we to do?' Stalin asked.

Nobody answered.

Timoshenko said that a directive must be issued immediately to alert all troops in the border districts.

'Read it!' said Stalin.

Zhukov read out the draft directive.

Stalin responded: 'It's too early to issue such a directive – perhaps the question can still be settled peacefully. We must prepare a short directive stating that an attack may begin with provocative actions by the German forces. The troops of the border districts must not fall for any provocations, and avoid complications.'

At this point, Zhukov and Vatutin were sent off to the next room where they quickly drew up a draft of the directive to be sent to the border districts. Returning to Stalin's office they asked for permission to read the directive. Stalin listened to it, read it over again, and made amendments. It was then signed by Timoshenko and Zhukov.

German armies attacked before dawn on 22 June 1941, moving in three main directions. Zhukov says categorically that reports which circulated after the war that some commanders were either peacefully asleep or making merry without suspecting that a calamity was about to fall on their country, are untrue. What is undisputed among historians is that the first blows on 22 June caught the Soviet Union by surprise.

The blows, on the ground and in the air, were staggering. So many hundreds of Soviet planes were knocked out of the air that Field Marshal Albert Kesselring described the swelling number of kills of Russian pilots as 'sheer infanticide'.

On the afternoon of invasion day Zhukov received his first post-invasion assignment. Stalin phoned him, saying: 'Our front commanders lack combat experience and are evidently a bit confused.' He said a decision had already been taken to send Zhukov to the South-Western Front and that he would have to leave his job as Chief of the General Staff and fly to the endangered city of Kiev at once. Stalin was piqued when Zhukov asked who would be his replacement at the General Staff. 'Don't lose time!' he snapped, adding that Zhukov should leave Vatutin in his place.

'I phoned my family to tell them not to wait for me,' says Zhukov, 'and in 40 minutes I was airborne. Only then did I remember that I had had nothing to eat since yesterday. The flyers helped out, treating me to strong tea and sandwiches.'

So began the war for Zhukov, a war that lasted 1,418 days and nights.

Life for Zhukov, during the first weeks and months of the war, was especially demanding. He was often on the job for 20 hours. To keep awake he drank cups of strong coffee and when the snows fell and he was on the field of battle he would take a 15-minute workout on skis. He spent countless hours pouring over maps, telegraphing front-line commanders, drawing up orders for the troops, discussing tactics with senior staff officers, dressing down some of them, demoting or relieving those he felt were ineffectual. He flew out to one battlefield after another, speaking sharply to officers who seemed to be floundering

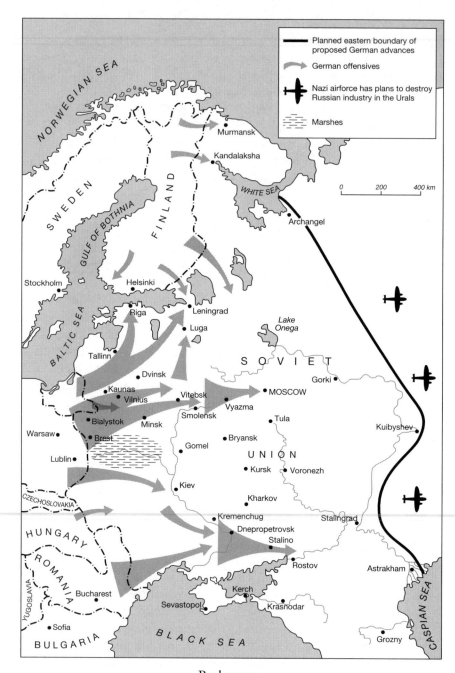

Barbarossa

and, it is said, ordering deserters or cowards to be shot at once. (His mobile bodyguard was said to double as a firing squad.) Often the fact of his presence inspired confidence in the troops. Meanwhile, he had frequent meetings with Stalin, a man whom he had once held in awe but whose lofty reputation was not sustained in his eyes. Zhukov soon learned that the Great Leader was not infallible. On occasion other officers waiting to see Stalin in the Kremlin were horrified to hear Zhukov and Stalin screeching at each other. But there were a handful of ranking generals brave enough to stand up to Stalin and survive; foremost among them was Zhukov. The pair maintained a working relationship throughout the war, each earning a measure of respect from the other, although the relationship never developed into one of friendship. Stalin, Zhukov discovered, had widely contrasting moods and a despotic temper; he learned to identify the mood by the way the Supreme Commander-in-Chief held his Dunhill pipe, and whether it was lit or not; whether he smoothed his moustache, or even by which tunic Stalin wore.

At the start, it was clear that the Red Army was outclassed by a stronger, better-equipped, more combat-experienced foe. The invasion army was qualitatively superior to the defenders. It had 190 divisions with about 5½ million men, almost 5,000 tanks, 47,000 artillery systems and mortars, 4,500 combat planes and almost 200 warships. Opposing this juggernaut were about 170 divisions comprising some 3 million men, nearly 14,000 tanks and over 10,000 aircraft. But in quality the Russian equipment left much to be desired.

Tempers flared often early in the Blitzkrieg and Zhukov records that a week after the invasion Stalin on two occasions 'reacted violently' to alarming events in the war.

The disaster falling on the USSR in the opening weeks and months of the war has been written about in thousands of books and articles. Many experts believe Russia's combat readiness was badly affected by poor analysis of the situation when German forces were massing on the border in readiness for invasion. It is officially admitted that at least some Russian border units were at peacetime levels of alert. Also, far too many officers were inexperienced and ill-trained. A potent reason was the legacy of Stalin's repressions within the military. In 1941 the Soviet Army was still having difficulty coping with the Great Purge of the late thirties when thousands of senior officers were executed or imprisoned. Zhukov, clearly embittered, cites the repressions in his memoirs, recalling several high-ranking officers he knew personally who were shot. One is Marshal Mikhail Tukhachevsky, a man he fondly remembers as 'an ace of military thinking, a star of the first magnitude'. Already in the 1930s, says Zhukov, Tukhachevsky 'warned that our Number One enemy was Germany'.

Zhukov cites Stalin's failures prior to the invasion. He says, for example: 'In the last few prewar months the leadership did not call for any steps that should have been taken when the threat of war was particularly great.' In addition although he does not explicitly attack Stalin for the repressions, he doesn't have to: his focus on the loss of Tukhachevsky and other high-ranking officers is a strong indictment of Stalin and his despotic power. But in his opinion Stalin did well in the political field, since Stalin had kept Russia out of a war with Hitler's Germany for almost two years, giving the entire nation, including the army, time to build up its strength; and for the army in particular time to undergo reorganization, even though this wasn't completed by invasion day.

Zhukov is self-critical. He reproaches himself and the military for their shortcomings in the prewar era. He does however explain that before the invasion he was only in the high post of Chief of the General Staff for less than five months and that it was impossible to achieve much in that short period. But he is unequivocal: 'I want to say loud and clear . . . that the errors made by the leadership do not lift the blame for blunders and misjudgements from the military command at all levels.'

As the Wehrmacht continued its remarkable offensive, moving a sizeable force and hundreds of panzers taken from strategic reserves to replenish losses, a few German generals began to realize that the road ahead was not going to be all downhill. Shortly after the invasion, Franz Halder, the German Chief of Staff of the Land Forces jotted in his diary: 'The enemy keeps bringing up new and fresh forces from the rear against our tank thrust . . . As was expected, the enemy has passed into an offensive in considerable tank strength . . . Troop movement has been registered on several sectors.' Another German officer, Panzer General Hermann Hoth, looking back at the first weeks of he invasion, said: 'A formidable obstacle hindering the advance of German forces were powerful enemy counterblows.'

And here is what German Field Marshal Erich von Manstein says in his book, *Lost Victories* during the period when the Russian side continued to suffer big reverses: 'Soon we were forced to defend ourselves on the northern bank of the Dvina river [west of Moscow] against enemy attacks supported by one tank division. On some sectors things were becoming critical.'

Although Zhukov concedes that in the first few weeks his troops were unable to smash the enemy and arrest their advance, he says that they had done 'the main job' – the enemy shock force heading for Kiev had been held up. However, Zhukov says that in spite of the heroism of the officers and men, in spite of the staying power of the commanding officers the situation in all sectors of the Western Front continued to worsen. After nightfall on the last days of June, Russian troops withdrew from Minsk, the capital of Belorussia (today the Republic of Belarus). Zhukov records: 'Breaking into the city the Nazi units began a savage massacre of its inhabitants, burning and destroying buildings and works of cultural value including historical monuments.'

While Russian unpreparedness and chaos on the military front is well known, a different picture emerges on the domestic front, especially concerning heavy industry, including the war industry. Before the invasion Russia had wisely built up a second industrial-war base in the Volga region, the Urals and in Siberia, far from the border. By the summer of 1941 almost a quarter of the country's munitions factories had been located in these areas. After the war began hundreds of factories that once stood in the European parts of Russia were relocated east of the Volga. This immense task was decisive to the war effort.

In his memoirs, written several decades after the war, Zhukov discusses the status of the army before invasion:

> The morale and fighting spirit of the troops and their political consciousness and maturity were always exceptionally high ... But today I cannot name a single major trend in the development of our armed forces that should have been written off, jettisoned or repealed. The period between 1939 and the middle of 1941 [when a non-aggression pact existed between Berlin and Moscow] was marked on the whole by transformations which gave the Soviet Union a brilliant army, and readied it well for defence.

Does Zhukov exaggerate? Should other states have done more to resist Hitler at the start of the Second World War? Dr Vladimir Zolotarev, head of Russia's Institute of Military History, said in May 2001 that, although the Soviet armies were battered in the opening months of invasion they continued to resist stubbornly. But he notes that after Hitler invaded Poland and occupied several other European countries, France with the second biggest army in Europe capitulated 'without any resistance to speak of' in June 1940.

This is how Zhukov sums up: 'History gave us too small a period of peace to get everything organized as it should be. We began many things correctly, and many other things we had had no time to complete. Our miscalculation regarding the possible time of Nazi Germany's attack had a telling effect. It lay at the root of the flaws in the preparations to repulse the first enemy onslaught.'

As the war progressed, Zhukov was constantly talking to or visiting commanders in the field. On the last day of June, Zhukov conferred by telegraph with Front Commander, General of the Army Pavlov. 'I realized,' he says, 'that the commander himself was not sufficiently familiar with the situation.'

What follows is an extract from Zhukov's conversation with Pavlov, typical of countless others he had with commanders during the war, when he wasn't immediately able to meet the front-line officers face to face. Those who knew Zhukov say that although as a military leader Zhukov often had to crack the whip, that he could display a hot temper and curse wildly when facing incompetent or disobedient commanders, nevertheless, except for his dealings with these officers, he kept his head in the most critical situations. On this particular occasion Zhukov knew that even a slight loss of control of his army by Pavlov meant a rise in casualties. It seems this was the case with Pavlov.

Zhukov: We can take no decision on the Western Front without knowing what is going on in the Minsk, Bobruisk and Slutsk areas. Please report on the substance of the matter.

Pavlov: In the Minsk area, the 44th Rifle Corps is pulling back south of the Mogilev highway ... In the Slutsk area, according to air observers, the 210th Motorized Rifle Division was engaged in fierce fighting yesterday ... In the Bobruisk area, the enemy built a bridge at 0400 hours today with 12 panzers crossing the river.

Zhukov: The Germans have announced over the radio that they have surrounded two armies east of Belostok. There is evidently some measure of truth in this. Why has your Headquarters failed to send out liaison men to locate the troops? Where are [Generals] Kulik, Boldin and Kuznetsov? Where is the cavalry corps? Surely, air observers have sighted the cavalry.

Pavlov: Yes, a large measure of truth ...

Zhukov: Your main mission is to locate the units as quickly as possible and withdraw them behind the Berezina river. Supervise personally and pick capable commanders for the task. The High Command wants you to assemble all troops of the Front promptly, and to ready them for action. In no event should an enemy breakthrough be permitted in the Bobruisk and Borisov areas.

But Zhukov says that the situation in Pavlov's sector did not improve. On 30 June Stalin called Zhukov at the General Staff and ordered him to summon Pavlov to Moscow where he was put on trial.

'I could hardly recognize him,' he says of Pavlov. 'He had changed so much in eight days of the war.'

The only cheering news at the start of the war had come from the Black Sea where warships under Admiral Filipp Oktyabrsky had used their anti-aircraft guns to beat off a Nazi air armada, and at the frontier fortress of Brest, which was still fighting back after a month of being completely surrounded. Its heroic defenders, including some women doctors and nurses, held out until the end, refusing to surrender.

The first major encounter with the enemy after several weeks of fighting was the Battle of Smolensk (10 July–10 September 1941). This battle occupies an important place among all the operations during the first summer of war. Zhukov writes that many German divisions and regiments which had planned to march through the streets of Moscow perished on the land around this ancient Russian city located some 300 kilometres west of Moscow.

Even though the Red Army was unable to hold Smolensk, Zhukov calls the battle a strategic success. 'The enemy aimed to cut our Western Front in two by committing powerful shock forces against it, to encircle the main Soviet force at Smolensk, and thereby open the road to Moscow.' He adds: 'A furious battle ensued beside the walls ... of Smolensk, which had once risen as a next-to-impregnable obstacle to Napoleon's armies heading for Moscow.' In Smolensk, he says, 'heavy fighting developed round every house and street, and inhabited locality'. He adds that his armies were able to stop the Wehrmacht for a short time but that this enabled the Soviet Army to gain time and permit the buildup of strategic reserves, and also allowed time to carry out defensive works on the Moscow sector.[3]

Zhukov says that, although it had been impossible to smash the enemy at Smolensk, as the Soviet High Command had planned, the enemy's shock forces were 'worn to a frazzle and visibly weakened'. (Incidentally, it was at the Battle of Smolensk that a new weapon, multiple rocket launchers – christened Katyushas – were used by Russian soldiers for the first time.) The Wehrmacht admitted that at Smolensk it lost 250,000 officers and men. On 30 July the Nazi command ordered Army Group Centre to take up defensive positions.

In conclusion Zhukov says the Battle of Smolensk plus the mounting activity and resistance of the Soviet troops of the Northern and North-Western Fronts as well as the Baltic Fleet and the air force, caused a sizeable breach in Plan Barbarossa. Zhukov evinces joy over the Smolensk battle because he says the fact that the German offensive was halted, even for a short while, was 'an important strategic success'. It is now generally agreed that at Smolensk Hitler's Blitzkrieg doctrine suffered its first serious blow since Poland was overrun in 1939.

Notes

1. At the Nuremberg International Military Tribunal in 1946, Hans Fritzsche, chief of the Home Press Department of Goebbels' Ministry of Propaganda, told the court that Germany had no reason for accusing Moscow of preparing an armed attack. Also, German historian Professor Gerhard Ritter has written: 'It is high time to abandon the Nazi legend that the war against Russia was a preventive one, that it was a defensive move against an anticipated attack . . . It was not a war to defend Europe but rather to seize power over the whole continent.' *(Stuttgarter Zeitung*, 22 June 1951.)

   Ten years before the Nuremberg trials, Hitler declared, also in Nuremberg (12 September 1936): 'If I had Russia's Ural Mountains with their incalculable store of treasures in raw materials, Siberia with its vast forests, and the Ukraine with its tremendous wheat fields, Germany and the National Socialist leadership would swim in plenty.' From Hitler's *My New Order*, New York, 1941.

2. Under Hitler's plans, Britain and France, two nations generally applauded for making tremendous contributions to world culture, were doomed. Had Germany won the war the future for Britain was spelled out by Walter Darre, a Nazi racial expert: 'As soon as we beat England we shall make an end of Englishmen once and for all. Able-bodied men will be exported to the continent. The old and weak will be exterminated.' As for France, Hitler said it was a 'country of negroids' which would fall into decline and that the French were a 'degenerate, voluptuous nation' that could not be Germanized. But these doomsday plans for Britain and France hinged on a successful campaign in Russia.

3. Shortly after the invasion General Gunther von Kluge and other German officers began to read histories of Napoleon's ill-starred invasion of Russia in 1812. Hitler also studied Napoleon's campaign in Russia. 'I will not make the same mistake as Napoleon,' he said. General Gunther Blumentritt says that in addition to Kluge, Generals Brauchitsch, Halder, Jodl and Rundstedt read Caulaincourt's account of Napoleon's Russian campaign with the greatest

attention. But during Christmas 1941, six months after the invasion, when Nazi troops lived under the shadow of Napoleon's retreat from the burned-out city of Moscow, it is reported that a Nazi order went out banning the circulation among officers of all books dealing with Napoleon.

7

MOSCOW IN DANGER

Moscow: those syllables can start
A tumult in the Russian heart.

ALEXANDER PUSHKIN

In five nights of raids on Moscow the Luftwaffe has accomplished little more than the entire Swiss Navy accomplished in World War One.

ERSKINE CALDWELL, author of Tobacco Road, in Moscow, July 1941

By that time [October 1941] Zhukov had already been recalled from Leningrad to Moscow and on the GHQ's orders was on his way to join the troops defending the capital.

ALEXANDER VASILEVSKY, A Lifelong Cause, 1978

The Nazi elite had not the slightest doubt that their army's Moscow offensive would succeed. Dr Goebbels, the propaganda chief, even ordered all Berlin newspapers to reserve space in their 12 October issue for 'last-minute reports' about the fall of Moscow. Nazi generals, meanwhile, had plans to demolish the ancient city. At a conference in the headquarters of Army Group Centre, Hitler spelled out the fate in store for Moscow:

> The city is to be surrounded. No Russian soldier, or civilian, man, woman or child, must leave the city. Every attempt to do so is to be frustrated by force. Preparations have been made to flood Moscow and its environs by means of giant installations, and to drown it in water. Where Moscow stands today, there will be a vast sea to hide the metropolis of the Russian people forever from the gaze of the civilized world.[1]

The Battle of Moscow comprised a whole series of diverse but extremely intense operations over a vast area, and was fought without interruption all through the autumn of 1941 and winter of 1941–42. The combatants employed over 2 million men, about 2,500 tanks, 1,850 aircraft and some 30,000 artillery pieces and mortars.

By midsummer of 1941, three months after the invasion, it was apparent that the German High Command had underestimated the resistance capability of the Russians. The German operations outside Leningrad, in the Ukraine and outside Moscow were remarkably successful on the face of it, but who could tell what the final reckoning would be? Hitler's generals had to admit that these successes did not bring about the rapid destruction of all enemy fighting forces or crush the fighting spirit of the defenders.

In early September, following the Battle of Smolensk, Hitler's armies on the central sector of the front were compelled to halt their offensive. But a major assault against Moscow was yet to come.

The first general offensive, with the aim of capturing Moscow – codenamed Typhoon – began on 30 September. Hitler's forces intended to envelop Moscow from north and south by means of powerful panzer and motorized assaults via the cities of Kalinin and Tula, while infantry formations were to advance frontally from the west. Spearheading the attack was General Heinz Guderian's tank group and the 2nd Army. On 2 October the enemy dealt powerful blows at the troops of the Western and Reserve Fronts. Zhukov says an 'extremely grave situation' developed south of Moscow where two Soviet armies found themselves faced with the threat of encirclement.

On orders of the Supreme Command a reinforced 1st Guards Rifle Corps was formed with its mission to hold up the enemy advance south of Moscow and enable the two threatened armies to withdraw.

Here are the recollections of Guderian, sometimes called 'the god of tank warfare':

> 2nd October . . . Simultaneously in the operational zone of the 24th Panzer Corps near Mtsensk, northeast of Orel, bitter fighting broke out, involving the 4th Panzer Division . . . A large number of Russian T-34 tanks were engaged in the battle, causing considerable losses to our panzers. The superiority that our panzers had so far was now lost and seized by the adversary. This wiped out the chances of a rapid and uninterrupted success.

Guderian added: 'The planned swift offensive on Tula has had to be put off.'

At 2:30 in the morning of 8 October Zhukov phoned Stalin who was still up and working. After outlining the situation outside Moscow, he said:

'The main danger now lies in the weak Mozhaisk defence line. Because of this, enemy armoured troops may suddenly appear near

Moscow. We must bring up forces quickly from every place possible to the Mozhaisk line.'

'Where are the 19th and 20th armies, and Boldin's group of the Western Front?' Stalin asked. 'Where are the 24th and 32nd armies of the Reserve Front?'

'They've been encircled to the west and northwest of Vyazma,' Zhukov replied.

'What do you propose to do?'

'I'm leaving at once for the Reserve Front to see Budenny.'

'Do you know where the Front's headquarters is?'

'I'll look for it in the neighbourhood of Maloyaroslavets.'

'All right. Go to Budenny and call me from there.'

Budenny, the moustachioed hero of Civil War days and perhaps the best known veteran in the Red Army, would have been a prize captive for Hitler. But Zhukov found him, apparently unconcerned, pouring over a map. Intense fighting was raging around Kaluga, some 200 kilometres southwest of Moscow. Zhukov says that few men were left alive after five days of bitter fighting 'but heroic self-sacrifice frustrated the enemy plans . . . and enabled our troops to gain time and organize defences at the approaches to Moscow'. At the same time students from the artillery and machine-gunners' schools arrived in the area where they took up positions to strengthen the sector.

On 10 October, after arriving at the tiny village of Krasnovidovo, where the Western Front Headquarters were located, a phone call came for Zhukov. Stalin was on the line.

'The supreme command has decided to appoint you Commander of the Western Front. Konev will be your deputy. Any objections?'

'No, what objections can there be? I think Konev should be put in command of the forces on the Kalinin sector. That sector is far too isolated, and we've got to make it a secondary division of the Front.'

'Very well,' Stalin agreed. 'The remaining units of the Reserve Front, the troops of the Mozhaisk defence line, are to come under your command. Assume control of the Western Front and act quickly. I've already signed the order, and it has been sent to the Fronts.'

'I'll act on your instructions right away, but I'm asking for larger reserves to be sent as soon as possible, since we may expect an intensification of the enemy thrust towards Moscow anytime now.'

Constantly on the move, from one headquarters to another, Zhukov was nevertheless in his element; his optimism and confidence in himself never wavered despite the critical situations that kept cropping up on practically all sectors of the front. One reason for his optimism was his knowledge of the ranking generals under his command. 'They were all experienced military leaders and we had full confidence in them,' he says. 'We were sure that, at the head of their troops, they would do everything possible to stop the enemy advance on Moscow.' In his memoirs, Zhukov pauses to heap praise on Generals Rokossovsky, Sokolovsky, Lobachev, Malinin and Psurtsev. He identifies the last officer as 'an energetic signal troops commander' who provided adequate communications for the troops at the Front.

But the situation was grim for hundreds of thousands of encircled Red Army men. Zhukov minces no words:

> West and northwest of Vyazma, our troops continued to fight heroically behind enemy lines, trying to break out of encirclement ... but all their attempts were futile. The Command of the Front and the Supreme Command helped the surrounded troops by bombing the enemy battle formations and by air-dropping provisions and ammunition. But this was all they could do, since they lacked both manpower and equipment.

Once again, Zhukov claims that their sacrifices were decisive. 'Having found themselves surrounded by the enemy, the troops did not lay down their arms but continued to fight courageously. In this way they pinned down the main forces of the enemy, and did not allow the offensive towards Moscow to gather momentum.'

It is estimated that 662,000 Soviet officers and men were taken prisoner by the Wehrmacht in the vicinity of Vyazma in October 1941. Only a few escaped capture. One who escaped, the former commander of the 45th Cavalry Division, Stuchenko, told Zhukov:

> What was left of our division broke out of encirclement in order to link up with the Front. We engaged the Germans whenever we could afford to, killing several thousands of them. Around the middle of October there was hardly a day without a fight, each new encounter more fierce than the last. Many outstanding commanders, commissars [political officers], and soldiers were killed.

Meanwhile, air raids on Moscow intensified. The alarm was sounded nearly every night. Authorities announced a state of siege in the city. Zhukov says that 'stern measures were introduced to prevent any possible breach of discipline'. Moscow residents 'quickly cut short any "panic-mongers"' whom Zhukov described as 'accomplices of the enemy'.

To repel the bombers the Supreme Command concentrated large

groups of fighters and bombers in the Moscow area. The air defence must have been effective because an American novelist, Erskine Caldwell, who was in Moscow at the time of the air raids describes watching several German air attacks from his hotel rooftop: 'In five nights of raiding the Germans accomplished little more than the entire Swiss Navy accomplished in the First World War,' Caldwell said, adding that few enemy planes were able to penetrate Moscow's air defence. The number of planes over the city at any one time was never more than six or seven, he says. A total of 132 raids on Moscow were reported between July and December 1941. An official announcement said hundreds of enemy planes were shot down on the approaches to the city.[2]

Not only was there a striking number of anti-aircraft guns and balloons with steel wires hanging beneath, but the air force kept the bulk of the attacking planes outside the capital. In addition, the Russians had something 'up their sleeve': hundreds of pilots who, to stop the approaching planes, got close enough to use their propeller to cut into a wing or tail of the attacker. Needless to say the rammers often themselves ended up in a fiery death. While many voluntarily chose to ram an enemy plane, there were actual orders issued, telling pilots when it was necessary to ram (if an incoming plane was headed for a vital target, etc.), and how to ram and survive. Some pilots survived more than one ramming. Luftwaffe pilots, meanwhile, were understandably jittery when approaching the skies over Moscow.

Zhukov describes the enormous preparations the civilian population of Moscow made to protect the approaches to their city. He says that some 250,000 Muscovites (mostly women and teenagers) erected an interior 'defensive perimeter' in October and November. They built 72,000 metres of anti-tank ditches, 52,500 metres of other anti-tank obstacles, and dug 128,000 metres of communication and other trenches. Volunteers made up the nucleus of many special scout and ski squads and were active in partisan detachments. Also, twelve people's volunteer divisions were formed made up of workers, engineers, scientists, artists and writers. None of them, says Zhukov, were skilled soldiers and 'what they learned of warcraft they picked up directly on the battlefield'.

Troops of the Western Front read the following appeal during the critical days of October:

Comrades! In this grim hour of mortal danger to our State, the life of every soldier belongs to the Motherland. She demands of each of us the utmost effort, courage, fortitude and heroism. The Motherland calls on us to rise like an unbreakable wall in the way of the fascist hordes and to defend our beloved Moscow. Vigilance, iron discipline, organization, resolute action, an unbending will to win and readiness for self-sacrifice are required today more than ever before.

The Wehrmacht did all it could to capture Tula, some 200 kilometres south of Moscow. Tank commander Guderian counted on taking Tula on the march and then moving on to Moscow from the south. But he failed to do so. Defending Tula was a handful of badly damaged Red army divisions that were down to 1,500 combatants or less. At full strength they would have had at least 5,000 men. Armed workers' detachments and a workers' regiment fought alongside regular troops.

The city of Tula, says Zhukov, and its people 'played an important role in defeating the Germans at the approaches to Moscow'.

Guderian reported on 6 November 1941: 'It is a torture for our troops and a disaster for our cause, because our opponent is winning time and we, with all our plans, face the inevitable prospect of winter warfare . . . An excellent opportunity of dealing a powerful blow is slipping out of our hands, and I don't know whether we'll ever have another.' Hitler himself was uneasy. He told Italian Foreign Minister Ciano that if he had known 'what was in store he might never have started at all'.[3]

The survival of Moscow hung in the balance in the autumn of 1941.

On the morning of 5 October 1941, Zhukov received a message from General Headquarters: 'Stalin wants to speak with the Front Commander.'

Zhukov telegraphed General Headquarters: 'Zhukov here.'

In less than two minutes there was reply:

Stalin: Greetings to you.

Zhukov: And greetings to you.

Stalin: Comrade Zhukov, can you get on a plane and immediately come to Moscow? The Stavka would like to discuss with you the necessary measures to rectify the situation on the left wing of the Reserve Front in the vicinity of Yuknov. Leave someone in your place – Khozin, perhaps. [The Stavka was a shortened name for the Soviet Main Headquarters, or *Stavka Glavnogo Komandovania*.]

Zhukov: May I fly out early in the morning of 6 October?

Stalin: Excellent. We'll expect you in Moscow tomorrow.

However, Zhukov says that 'certain important events' in the sector of the 54th Army made it impossible for him to leave the next morning and, with the Supreme Commander's permission, his flight was postponed.

On the evening of that day, Stalin again telegraphed: 'How are things with you? What's new concerning enemy actions?'

Zhukov reported:

German pressure has slackened. According to what prisoners say, German troops sustained heavy losses in September and are taking up defensive positions near Leningrad. Artillery is shelling the city, and it is being bombed from the air. Our aerial reconnaissance has detected large columns of motorized infantry and tanks moving southward from the Leningrad area – evidently in the direction of Moscow.

After his report, Zhukov asked Stalin if his order to fly to Moscow still stood.

'Leave General Khozin or Fedyuninsky in your place,' Stalin repeated, 'and fly to Moscow.'

The gravity of Moscow's predicament in the autumn of 1941 is seen in this blunt, often quoted Stalin–Zhukov exchange that took place in October. Hitler's forces were indeed coming up to the gates of the city. Stalin asked Zhukov:

'Are you sure we'll hold Moscow? I ask you this with pain in my heart. Speak honestly, as a Communist.'

Zhukov's reply:

'We'll hold Moscow all right. But we need at least two more armies and some 200 tanks.'

Alexander Vasilevsky, a wartime marshal who held some of the highest offices in the defence establishment, has commented on this famous exchange: 'Here you see Zhukov's special military style – his faith in the strength and heroism of his troops, his confidence in the support the troops would get from the country, his trust in the indestructible spirit of the people.'[4]

Although enemy units had advanced, some of them close enough to see the onion domes of some of Moscow's churches through their binoculars, by the latter part of October the enemy's strike forces in front of the capital had been greatly dissipated; and towards the close of November the Soviet Command began preparing a counter-offensive at Moscow.

The main operation of the counter-offensive was directed by Zhukov who reported that on the first day of the assault the forces of the Kalinin Front, commanded by General Ivan Konev, penetrated the German forward line of defence but could not topple the enemy; that it was only after ten days of bitter fighting and changing of tactics that the troops began pushing forward; that they were helped by other Fronts (like the Western) which smashed up a large enemy grouping.

Meanwhile, a gargantuan effort was taking place to move whole factories to the rear from evacuated areas in the European part of Russia. By November 1941, before Zhukov's counter-offensive in front of Moscow, over 700 large factories had been moved on railway flat cars to the Ural Mountains, over 300 other large enterprises were transferred to Siberia and nearly 400 others were moved to the area behind the Volga river. It was an unprecedented wartime transfer.

Not surprisingly, Zhukov's armies were short of arms, munitions, fuel and other matériel. Mainly it was the shortage of weapons that made it doubly difficult to wrest the strategic initiative from the Wehrmacht. But despite these problems the Stavka decided to take advantage of the exhaustion shown by the enemy. In this case the large reserves behind Moscow would prove decisive in the counter-offensive.

In early December, despite being hampered by deep snow, the Russian counter-offensive began, led by troops of the Western and Kalinin Fronts. Ski units, cavalry and airborne troops were used to help batter the retreating enemy. In one bitter clash the 2nd Panzer Army commanded by the famed German tank general, Guderian, reportedly lost 70 tanks. During the winter offensive, Hitler's troops were rolled back between 150 and 300 kilometres from Moscow. Zhukov says it was the first major defeat of the Wehrmacht in the six months since the war began. In Zhukov's eyes the success of the winter offensive showed that the German armies could be defeated 'provided things were made difficult for them'.

Hitler's generals testify that the counter-offensive caught them unawares. General Tippelskirch writes that 'the German Army, which had strained all its forces and was neither morally nor materially prepared for a war of manoeuvre in winter, was caught off its guard by the Russian counter-offensive. The impact of the Russian blow and the scale of the counter-offensive were so great that they shook up the front along a considerable length and nearly brought about a complete disaster.'[5]

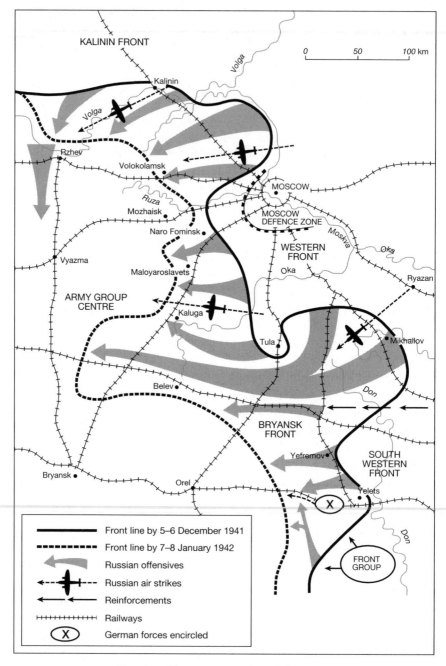

Russian Counter-attack at Moscow

Tippelskirch adds a mournful note: 'The sword of retribution was drawn.'

Asked at the Nuremberg International Tribunal when it was that he began to realize that Plan Barbarossa was failing, Field Marshal Wilhelm Keitel, Chief of Staff of the German High Command, uttered one word: 'Moscow.'

It wasn't too long, though, before Hitler's High Command began explaining away its failure to take Moscow, saying that the harshness of the winter had impeded its advance and favoured the Russians. But the realities of war on the Eastern front were beginning to be learned. Count Ciano, Italy's Foreign Minister, wrote in his diary: 'The vicissitudes of the war, particulalry the recent fighting, have convinced Hitler that Russia, that ocean of land, may have innumerable surprises in store.'

Did Hitler have a chance of taking Moscow in the summer of 1941, as some Wehrmacht generals claim? Averell Harriman, who was the US ambassador to Moscow during the war and spent more hours with Stalin than any other foreigner, had this to say:

> Stalin told me that the Germans had made a great mistake. They tried a three-pronged drive, remember, one at Leningrad, one at Moscow and one in the south. Stalin said that if they had concentrated on the drive towards Moscow they could have taken Moscow; and Moscow was the nerve centre of the Soviet Union and this would have broken that nerve centre and it would have been very difficult to conduct a major operation if Moscow had been lost. He said the Germans had made that kind of mistake in World War One – by not going to Paris. So Stalin said they were going to hold Moscow at all costs. And Stalin gave us details of his plans and I made up my mind they would be able to do it and reported this to President Roosevelt. That was not the general view. Our military attaché was quite positive that it was only a matter of a few days before the Germans would be in Moscow. And that was the view of all our military attachés. This was no particular wisdom on my part, but Beaverbrook [Lord Beaverbrook, Churchill's representative, accompanied Harriman to Moscow in 1941 when Harriman was on a special mission and was not yet ambassador] and I did have an opportunity to hear Stalin explain his programme and we accepted it.[6]

Two decades after the war, General Adolf Heusinger, who had served on Hitler's General Staff, stated baldly (in 1966) that the Germans could have taken Moscow in the summer of 1941 – that is, if Hitler had not stopped the offensive but continued the drive on Moscow in August. Some of his colleagues agreed with him.

What do Zhukov and his comrades-in-arms say? The following are questions that were put to three victorious marshals almost a quarter of a century after the war:[7]

Marshal Georgi Zhukov:

Q: What would have happened if the Germans had continued their offensive against Moscow in August?

Zhukov: That's not an easy question to answer. [The Marshal pauses for a moment.] There were many attendant circumstances of importance to us and the enemy alike.

For a number of reasons the war began in a situation highly unfavourable for us. The troops of the frontier military districts were forced to retreat, suffering heavy losses. Nevertheless, the Soviet fronts succeeded in organizing a stiff defence in July and inflicted telling reverses on the enemy in several sectors. As a consequence the German Command in August had neither the forces nor the means for a simultaneous advance in all strategic directions. On the other hand the Soviet Command was continuing to consolidate its defences.

Q: What view was taken at that time of the enemy's intentions?

Zhukov: The prevailing opinion was that the Germans would continue their push towards Moscow. But, as it became known later, the German High Command was seriously concerned about the situation in the Ukraine where the armies of the South were unable to disrupt the Soviet defences. Also the armies of the [German] Centre were in imminent danger of attack on the flank by the forces of our Central and Southwest Fronts. Along with that the Germans had come up against stubborn resistance in the Luga sector, and not only failed to break through our defences in the Leningrad direction but also came under a strong counter-attack at Lake Ilmen. To counteract our offensive and reinforce the armies of the North, the German Command was compelled to rush in the 39th Mechanized Corps from the Smolensk sector, which weakened the Centre armies. The emergency shift of the 2nd Panzer Formation and the 2nd Army to the south and southeastwards, as well as the offensive operations launched by the Soviet Reserve Front at Yelnya and by the Western Front in the Dukhovshchina sector forced the armies of the German Centre to assume the defensive and call off their drive on Moscow.

Q: So your conclusion is . . .?

Zhukov: It was beyond the power of the German troops to take Moscow in their stride in August 1941 as some German generals had hoped. But if they had persisted in their offensive they might have found themselves in a situation still worse than that of November and December

1941. Besides meeting with fierce resistance from our troops at the approaches to Moscow, the armies of the enemy Centre might have received a staggering counterblow from the forces of our Southwest Front. Consequently, attempts by German generals and certain historians in the West to put the blame for the defeat at Moscow on Adolf Hitler are as untenable as the fascists' entire military and political strategy.

Marshal Konstantin Rokossovsky:

I think Adolf Heusinger places the question in a shallow and trivial light. How could there be any thought of continuing the Moscow offensive when the German rear was so drawn out and there were such strong Soviet formations on the flanks of the advancing troops? Take the Yelnya salient, for example. The Germans had made a deep thrust there but they had extended their communications too far, and the Soviet troops were able to deliver a counterblow, notwithstanding the great difficulties. There the Germans were forced to retreat. How can anyone assert that General Ludwig von Beck could have continued the drive on Moscow in August? No, that viewpoint is not serious.

Marshal Vasily Sokolovsky:

From the very beginning the war against the Soviet Union was a gamble, and one battle like the Battle of Moscow could not be decisive. As to the situation on the Western Front in August 1941, the Soviet Supreme Command had organized a Reserve Front which had taken up positions behind the Western Front. The Germans would have come up against it, and at a time when it was still at full strength. Actually the decision to form the Reserve Front was taken on 30 June 1941. The Front consisted of six armies. This was clearly a substantial force.

Notes

1. From Fabian von Schlabrendorff, *Offiziere gegen Hitler*, Zurich, 1946.
2. From Erskine Caldwell, *Moscow Under Fire*, London, 1942.
3. Heinz Guderian, *Reminiscences of a Soldier*, New York, 1953; Ciano's *Diplomatic Papers*, London, 1948.
4. Vasilevsky's remarks on the 1941 Stalin–Zhukov exchange appear in the introduction to Zhukov's *Reminiscences and Reflections.*
5. Tippelskirch, *History of the Second World War*, 1949.
6. Averell Harriman made these remarks in Moscow in May 1975. The author met Harriman at that time and put several questions to him about the battle of Moscow and the overall course of the war. Not all US officers who had served in Moscow were so negative. One, Col. Philip Faymonville, believed in Russia's ability to hold back the enemy.
7. Marshals Zhukov, Rokossovsky and Sokolosky gave their comments on the Battle of Moscow in interviews that appeared in the May 1967 issue of the journal, *Sputnik.*

8

'WE WERE *EATING* THE PARK'

All of us are soldiers today, and those who work in the field of culture and the arts are doing their duty on a par with all the other citizens of Leningrad.

DMITRI SHOSTAKOVICH, the composer, in a radio broadcast from
Leningrad, August 1941

It was here that Pushkin had written *The Gypsies* and *Boris Godunov* and many lyrical poems ... [but] the Pushkin family mansion, once a museum, had been burnt down.

GENERAL S.M. SHTEMENKO, 1944

The first violin is dying, the drum died on his way to work, the French horn is at death's door ...

From a report by Y. BABUSHKIN on the state of Leningrad's orchestra,
January 1942

At Moscow's Central Airfield the weather was cool and overcast on the morning of 10 September 1941. Georgi Zhukov, then a general, had come to board a plane for beleaguered Leningrad, and three men – two generals and the pilot – stood beside the plane on the tarmac. To reach Leningrad the plane would have to fly over enemy lines. The men looked at the sky where the clouds hung dense and low.

'We'll slip by,' the pilot said smiling. 'The weather couldn't be better for crossing enemy lines.' Zhukov arrived safely, but just before his plane (which was without fighter escort) reached the city two Messerschmitt fighters spotted it. His plane finally landed within the city and Zhukov doesn't say much about the enemy planes, but he appears to have had a narrow escape.

In September 1941 the 'noose of the blockade' tightened on Leningrad's throat as Hitler's Army Group North under Field Marshal von Leeb managed to capture a substantial portion of the region around the city. With the capture of Schlusselburg (to the east, on Lake Ladoga) on 8 September, the enemy had cut the last overland link with the rest of the country. Leningrad was now effectively blockaded.

On the Karelian Isthmus, Finnish troops had emerged on the old national border and tried to advance further but were halted. Now they were waiting for a favourable chance to lunge at Leningrad from the north. With the fall of Schlusselburg the city's position became precarious. The only road in and out of the city, essential for ammunition and equipment, not to mention food, was across Lake Ladoga – or by air under cover of fighter planes. Now Hitler's forces had begun bombing and shelling the city.

Zhukov calls the attacks 'merciless and barbaric'. The Germans battered away at the city from all sides. Meantime a large mass of panzer and motorized troops had crashed through to the near approaches to the city, to Uritsk, the Pulkovo Heights and Slutsk. There was, says Zhukov, 'every evidence that the enemy was taking up positions for a final assault'.

Each day, almost each hour, the situation became more critical. In this situation, the Supreme High Command ordered Zhukov to do everything possible to save the city and he was determined to save it to prevent 'the city that Peter the Great built' from suffering the disaster that Hitler had in mind for Leningrad. Hitler had decided to erase Leningrad from the face of the earth. 'It is proposed to approach near to the city and to destroy it with the aid of an artillery barrage from weapons of different calibres and with long-range air attacks' [from the Directive of German Naval Headquarters of 22 September 1941].

Among the objectives for destruction marked on German maps one reads: 'No. 9–the Hermitage [one of the great art museums ranking with the British Museum, the Louvre, the Prado, Washington's National Gallery of Art and Dresden's Gemaldegalerie] ... No. 192–Young Pioneers' Palace ... No. 708–Institute for Mother and Child Care ... No. 736–School'.[1]

Leningrad was Hitler's chief objective on the northern flank. In July the Germans made their first attempt to capture the city but it was foiled by the stubborn resistance of the Leningrad garrison. A second attempt made in August also failed. Early in September 1941 the Wehrmacht made an all-out assault, preceded by a ferocious artillery bombardment and air attack. Here is how one witness describes it:

The houses, streets, bridges and people, plunged in darkness only a second earlier, were suddenly illuminated by sinister flames. Dense clouds of black smoke rose slowly to the sky, filling the air with an acrid smell. Fire brigades, self-defence groups and thousands of workers fought the fires in spite of fatigue after a full working day. Their efforts tamed the flames gradually, and the fires died out. But the Badayev warehouses, where the city's food supplies were stocked, continued to burn. The fire there raged for more than 5 hours.

Towards nightfall on 11 September by the authority of a note from the Supreme Commander, Zhukov took over command of the Leningrad Front. Until the morning hours of the next day he discussed the situation in the city and what additional measures could be taken to protect Leningrad. Taking part in the discussions were Marshal K.Y. Voroshilov, Admiral Ivan Isakov, who was in charge of the Baltic Fleet and some other units of the Front, and Andrei Zhdanov, the city's party leader.

> I knew the city and its environs well because I had studied there some years before at a school for cavalry commanders [says Zhukov]. Much had changed since then but I still had a good idea of the battle zone.
>
> I learned of the acute shortage of anti-tank guns all along the front. To make up for it we decided to use some of the anti-aircraft guns that could pierce armour. They were immediately moved from the city squares and streets and stationed at the most dangerous points. We also planned to form five or six rifle brigades made up of Baltic Fleet sailors and Leningrad students. They were to be activated within a week.

The main task was to supply the troops with arms, ammunition and other military equipment. These were manufactured inside the city under continuous enemy shelling and ceaseless air raids. The Kirov plant, for instance, which made heavy KV tanks, was turned into a major centre of defence. Many of its workers joined the *opolcheniye*, or peoples' volunteer army and their places were taken by boys, girls, women and old men. The workers slept on the premises, not leaving the plant for days on end.

A German POW later testified at the Nuremberg International Tribunal that the Wehrmacht shelled the city in the morning from 8 to 9, then from 11 to 12, in the afternoon from 5 to 6, and in the evening from 8 to 10; this way the shelling would kill as many people as possible, destroy factories and the vital buildings and, at the same time, destroy the morale of Leningraders.

On 11 September the Nazis had renewed their offensive and the next day General Halder, Chief of the General Staff of the German ground forces, jotted in his diary: 'The offensive on Leningrad of the 41st Motorized and 38th Army Corps is developing quite satisfactorily. A great achievement!'

Bitter and costly battles continued for a week. Zhukov reveals one of the measures used to defend against a superior enemy:

> Energetic and resolute action was called for. It was essential that we use even the least opportunity to counter-attack day or night, fatiguing the enemy, inflicting losses in men and arms, and frustrating his offensive actions. The strictest order and discipline had to be maintained. Troop control had to be tightened. We were working to stabilize conditions in the blockaded city which was in a most complicated situation.

A critical situation developed on 13 September when the Wehrmacht captured three small towns close to Leningrad. General Halder noted in his diary: 'Considerable successes at Leningrad. The emergence of our troops at the "internal fortified perimeter" may be considered complete.'

Zhukov remembers: 'A desperate situation had arisen. To eliminate the danger, the Front's military council decided to commit our last reserve, the 10th Rifle Division. This was a tremendous risk, but we had no other choice.'

The city's predicament may be gauged from Zhukov's telegraphic conversation with Marshal Saposhnikov (the Chief of the General Staff) on 14 September:

Shaposhnikov: Greetings, Georgi Konstantinovich. Please report on the situation and tell me what measures you are taking.

Zhukov: Greetings, Boris Mikhailovich. The situation in the southern sector is much more complicated than the General Staff had thought. This evening the enemy is attacking with 3 or 4 infantry divisions and two panzer divisions ... The situation is extremely serious. What makes matters worse is the absence of any reserves in the Leningrad area. We are resisting the enemy's offensive with whatever we can marshal – odd detachments, separate regiments, and newly activated workers' *opolcheniye* divisions.

Shaposhnikov: What measures have been taken?

Zhukov: This evening we organized a system of artillery fire including naval, anti-aircraft, and other artillery, to shell the roads used by the enemy. We're taking stock of our mortars, and I think that by morning we'll manage to put up a dense barrage in the main sectors to back up our infantry ... We are marshalling all aircraft of the Leningrad Front and the Baltic Fleet, and also something like 100 tanks ... Although we have 268 aircraft, only 163 are in working order. We need more planes.

Shaposhnikov: I think your plan of first organizing an artillery barrage is absolutely correct. The Leningrad Front has enough guns to put up such a barrage.

Zhukov: Splendid.

Zhukov also explained that he needed immediate help from the 54th Army of the Volkhov Front located to the east of the city in order to try and break the blockade.

When Zhukov got in touch with Marshal G.I. Kulik, the commander of the 54th, he became thoroughly exasperated when Kulik said he could not offer any help very soon, that he expected an enemy attack on his front. Zhukov could not, he says in his memoirs, hide his annoyance any longer. He said in a telegraphic message to Kulik:

> The enemy has not mounted an attack [against you], he was merely reconnoitring in force. Unfortunately some people mistake reconnaissance and skirmishes for an offensive ... It is clear to me that you are above all worried about the welfare of the 54th Army, and evidently insufficiently worried about the situation in Leningrad. I want you to know that I am having to send people from the factories to meet the attacking enemy, and have no time to practice joint action on site. I have underestood that I cannot count on any active manoeuvre by your Army. I will rely on myself only. Let me add that I am astonished at the lack of cooperation between your group and the Front. It seems to me that Suvorov [the eighteenth century Russian military wizard], if he were in your place, would have acted differently. Pardon me for speaking my mind, but I have no time for diplomacy. Best wishes.

Zhukov reveals that in his next conversation with Stalin he did not hold back the contents of the message he sent to the reluctant commander of the 54th Army.

Despite everything that Zhukov could do, he admits that the situation in and around Leningrad continued to deteriorate. Field Marshal von Leeb was evidently doing his utmost to carry out Hitler's order and complete the destruction of Leningrad at any cost before the Germans launched their offensive against Moscow.

On 17 September the fighting reached its peak. On that day six German divisions strongly supported by the air force of Army Group North mounted a new attempt to break through to Leningrad from the south. 'The city's defenders fought stoutly for every metre of soil, and continuously counter-attacked,' says Zhukov. 'The artillery of the Leningrad Front and the guns of the Baltic Fleet rained shells upon the advancing enemy, while army and navy aircraft rendered all possible support to our ground forces.'

A strict order went out saying that vital defence lines 'may not be abandoned under any circumstances'. The meaning for defenders was all too clear. Time and again, says Zhukov, entire artillery battalions, sometimes even regiments, took up combat positions in the open and fired on the attacking enemy at point-blank range, wreaking havoc upon the enemy. In just one sector more than 500 artillery pieces were positioned for direct fire.

At the height of the fighting for the towns of Pulkovo and Pushkino, the Wehrmacht delivered one of the most powerful artillery and air blows on Leningrad, trying to break the will of the people and of the army that was defending the mauled city. On 19 September the shelling of the city lasted without interruption for 18 hours – from 0105 hours to 1900 hours. During this period, the Luftwaffe mounted six massive air raids on the city, with as many as 275 bombers breaking through to Leningrad.

The well-known poet Olga Bergholts, working at the studio of Radio Leningrad had a visitor that day, the 19th, the day of the savage air raid. The visitor to the studio was a woman named Moskovskaya who lived on Sremyannaya Street and she had just lost her two children after a bomb fell on her house. She had never spoken over the radio before but she begged Olga: 'Let me speak over the radio . . . Please, I want to speak!' She got her wish and the woman told listeners what had happened to her children an hour before.

But what everyone who heard her remembered most was not so much her words as her breathing. It was, said the poet, the heavy, laboured breathing of a person who is all the time keeping down a scream, suppressing a fit of violent sobbing.

> This breathing, amplified by the loudspeakers came into the houses of Leningrad and into the trenches on the approaches to the city, and city dwellers and soldiers listened to a mother's story of how her little boy and girl had died in Sremyannaya Street, listened to her breathing, the breathing of boundless grief and boundless courage. They all remembered this breathing and it helped them to hold out.[2]

Not so very long before the woman's broadcast, the composer Dmitri Shostakovich appeared at the same studio and gave a radio address. It was the day the main city newspaper carried the bold headline: 'The Enemy is at Our Gates.' Shostakovich stayed in the stricken city for several months until he was evacuated. But while he remained he put on a fire-warden's uniform, doing his duty at the conservatoire where he was teaching. On the radio he spoke with great emotion in a clear voice about his new symphony, later to be known as 'The Leningrad Symphony':

> An hour ago I completed the second part of my new work. If I manage to complete the third and fourh parts of this composition and if it turns out well, I shall be able to call it the Seventh Symphony ... Despite the wartime conditions, despite the danger which is threatening Leningrad, I have written the first two movements in a comparatively short time. Why am I telling you this? I am telling you so that listeners tuned in to me now should know that life in our city is normal. All of us are soldiers today, and those who work in the field of culture and the arts are doing their duty on a par with all the other citizens of Leningrad.

Advancing towards Leningrad, Hitler's armies on 18 September had seized the town of Pushkin, where the legendary Russian poet had lived and created some of his timeless poems and prose works. All Russians (and many non-Russians) revere the name of Pushkin, and when General S.M. Shtemenko who saw the town of Pushkin after Hitler's troops got through with it and were forced back in the summer of 1944, he wrote the following in his memoir:

> The tomb of the great poet was in the former Svyatogorsk Monastery. It was here that Pushkin had written *The Gypsies* and *Boris Godunov* and many lyrical poems that were afterwards set to music. They had all become an inseparable part of our culture, of the Russian character. How could we pass by such a place?

Then he describes the wanton destruction: the monastery had been partly blown up, its dome was gone. The Pushkin family mansion, once a museum, had been burnt down. 'We left this scene of destruction with bitter feelings.'[3]

Later it was learned that the German Army Group North commanded by von Leeb was being hurried by Hitler to lose no more time and crush the resistance of the defenders of Leningrad in order to join hands with Finnish troops in Karelia. But despite these attempts the invaders failed to break through to Leningrad. Zhukov says that thanks to the measures taken by the Front Command (he is being modest; Zhukov was a major part of the command), a 'dependable deeply echeloned and insurmountable line of defence had been put up at the northern, southern and southeastern approaches to Leningrad by the end of September'.

Zhukov continues: 'Suffice it to say that when we stabilized the situation on the Leningrad Front, our defences in the main sectors were of two lines. A rifle division with plenty of anti-tank weapons held a line of no more than 10 to 12 kilometres.'

But Zhukov says the defence had now become invulnerable because his Front had put up a solid network of fortifications, and because army and naval artillery was being put to good use. There was also effective cooperation between ground troops and air force, as well as a dense, well-organized air defence of the city and the troops.

Despite the heavy assault on the city, except for those who joined the soldiers on the front lines, the workers did not leave their work places; and between July 1941 and the end of the year they produced 713 tanks, 480 armoured vehicles, 58 armoured trains, more than 3,000 anti-tank guns, nearly 10,000 mortars and over 3 million shells and mines.

During the 900-day blockade of Leningrad, many children were evacuated to the town of Karpinsk in the Ural mountains. The first thing they did when they arrived was run to the local park. Anya, who was aged 12 in 1942, recalls: 'But we didn't go for a walk in the park – we ate it. That's how hungry we were! We especially loved larches: their soft needles seemed a delicacy. We ate young sprouts of small pines, and chewed mouthfuls of grass ... So ever since the siege I have come to know all the edible plants.'[4]

Famine came to the city in the autumn of 1941. On 20 November daily bread rations were cut down to 250 grams for workers, engineers and technicians, and 125 grams for office workers, dependants and children. This norm was the lowest during the entire Nazi blockade and existed for 35 days, until 25 December 1941. Meat, fats or sugar were unheard of in those days.

Before the war Leningrad had a population of 3,100,000. As many as 1,700,000, including 414,000 children, were evacuated between June 1941 and March 1943. Nevertheless many civilians perished from hunger. During the first and most severe winter of the blockade, the winter of 1941–42, more than 263,000 people starved to death in the city. In all, more than 600,000 inhabitants died of starvation and lie in the city's Piskarevskoye Cemetery.

A diary which was kept by a schoolgirl, Tanya Savichev, who lived in Leningrad during the blockade, opens the stark exposition of the museum at the Piskarevskoye Memorial Cemetery.

> Zhenya died at 12:30 p.m. on 28 December 1941.
> Granny died at 3:00 p.m. on 25 January 1942.
> Lyoka died at 5:00 a.m. on 17 March 1942.
> Uncle Vasya died at 2:00 a.m. on 13 April 1942.
> Uncle Lyosha at 4:00 p.m. on 10 May 1942.
> Mother at 7:30 a.m. on 13 May 1942.

The last entry: 'The Savichevs have died. They all have died. I am all alone.' Tanya was evacuated shortly afterwards but being already extremely weak she died in 1943.

In early October Zhukov's scouts reported that the Germans were building dugouts, making bunkers and pillboxes, and laying mines and other obstacles to protect their battle lines. Zhukov's intelligence unit drew the conclusion that the enemy was digging in for the winter, and prisoners confirmed this. 'For the first time in many days we could tangibly feel that the Front had fulfilled its mission and had halted the Nazi offensive on Leningrad.'

At the end of the year the situation on the various fronts improved, and a build-up of Supreme Command reserves was taking place in the country's rear. 'The enemy was gradually losing superiority in arms and manpower that he had had at the begining of the war.' To make the most of the favourable situation, says Zhukov, the Supreme Command decided to mount an offensive operation in the Lake Ladoga sector and break the blockade of the city. The operation was code-named Iskra (Spark).

Zhukov adds that as the operation unfolded his troops captured Schlusselburg and a number of other points which the Nazis had turned into mighty centres of resistance. On 18 January the advancing units of the two Fronts made contact. The siege of Leningrad was lifted.

Notes

1. From the first days of the Nazi invasion of Russia, preparations were made for the evacuation of the most valuable possessions of the Hermitage including the

two Madonnas by Leonardo da Vinci and the Madonna by Raphael. In July 1941 several special trains departed from Leningrad headed for Siberia. One of them had 20 cars carrying 1,422 boxes containing over 700,000 showpieces from the Hermitage. The most valuable works of art were placed in an armoured car provided by the railway. Many valuable exhibits remained at the museum and 'lived' through the war and blockade along with the citizens. (Some of this information comes from a booklet, *Boris Piotrovsky, The Chief Curator of the Hermitage Treasures*, by Yuri Alyansky, Moscow, 1988.)

2. Vladimir Sevruk (Editor), *Moscow – Leningrad*, Moscow, 1974. Olga Bergholts, who wrote dramatic works for stage and screen, in addition to poetry, remained in Leningrad throughout the blockade. Her Radio Leningrad broadcasts were heard by the soldiers of the various fronts, in addition to Leningraders, until the radio fell silent in early 1942.

3. S.M. Shtemenko, *The Soviet General Staff at War*, Moscow, 1970.

4. From *Sputnik*, May 1990.

9

'A POCKET EDITION OF HELL'

Stop! Bow low in tribute – you are standing on sacred ground.

LILIA KIRSHINA, Volgograd, 1967

Manstein's plans to rescue the encircled forces at Stalingrad ... were not destined to succeed.

G.K. ZHUKOV, *Reminiscences and Reflections*

Hitler's war plans set the objective of advancing to the A–A (Archangelsk–Astrakhan) line, that is from the White Sea in the far north to the Caspian Sea in the south. Stalingrad was often mentioned in 1941 and again in 1942 when the German armies were drafting operations on the Eastern Front for the spring and summer. Of course the fact that the city was named after Stalin is said to have further vexed the Fuehrer, as did the name of Leningrad, which he always called St Petersburg. At the beginning of November Hitler took it for granted that the city was almost or already in German hands. 'We are there,' he said in a speech broadcast on 8 November 1942 which was picked up by Russian radio intelligence.

By the end of the autumn of 1942 Hitler's forces on the Soviet–German front were composed of slightly more than 250 divisions with a total strength of some 6.2 million officers and men, around 51,000 guns and mortars, 5,000 tanks and assault weapons, 3,500 aircraft and close to 200 warships.

By comparison, the Soviet Union had in the field approximately 6.6 million officers and men, 77,000 guns and mortars, 7,000 tanks and 4,500 aircraft. Crucially, says Zhukov, the Soviet High Command had a strategic reserve of 27 rifle divisions, 5 independent tank and mechanized corps, and 6 independent rifle brigades.

Sizing up the strength of both sides, Zhukov says that by the end of the 'first period of the war' the balance of forces began to tilt in Russia's favour. But he adds another dimension to the war in the East, saying that the Soviet side had learned to conceal its plans and to misinform and confuse the enemy on a large scale. 'Because of well-camouflaged regroupings and troop concentrations we were able to make surprise attacks.'

An example of the Wehrmacht being misinformed was a statement by the German High Command, after fierce fighting in the south, in Stalingrad and in the Northern Caucasus, that it believed Soviet forces would not be able to launch a major offensive on these fronts. A German Ground Forces High Command order dated 14 October 1942 stated: 'The Russians have been badly exhausted in recent combat actions. In the winter of 1942–43 they will not be able to raise forces as strong as they had last winter.'

This, says Marshal Zhukov, was far from true.

The summer of 1942 was a busy time for Moscow and not only on the battlefront. In August Winston Churchill flew to Moscow to deliver the bad news that America and Britain would be unable to open a Second Front that year. In the plane Churchill made the following entry in his diary: 'I pondered on my mission to this ... Bolshevik State I had once tried so hard to strangle at its birth ... What was it my duty to say to them now? General Wavell, who had literary inclinations, summed it all up in a poem ... There were several verses, and the last line of each was, "No Second Front in nineteen forty-two".'

Although the Russians were never persuaded that North Africa, the Far East and the war in the Atlantic were major theatres, it is arguable that D-Day in 1944 was so late as to raise the suspicion of 'a political motive' aimed at the Kremlin. Nevertheless, there is little doubt that to have seriously hoped for a Second Front as early as 1942 was unrealistic.

After informing Stalin about this during a very unpleasant meeting between the two leaders, Churchill was handed a memorandum which said:

> The British Government's refusal to open a second front in Europe in 1942 delivers a mortal blow to Soviet public opinion, which had hoped that the second front would be opened, complicates the position of the Red Army at the front and injures the plans of the Soviet High Command. The difficulties in which the Red Army is involved through the refusal to open a Second Front in 1942 are bound to impair the military position of Britain and the other Allies.[1]

Zhukov reveals some of the thinking behind the planning of the

Soviet offensive at Stalingrad: 'According to the Supreme Command's plan, the westward thrust our forces undertook in the summer and autumn of 1942 against the Nazi Army Group Centre was to disorient the enemy, to make the German Command think it was precisely at this point and nowhere else, that we were preparing for a major winter operation. This is why in October the Nazi Command began building up large forces against our western fronts.' He mentions that three divisions – armoured, motorized and infantry – were moved from the Leningrad area to the north of Smolensk, and another seven divisions were rushed from France and Germany to the west of Moscow (also in the vicinity of Smolensk). Thus by early November the Nazi Army Group Centre had gained 12 divisions, plus other reinforcements.

Zhukov claims that the Germans were guilty of operational blunders and that they were aggravated by poor intelligence; that they failed to spot preparations for the major counter-offensive at Stalingrad where there were 10 field, 1 tank and 4 air armies, and other units.

This claim is backed by German General Jodl who admitted to the Nuremberg International Tribunal after the war that the Wehrmacht had no idea of Russia's actual strength in the Stalingrad area, and that German troops were caught by surprise when a powerful blow was struck – one that 'proved decisive'.

In the autumn of 1942 the Germans, says Zhukov, found themselves in a 'complicated position'. First, he says, they had not achieved their strategic objectives. Second, they were faced with an overextended front from the Black Sea through the Northern Caucasus, Stalingrad, the Don area and up to the Barents Sea. Third, they had no strategic reserves in the front and in the rear. Fourth, they had to deal with low morale among the troops.

Meanwhile fierce fighting proceeded on the Soviet–German front. On 28 June 1942 the Germans took the offensive. The Wehrmacht attempt to crush the Soviet left flank south of Orel failed. But the Red Army was forced to retreat across the Don, fighting delaying actions against superior German forces. On 6 July Hitler's armies were stopped short near Voronezh by counter-attacks from the north. The intial German plan was frustrated. The pivot of the fighting then shifted south, to the Volga sector. On 12 July the Soviet High Command established the Volga Front under General Andrei Eremenko. For four gruelling months the opposing armies fought it out, one of them pushing the other back, the retreating Russians putting up a stiff defence. In July the Geman Command launched its

'Plan Edelweiss' aimed at seizing the Caucasus. Field Marshal Ewald von Kleist, Commander of Army Group A, remarked later: 'We might still have reached our goal if my armies had not been drained off unit after unit to prop up the offensive on Stalingrad.'

On 21 August under heavy pressure the Soviet forces withdrew from the outer ring of defences to the inner ring in Stalingrad. Two days later the Luftwaffe sent hundreds of planes to bomb the city. General (later Marshal) Eremenko provides a graphic description of this attack in his book on the embattled city:

> The earth of Stalingrad seemed to bristle and turned black. It seemed as though a monstrous hurricane had fallen upon the city, raised it into the air and then flung back the ruins of its houses upon the squares and streets. The air grew hot, acrid and bitter. It became difficult to breathe. The din was indescribable. It jarred on the ears with the hellish disharmony of diverse noises. The screech of dropping bombs mixed with the boom of the explosions, and the clatter of toppling houses with the crackle of the flames. And in this chaos of sounds we distinctly heard the groans and curses of the dying, the weeping and pleading of the children, the sobbing of the women. Our hearts contracted from pity for the innocent victims of this Nazi brutality. The mind would not suffer the thought that it was impossible to prevent the pain of hundreds of peaceful people, especially the children.[2]

In mid-September the fighting shifted inside the city. Nazi propaganda broadcasts several times announced its fall. But this was premature as the invaders met what Siberian General A.P. Beloborodov calls a 'collision with Russian tenacity'. Throughout the autumn and winter of 1942–43, the city was the focus of all operations on the Soviet–German front. The city of Stalingrad, a major industrial and communications centre, was desired by the German Command in order to cut the Volga and set the stage for capturing and holding the Caucasus.

The following true-to-life story is included here not as mere relief from the gore of battle but to show that even where street fighting was hottest, humanity could show its face:

> Stalingrad – at first the Germans called the city a pocket edition of Hell. Then they changed the metaphor and began calling Hell a pocket edition of Stalingrad.
>
> Almost miraculously, despite hundreds of thousands having been evacuated to the rear, a crowd of civilians, mainly bedraggled women and

children, remained in Stalingrad during the siege of the city, surviving precariously on the tall banks of the Volga river, in shell holes and gullies that ran into the city.

On Lenin Street the Russian trench-mortar positions ran through the upper floor of Building No. 36. On the opposite side of the road the Germans held onto a basement, and between these two buildings every square foot of space was under fire. It was taken for granted that no one could possibly survive in this no man's land and, except for fighting men, most civilians had fled from the city. It was said that even the bats in this building had decamped.

But on this particular street one civilian remained. At dusk, a wraith-like creature would lift the lid of a manhole right in the middle of the street, almost exactly between the two firing lines. Her elderly hand would toss out bits and pieces of rubbish, then lower the lid and return to her subterranean home. She was living (perhaps existing is a truer word) in a cast-iron drainpipe in the city's underground maze. Russian soldiers remembered that she wore an old-fashioned winter coat with a frayed fox collar. The soldiers had become increasingly fond of her because she would creep across the street in the blackness of a moonless evening, when relative quiet reigned, climb the half-ruined charred staircase, bringing the smoke-begrimed gunners freshly washed foot cloths, or a newly darned shirt or trousers, or warm porridge.

In her underground home she had a small kerosene stove which hummed away quietly amid the thunder of battle.

Soap was a luxury but the woman – Maria Gavrilovna – would produce a small bar when the men needed it. When the battery commander complained of an awful toothache one day, she gave him a hot potion of some kind to ease the pain. Gradually the soldiers began to address her as 'Mother'.

One morning Maria Gavrilovna told her 'sons' that today she would give them a feast – hot cabbage soup. Where she managed to find a head of cabbage nobody knows. But the cabbage soup in combination with tinned beef promised to be a special treat for the men. At dusk, when the firing slackened, the well-known figure lifted the manhole cover, climbed out and waddled acoss the street, carrying a piping pot of cabbage soup.

All of a sudden the men heard the deadly crackle of enemy fire; but they saw Maria Gavrilovna continue to walk calmly, not hurrying, so as not to spill the soup. The Russians returned the fire in order to defend their much-treasured visitor. But when she climbed the stairs, without spilling a drop of soup, the men noticed blood forming beneath her kerchief. Putting down the pot of soup she sank to the floor without saying a word. She never regained consciousness. the soldiers buried her that night in the enclosed courtyard of House No. 36.

On her grave they wrote:

'Here lies Maria Gavrilovna Timofeyeva, Mother of the 12th Trench Mortar Battalion.'[3]

On 10 November 1942, Zhukov arrived at the Stalingrad Front to help finalize plans for the great counter-offensive that would begin shortly and lead to a victory that would stun the entire German nation. Two days later Zhukov was in Moscow discussing the pending operation with Stalin. In two more days he was back in Stalingrad with orders to 'check once again troop and command readiness for the start of the operation'. The operation had as its goal the encirclement of an entire German army.

On 11 November after inspecting, with other generals, the terrain in front of several key armies that were to develop the offensive, Zhukov used the Baudot printer to report to the Supreme Commander.

His report began:

Spent two days with [General A.I.] Eremenko. Personally inspected enemy positions confronting 51st and 57th armies. Ironed out details of pending objectives of Operation Uranus with divisional, corps and army commanders. Inspection showed [General F.I.] Tolbukhin ahead in preparations ... Have ordered battle reconnaissance and finalization of combat plan and Army Commander's orders on the basis of intelligence thus acquired. [General M.M.] Popov working well, knows what he is doing.

Zhukov informed Stalin of a number of shortcomings, including failure of arrival of transport and horses for two infantry divisions, a shortage of shells for the coming operation, and the urgent need for 100 tons of antifreeze ('without which advance of mechanized units impossible') and winter gear for the two armies he had visited.

Zhukov also reported that the operation would be delayed but added: 'Have ordered readiness by 15 November 1942.'

In his memoirs Zhukov offers these excerpts from the diary of an officer from a Romanian artillery brigade that fought the Russians at Stalingrad:

19 November
Russians are fiercely shelling the left flank of our 5th Division. I've never been under such fire ... Gunfire so heavy the ground shudders and windows shatter.

20 November
... No communication with higher command. 6th division received

orders to hold out to last man. Currently we are encircled by enemy troops . . .

21 November

We are surrounded . . . Great confusion . . . Friends staring at snapshots of their loved ones, wives and children. It hurts to think of my mother, brother, sisters and relatives. We're putting on our best clothing, even two sets of underclothes. We figure very tragic end in store . . . Two alternatives discussed among ourselves:

1) Try to break out.

2) Surrender.

After a long discussion the decision is – surrender.

We hear the Russians have sent a truce envoy with surrender proposals.

The diary ends at this point. Zhukov says the entire group of Romanians surrendered.

In early summer 1942 Hitler still had large forces that he could freely manoeuvre. Since the beginning of the year German military thinking was built on the assumption that seizure of the important economic regions in Russia's south would weaken the enemy and strengthen the Third Reich to the extent that it would decide the outcome of the war. The Caucasian oil fields were also a prime target as there was beginning to be oil as well as food shortages in Germany. But seizure of Moscow remained a major goal. Thus, the Wehrmacht still concentrated a large force in the Moscow sector.

Hitler, in a speech on 9 September 1942, dwelt in detail on Directive 41 which spelled out the basic tasks for the summer campaign. The Fuehrer explained the concept that Directive 41 was built upon. 'What we aim at,' he said, 'is first, to capture the enemy's last remaining grain areas; second, to capture his last remaining coal, which we can make into coke; third, to move closer to his oilfields, to capture them or, at least, cut them off from the rest of the country, and fourth, to extend the offensive and take control of the Volga, the enemy's last major waterway.' The German plan revealed the true goals pursued in Russia. As Joseph Goebbels had said, 'It is not a war for the throne or altar. It is a war for grain and bread, for a well-stocked dinner-table, for full breakfasts and suppers . . . a war for raw materials, rubber, steel and iron ore.'

Zhukov says he and Vasilevsky discussed the planned counter-offensive by three fronts, set the date for the second half of November, and got

Stalin's endorsement. Already at the beginning of the month the temperature dropped sharply and ice began to appear on the Volga river. Needless to say, the winter would be a negative factor for Hitler's armies. Since food was running out the German Army would soon permit the slaughtering of horses. (In fact, the only meat thousands of German soldiers would enjoy for their Christmas dinner was horse meat. Thousands were slaughtered for this purpose.)

Zhukov gives this description of the opening of the operation:

> At 07:30 on 19 November the troops of the South-Western Front struck a telling blow, breaking the defences of the 3rd Romanian Army on two sectors simultaneously ... The enemy buckled and, panic-stricken, fled or surrendered. German units holding positions behind the Romanian forces, mounted a powerful counter-attack in an attempt to check our advance, but were crushed by the 1st and 26th Tank Corps. The tactical breakthrough on the South-Western Front was now an accomplished fact.

Quickly breaching the German defences the Red Army advanced up to 50 kilometres, trapping the enemy in a giant pocket. On New Year's Eve, the outer front of the encirclement was 240 to 320 kilometres west of Stalingrad. Unsuccessful efforts were made to extricate the army of 250,000 officers and men, and a major rescue attempt by Manstein from the southwest also failed. Twice in January Friedrich Paulus, the German commander of the German Sixth Army was asked to surrender and thus save lives. He declined. The German soldiers were now condemned men without hope of rescue or supply by air. Paulus, whom Hitler promoted to Field Marshal at the end of January, finally surrendered on 2 February with some 90,000 troops.

The casualties at Stalingrad were enormous. For the first time in the war Germany suffered heavy losses: perhaps 150,000 dead and 90,000 taken prisoner. The Red Army lost more than half a million men in the struggle. An idea of the harsh discipline imposed by Red Army commanders under Zhukov is given by a statistic released in 1995 by the Russian Defence Ministry. At Stalingrad 13,500 soldiers were executed for cowardice and desertion.

The city never fell into German hands although some of Hitler's soldiers managed to set foot on stretches of the Volga river's western bank. It is said that the Russian people link many aspects of their history with the historic city of Stalingrad, now known as Volgograd. Today there is a 52-metre sculpture known as the Motherland

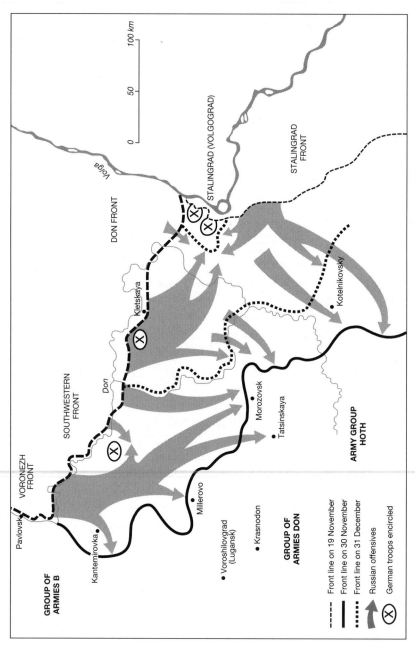

The Battle of Stalingrad

GROUP OF
ARMIES B

VORONEZH
FRONT

SOUTHWESTERN
FRONT

Pavlovsk

Kantemirovka

Millerovo

Voroshilovgrad
(Lugansk)

Krasnodon

GROUP OF
ARMIES DON

Morozovsk

Tatsinskaya

ARMY GROUP
HOTH

Kotelnikovsky

Don

Kletskaya

DON FRONT

Volga

STALINGRAD (VOLGOGRAD)

STALINGRAD
FRONT

100 km

50

0

Front line on 19 November
Front line on 30 November
Front line on 31 December
Russian offensives
German troops encircled

architectural ensemble that is is dedicated to the hundreds of thousands of Russians who followed the Kremlin order forbidding retreat. The order, No. 227, entitled 'Not a Single Step Back!' was issued when the existence of the Russian nation was under threat. Many of Stalin's generals called the order one of the most important documents of the war.

For his successful leadership at Stalingrad, Zhukov was awarded the Order of Suvorov 1st class. Other generals who received the same award for the Stalingrad battle included Vasilevsky, Voronov, Vatutin, Rokossovsky and Eremenko.

Here is how the German generals regard the defeat at Stalingrad:[4]

Stalingrad was the turning point of the Second World War. For Germany the Battle of Stalingrad was the worst defeat in its history, and for Russia, its greatest victory. None of its Allies in the war can boast of such a victory.

General Hans Doerr

The catastrophe at Stalingrad, the unheard-of surrender of an entire army along a huge front, the heavy losses caused by this national disaster, as well as the major defeat of our allies who were unable ... to hold the flanks attached to the Sixth Army – all this led to a serious crisis.'

General Heinz Guderian

The Battle of Stalingrad was the turning point in the history of the German people. In the Battle of Stalingrad itself and in the events which accompanied it we see the reflection, as in a drop of water, of all the problems of the Nazis' predatory war.

Field Marshal Friedrich Paulus

We did not have the slightest idea of the Russian strength in the area of Stalingrad. Previously, there had been nothing there and suddenly a powerful blow was struck, proving decisive.

General Alfred Jodl

For the German people this terrible defeat was a rude political awakening. This was mirrored most distinctly in the hearts of the prisoners of war taken at Stalingrad.

General Otto Korfes

After Field Marshal Paulus was captured (the first time a German Field Marshal had been taken prisoner) he said he had never expected a Soviet offensive on so massive a scale.

Zhukov is more blunt: German operational blunders were aggravated by poor intelligence; they failed to spot preparations for the major counter-offensive near Stalingrad where there were 10 field, 1 tank and 4 air armies, a number of independent tank, mechanized and cavalry corps, brigades and independent units, 15,500 guns and mortars, 1,460 tanks and armoured self-propelled guns and 1,350 combat aircraft. Zhukov says the victory 'turned the tide of war in favour of the Soviet Union and launched the massive efforts to drive the enemy off Soviet territory'. He says that after the battle the Soviet Supreme Command assumed the strategic initiative and held it until the end of the war. 'It was a jubilant, though hard-won victory not only for the fighting forces who destroyed the enemy, but also for the people at home working day and night to provide the army with the wherewithal to rout the enemy successfully.'[5]

In Moscow's view the Stalingrad offensive demonstrated to the world the inner strength of the country's economy and the morale of the people; in effect, their determination to win at all costs. As to the economy, by the autumn of 1942 the wartime economy had been built up to full blast.

After Stalin's death it was unclear who was the actual architect of the counter-offensive that led to the great victory on the Volga. Zhukov (like Vasilevsky) strives to prove that it was a collective effort: 'I would like to reiterate that the Supreme Command and the General Staff unquestionably played the decisive role in planning and effecting the counter-offensive at Stalingrad.' He goes on to say that the Supreme Command (of which Zhukov was a leading member) and the General Staff deserve credit for their ability to analyse with scientific accuracy all the factors involved in the enormous operation and predict its progress and final result. Therefore, he concludes, 'it is out of the question' to attribute this action to any particular individual.

Zhukov adds a personal note about his role in the Battle of Stalingrad. He says: 'For myself personally the defence of Stalingrad, the preparation of the counter-offensive and participation in deciding the main aspects of operations in the south were of special importance as now I had accumulated far more experience in mounting a counter-offensive than I had at Moscow in 1941 where limited forces did not permit a counter-offensive with the aim of encircling an enemy grouping.'

On 13 November 1942 Zhukov and Vasilevsky at a meeting with Stalin pointed out that as soon as Hitler's armies at Stalingrad found themselves in a tight spot the Nazi High Command would be compelled to move some of its forces from other sectors, particularly from

Vyazma, west of Moscow, to assist the forces at Stalingrad. To prevent this, it was essential to prepare a new offensive in front of Moscow, first to smash the Germans in the Rzhev Salient north of Vyazma.

Stalin agreed and asked which of the two men would take charge.

Zhukov replied: 'Plans for the Stalingrad offensive are complete and the operation is ready to begin.' So he suggested that Vasilevsky co-ordinate operations at Stalingrad while he take charge of preparations for an offensive in front of Moscow.

Zhukov also reports that the westward thrust in front of Moscow against the Wehrmacht's Army Group Centre was to confound the enemy – to make the German command think it was precisely there and nowhere else that the Red Army was preparing for a major winter operation. Believing this, the German Command began building up large forces west of Moscow. By November, says Zhukov, Army Group Centre had gained 12 divisions, including 2 panzer divisions plus other units from France and Germany.

While admitting that his troops failed to accomplish the task assigned by the Supreme Command – to eliminate the enemy salient west of Moscow – Zhukov convincingly shows that 'their vigorous actions prevented the German Command from rushing large re-inforcements from this sector to Stalingrad'. Also, the Wehrmacht was obliged to move additional panzer divisions towards the Rzhev salient. Zhukov gives reasons for the lack of success of the operation includ-ing the shortage of supporting armour, artillery and aircraft – which were necessarily concentrated at Stalingrad for the big counter-offensive there. But the main thing – prevention of reinforcements to the surrounded German troops at Stalingrad was not only accom-plished but led to one of the major triumphs in military history. Nevertheless there are a few voices who, because Zhukov failed to eliminate the 'Rzhev salient', go so far as to call his lack of success Zhukov's 'greatest defeat'. Professor Oleg Rzheshevsky, one of the world's foremost authorities on the war (he is chairman of the Russian Historians of the Second World War), has disposed of this argument in one lucid paragraph. (See Introduction.)

If anyone needs proof that the action in front of Moscow in the autumn of 1942 was a secondary operation, despite Zhukov's (tem-porary) presence, there is this fact: although Zhukov had left the Stalingrad area he not only kept in daily contact with his headquarters there, but he kept a hand in making the Stalingrad decisions. Here is an example: late at night on 28 November while at a command post west of Moscow he received a call from the Supreme Commander, asking him what action he thought should be taken to destroy the encircled Wehrmacht troops at Stalingrad. The following morning Zhukov telegraphed Stalin providing detailed advice. He suggested that the encircled German grouping should be cut in two, and then the weaker grouping be destroyed first. Afterwards, he recommended that 'with all our force' the stronger grouping should be eliminated.

Notes

1. At the time of the Battle on the Volga Churchill tried in vain to get Soviet consent for British troops to be sent to the Caucasus.
2. Eremenko, *Stalingrad* (in Russian), Moscow, 1961.
3. Variations of this story appeared in several military newspapers published during the war.
4. Some critics, for example Alan J. Levine (1985), question the importance of German defeats at Stalingrad and elsewhere, saying that Allied victories in these battles were not all that vital in the long run. It is a theoretical argument, and in light of the ramifications of the battle – and statements by an overwhelming number of experts, plus statements by many German commanders, including Paulus, Jodl, Guderian and Doerr – is untenable.
5. Russian historian Alexander Borisov takes a cynical point of view saying that, after Stalingrad, the most far-sighted political leaders in the West realized that the defeat of Nazi Germany was now just a matter of time; that by further postponing of the Second Front, the Western Allies were running the risk of arriving in Berlin 'too late'.

10

KURSK: THE NAZIS' WATERLOO

The spectre of inevitable disaster now arose for Nazi Germany.

G.K. ZHUKOV, *Reminiscences and Reflections*

As Hitler prepared for his new summer offensive in 1943, he announced a new slogan, *Festung Europa* (Fortress Europe), making it clear that Germany would cling to all the territories the Red Army had not yet liberated. But taking the offensive, the Wehrmacht, using large panzer groups, planned a double envelopment: to surround and wipe out Russian forces congregated inside the Kursk Bulge. A large force under Field Marshal Hans Gunter von Kluge was deployed to the staging area.

At the beginning of April 1943 Zhukov was already helping plan the Russian counter-action for the coming battle of Kursk which would take place in July of that year.

A key role in the frustrating of 'Citadel' – Hitler's code name for the battle – was played by tens of thousands of civilians who built trenches and other fortifications. The military historian Dr Leonid Yeremeyev says that the total length of Russian trenches dug at the Kursk Bulge equalled the distance from San Francisco to Washington to Montreal (about 6,000 kilometres).

Hitler's generals based their plans for Operation Citadel on the particular situation that had arisen at Kursk as a result of battles in the region during the winter of 1942–43. The front line had assumed contours which have gone down in history as the Kursk Bulge – or Kursk Salient. This was a huge area of 65,000 square kilometres and was held by Russian troops. Both in the north and south of the bulge were two wedges held by powerful German forces. Wehrmacht generals were eager to exploit the situation and launch pincer attacks at the base of the bulge, using the element of surprise. After their anticipated victory, they hoped to advance on Moscow and Leningrad.

The preparations for the Wehrmacht's offensive were almost completed and the assault was expected any day. Meanwhile, the governments of the United States and Britain were not so sure of Hitler's intentions.

On 19 June 1943, Prime Minister Churchill wrote to Stalin:

'We have some reason to believe that the unexpectedly rapid defeat of the Axis forces in North Africa has dislocated German strategy and that the consequent threat to Southern Europe has been an important factor in causing Hitler to hesitate and to delay his plans for a large-scale offensive against Russia this summer.'

On 27 June Churchill wrote again:

'You will not be heavily attacked this summer.'

No doubt Churchill was trying to be helpful to his Russian ally but in this case his prediction was faulty.

The Soviet Command had a good idea of what the Wehrmacht was up to. Strong and deep fortifications were raised, and strategic reserves were brought up. At key points the Red Army's defences were 100 kilometres deep. According to Zhukov, Supreme Headquarters worked out a very detailed plan for the Battle of the Kursk Bulge. Troops of two Fronts were to block the coming German offensive and sap its power. In the next stage the troops of five Fronts would mount a counter-offensive.

Zhukov was kept busy flying from one vital front to another, combined with frequent visits to Supreme Command Headquarters in Moscow. In the spring Stalin also asked him to attend a meeting at the Kremlin attended by managers of the biggest factories producing tanks and aircraft. 'Their reports clearly revealed the grave situation that still persisted in industry.' Zhukov adds that 'there were delays in the help under Lend–Lease from the USA'.[1]

In March Zhukov says that the situation on the Kursk Bulge had become stable and that both sides were preparing for a decisive encounter. In March and April he visited almost all the armies and other formations inside the bulge. He says he was 'anxious' about a particular division which he believed would be the recipient of the enemy's main blow, and therefore he and his generals resolved to reinforce that sector with plenty of artillery.

The following month Zhukov estimated the dimensions of the

coming battle at Kursk: 'At the present time, the enemy has as many as 12 tank divisions lined up along the Central and Voronezh Fronts and, by taking 3 or 4 tank divisions from other sectors, he could pitch as many as 15 or 16 tank divisions with some 2,500 tanks against our Kursk grouping.' Considering these facts, Zhukov said preparations should be made for a mammoth tank battle at the Kursk bulge.

Zhukov mentioned a factor which no doubt played a vital role in the Red Army's victory: all of the highest ranking officers involved in the operation agreed on the necessity of thorough reconnaissance of enemy positions on all the sectors of the armies involved. On 8 April 1942 Zhukov sent Stalin a preview of the battle that would take place 90 days later. It was, as might be expected of Zhukov, a job well done. (Zhukov calls it a 'forecast' of the great battle.)

It began: 'I hereby state my opinion on the possible movements of the enemy in the spring and summer of 1943 and our plans for defensive action in the coming months.'

Zhukov then listed six main points. Three times he mentioned Kursk. But first he pointed out that, having suffered serious losses in the winter campaign of 1942–43, Hitler's armies would not appear to be able to build up big reserves by the spring to resume the offensive in the Caucasus and to push forward to the Volga to make a wide enveloping movement around Moscow. He then said that in the first stage of the battle, having gathered as many of their forces as possible, including at least 13 to 15 tank divisions and large air support, the Germans would evidently deal the blow with an enveloping movement around Kursk from the northeast and southeast.

He also said that an additional attack on Kursk from the southwest aimed at dividing the Russian front 'must be expected'. He recommended that 'if the enemy is to be crushed by our defensive formations, besides those measures to build up the anti-tank defences on the Central and Voronezh Fronts, we must get together 30 anti-tank artillery regiments from the passive sectors as rapidly as possible and redeploy them as part of the Supreme Command's reserves in the areas threatened'.

Zhukov signed his report 'Konstantinov' – his code name.

Of paramount importance was whether to let the enemy attack first or to pre-empt such an attack. Zhukov passed along this advice: 'I do not believe it is necessary for our forces to mount a preventive offensive in the next few days. It will be better if we wear down the enemy in defensive action, destroy his tanks and then, taking in fresh reserves, by going over to an all-out offensive we will finish off the enemy's main grouping.'

Looking back, Zhukov's forecasts did not – and he is pleased to admit it – differ substantially from what the German High Command did.

Hitler's top secret orders to his commanding officers on 15 April 1943 included the followng instructions:

> As soon as weather conditions permit, I have decided to launch the Citadel offensive, the first offensive operation this year.
>
> Decisive importance is attached to this offensive. It should be carried out rapidly and with definite success. The offensive should give us the initiative for the whole of the spring and summer of this year.
>
> In this connection, all preparatory measures should be implemented with the greatest of care and energy. The best formations, the best armaments, the best commanding officers and a large amount of ammunition should be used where the main thrusts are being made. Each commanding officer, every soldier of the line must become thoroughly aware of the decisive significance of our new offensive. The victory near Kursk should be a torch for the whole world.[2]

Next, Hitler spelled out his expectations: 'The aim of the offensive is a concentrated thrust carried out decisively and rapidly by the forces of one main attack force from the area around Belgorod and of another from the area to the south of Orel to surround the forces in the Kursk area by a concentric offensive and destroy them.'

Because Zhukov had correctly foreseen the enemy's intentions and, much later, obtained a copy of Hitler's orders to his armies at Kursk, he was able to say with some satisfaction: 'Thus, having appraised the situation correctly, before the German offensive was launched, the Soviet commanding officers had precisely determined the probability and direction of the Nazi manoeuvres in the Kursk Bulge area.'

Zhukov's most able generals predicted that a German offensive could be expected in the second half of May. His Chief of Staff, General M.S. Malinin, suggested that to foil the enemy offensive operations, the forces inside the Kursk Bulge (the Central and Voronezh Fronts) should be reinforced with aircraft – mainly fighters – and anti-tank artillery, not less than 10 of these regiments to be sent to each front.

In the spring of 1943 Zhukov's wealth of experience since the beginning of the invasion clearly reaped benefits in his relationship with Stalin, never an easy one. Zhukov says for example that when he met Stalin on 12 April 'the Supreme Commander listened to our views more attentively than ever before. [Zhukov was accompanied by Vasilevsky and Antonov.] He agreed that the main forces should be concentrated in the Kursk area but just as before he was anxious about the Moscow sector.'

Zhukov says that by mid-April the Supreme Command had already taken a preliminary decision on deliberate defence.

> True, we repeatedly returned to that question but the final decision on deliberate defence was taken by the Supreme Command at the beginning of June. At that time the enemy's intention of launching a mighty offensive against the Voronezh and Central Fronts was, in actual fact, known; it was to involve the biggest tank groupings, using the new Tiger and Panther tanks and the self-propelled Ferdinand guns.
>
> Simultaneously with the plan for deliberate defence and counter-offensive, it was also decided to work out a plan for offensive operations, without waiting for the enemy offensive if he should postpone it for a long period.

Zhukov concludes by saying his forces' defences were in no way hasty measures but ones that were deliberately taken and, depending on the situation, the Supreme Command was to choose the 'moment for going over to the offensive'. It was borne in mind that 'things should not be done in too much of a hurry, nor should they be dragged out too much either'.

Meanwhile, Zhukov was instructed to fly to the North Caucasian Front where heavy action was being conducted to annihilate the Wehrmacht's 'Taman grouping', the core of which was formed by the well-equipped German 17th Army.

The elimination of the enemy on the Taman Peninsula was of great significance to the Supreme Command. Besides destroying a big enemy grouping of 14 to 16 divisions, numbering approximately 180,000 to 200,000 men in this sector, as a result of this operation the Soviet armies liberated the vital Black Sea port of Novorossisk. Since the first half of February the heroic detachment of men of the Soviet 18th Army and the sailors of the Black Sea Fleet had been fighting in the Taman area on a very small bridgehead.

Zhukov, who held the rank of marshal since the Stalingrad victory, and his party of generals and admirals arrived at the headquarters of the 18th Army. He says that after the group of experts had familiarized themselves with the situation, including the forces and resources of the army and the sailors of the Black Sea Fleet, 'we all came to the conclusion that it was impossible at that time to take any major steps to extend the Novorossisk bridgehead, which the troops called "The Little Land"'. Indeed, that bridgehead was no more than 30 square kilometres in area. Recalls Zhukov: 'At that time there was one question that particularly worried us, namely, whether the fighters would hold out in the face of the ordeals falling to their lot in an unequal struggle with an enemy who made air attacks day and night and subjected to artillery fire the defenders of this little bridgehead.'

Having told Stalin his views about the Novorossisk bridgehead, Zhukov set out for the 56th army on the North Caucasian Front which was commanded by General A.A. Grechko, who after the war was appointed Minister of Defence. In his book, *The Armed Forces of the Soviet Union* published in 1975, Grechko speaks of the fighting in the Caucasus at that time:

> In the North Caucasus, the Soviet forces wore down the attacking Nazi troops in bitter defensive operations. The enemy had been trying to break through to the oil port city of Baku and the port of Tuapse. Soviet forces later launched a counter-offensive and inflicted a decisive defeat on the enemy after fierce battles at Novorossisk and Taman, in the salt steppes and outside Rostov.

Before recounting the actual Kursk battle, Zhukov speaks in a confident tone about the state of the Red Army at that time: 'By the summer of 1943, just before the Battle of Kursk, our armed forces were, on the whole, both numerically and qualitatively superior to the Nazi armed forces. Now the Soviet Supreme Command had all the necessary means to crush the enemy forces decisively and firmly retain the strategic initiative in all the key directions and dictate its terms to the Wehrmacht.'

After defeating the Germans in the Kursk bulge area, the Supreme Command intended to liberate the Donbass (the Don Basin), a large part of the Ukraine, to eliminate the enemy's bridgehead on the Taman peninsula, liberate the eastern areas of Belorussia and create conditions for driving the invaders out of Russian territory altogether.

It is not hard to know what was in the minds of the German High Command just before the Kursk battle. Zhukov puts it into one short sentence: 'The enemy was preparing to wreak vengeance for their defeat at Stalingrad.'

The clash at the village of Prohkorovka was the biggest tank battle

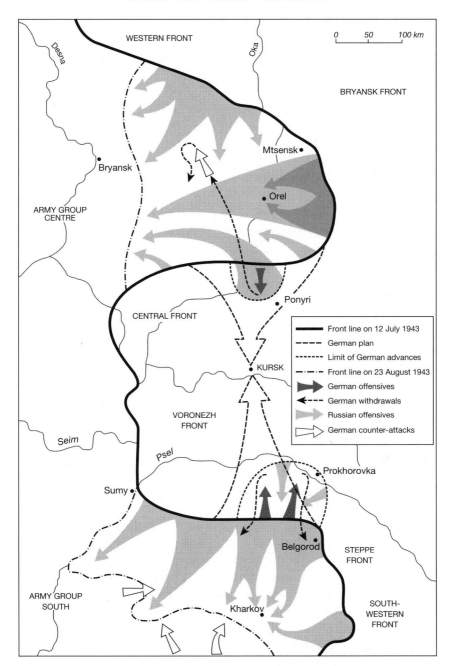

The Battle of the Kursk Bulge

of all time. The two sides flung between 800 and 1,000 tanks into the fray. The first day the Wehrmacht lost over 300 tanks and more than 10,000 men and officers. There were also fiercely fought aerial duels. Soviet pilot Ivan Kozhedub shot down more than 10 enemy planes. Fighter pilot Alexei Maresyev, who had lost both his legs in combat a year earlier, bagged three German planes in the early air battles over the Kursk Bulge.[3] Meanwhile, the French 'Normandie' squadron fought alongside the Soviet flyers. (Their pilots shot down 33 Luftwaffe planes at Kursk in July and August 1943.)

Some historians refer to the mammoth 60-day Battle of Kursk as the 'Waterloo of German Fascism'. One Western military expert calls it a 'titanic battle of modern war'. For the Russians it was one of their most important victories of the war. At Kursk there occurred another gigantic clash of armies as each side fielded an army of more than a million strong. In no other battle of the Second World War were more tanks, guns, mortars and aircraft engaged. The Kursk battle was note-worthy for the complete defeat of German tank formations. The mammoth clash of ironclads at Prokhorovka on 12 July involved a combined total of a thousand or more tanks and armoured vehicles. Hitler never recovered from his defeat at Kursk. Partly as a consequence of Soviet victories at Stalingad and Kursk – and Stalin's continued close involvement in Red Army strategy – Roosevelt and Churchill agreed to hold a summit close to Russia (in Tehran) at the end of 1943.

Historian Nikolai Yakovlev says that before the great battle of Kursk, Teutonic gigantomania lulled Hitler and his generals into believing they possessed the ultimate wonder weapons. They brought to Kursk all that was considered the best and the biggest in Nazi arsenals.

By early July 1943 they concentrated more than 900,000 men, about 10,000 cannon and mortars, 2,700 tanks and assault guns and some 2,000 planes in the Kursk direction.

Zhukov says that his armies at Kursk, as in other battles, were 'significantly helped' by partisans. He says that starting the previous year the Wehrmacht was forced to deploy 10 per cent of its ground forces, including SS and SD police forces, to cope with the partisans.

When the Kursk battle was over, the Germans had suffered one of their worst defeats of the war. The Wehrmacht never recovered from its loss at Kursk, which finally raised the spectre of inevitable disaster for Nazi Germany.

Georgi Zhukov as the victorious Commander of Russian–Mongolian forces in the summer of 1939 against a major Japanese incursion in Mongolia.

Zhukov with first wife, Alexandra Dievna and two youngest daughters, Era and Ella.

Zhukov off duty, playing the accordion with daughter Era.

Three Zhukov sisters (left to right) Maria, Era, Ella.

Georgi Zhukov with his mother, wife and daughters.

Zhukov, Eisenhower and Montogomery drinking a toast at Eisenhower's Headquarters in Frankfurt-am-Main in June 1945.

Marshal Zhukov in summer
uniform.

Portrait of Georgi Zhukov with three of
his gold hero medals.

Eisenhower and Montgomery are checking their diamond-studded Order of
Victory medals they have received from Zhukov. Andrei Vyshinsky (with glasses)
looks on.

Zhukov, Eisenhower,
Montgomery and Vyshinsky
enjoying a chat in Frankfurt,
Germany.

Zhukov, glittering with medals,
on horseback during Victory
Day parade in Voronezh, south
of Moscow.

Zhukov and Ike watch an Allied air show in Frankfurt on June 10, 1945.

From left, Air Marshal Sir Arthur Tedder, Montgomery, Eisenhower, Zhukov and Vyshinsky enjoy a stroll near Supreme Headquarters Allied Expeditionary Forces in Frankfurt.

Zhukov the pensioner enjoying fishing with an American rod and reel that had been presented to him by US President Dwight Eisenhower.

Zhukov's daughters, from left, Era and Ella, in Moscow, 2002.

Bronze statue of Marshal
Zhukov on horseback close to
Red Square.

Zhukov's place of interment in the Kremlin Wall, between Civil War
Commander Sergei Kamenev (left) and Marshal Alexander Vasilevsky.

Notes

1. The United States gave the USSR Lend–Lease assistance in the Second World War to the amount of $9,000 million which assisted the Soviet war effort.
2. Heinz Guderian, *Panzer Leader*, New York, 1952. G.K. Zhukov, *Reminiscences and Reflections*, Moscow, 1985.
3. The author met Alexei Maresyev ('Russia's Douglas Bader') in Moscow in 1997 and learned that when he was in the hospital thinking his flying days were over he read a line from Maxim Gorky's *Song of the Falcon* that kept his hope alive. It was: 'Those who are born to creep cannot fly.' Obviously, Alexei was not born to creep.

11

THE PARTISANS OF BELARUS[1]

The Belorussian Operation smashed the German Army Group Centre, which lost more than 30 divisions in various pockets.

From press reports in Moscow, August 1944

Our men enthusiastically welcomed the Second Front by our allies in Normandy, which brought the downfall of Fascism and the end of the war closer.

G.K. ZHUKOV, *Reminiscence and Reflections*

It seemed as if the whole earth of Belorussia (today Belarus) shook with explosions. It was the partisans who had attacked the railways strictly according to plan. For three nights running their mines and bombs ripped the silence with their blasts. This was a 'battle of the rails' of unprecedented scope. In fact the partisans carried out almost 40,000 explosions of tracks in all directions at the same time. This action paralysed the enemy's transport communications. At a moment that was most inopportune for the Nazis the partisans put out of action several main lines that were of crucial importance. Among these were the Minsk–Orsha, Minsk–Brest and Pinsk–Brest lines. Many of the bridges, telegraph and telephone and power transmission lines were also wrecked.

In the final stage of the Belorussian campaign, prior to the giant offensive on Belorussian soil, the partisans had effected 182,000 explosions of tracks, derailed 5,494 military trains carrying troops and supplies, demolished 1,101 rail and road bridges, destroyed 73 aircraft, 397 tanks and 2,510 motor vehicles.

Meanwhile, 2,400,000 officers and men, 36,400 guns and mortars, 5,200 tanks and self-propelled guns and 5,300 combat planes to the east of the front line were on battle alert.

It was 23 June 1944 and Operation Bagration was about to begin. Operation Bagration began on 23 June 1944 on the fields of

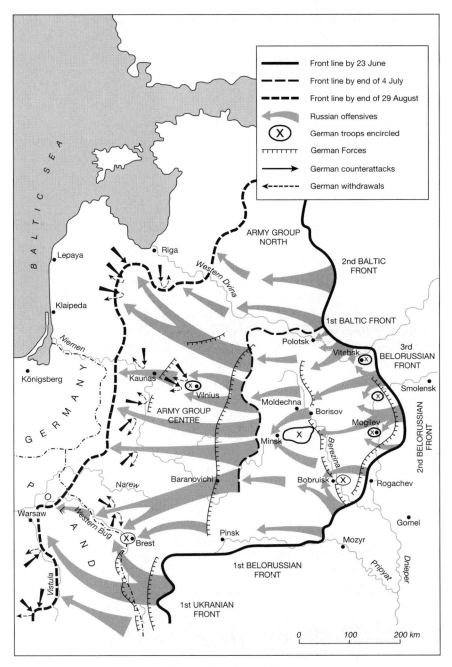

Operation Bagration

Belorussia (White Russia) and lasted 67 days and nights. This campaign was one of the largest offensive operations of the war and fundamentally changed the strategic situation on the entire Eastern Front. After Bagration the next most important objective was Berlin. Afanasy Beloborodov, one of the most acclaimed generals on the Eastern Front, says the Wehrmacht was forced to transport to Belorussia from other sectors more than 40 divisions and 4 brigades; that this led to the weakening of the German forces in Western Europe, making far easier the offensive of the Anglo-American troops in France.

In August 1943 the German High Command started to build what was called the Eastern Wall. The Nazis claimed it was far superior to the allegedly impregnable Atlantic Wall. The Eastern wall was to block the Red Army's way to the West. The so-called Belorussian Balcony was a giant salient stretched out around Minsk within which was spread Field Marshal Ernst von Busch's Army Group Centre. The Belorussian Balcony, as a component part of the Wall, was to cover the shortest routes to Germany and secure the Nazi forces' main lines of communication along the whole of the Eastern Front.

Military supplies and troops moved to the front mainly through Belorussia, because it was the shortest route. That was why the Wehrmacht High Command ordered its forces to defend Belorussia as they would defend Germany itself. To stiffen the defences further the cities of Vitebsk, Orsha, Mogilev, Bobruisk, Polotsk and of course Minsk, were declared fortified areas or fortresses. Powerful strongpoints were being built in other cities, towns and major inhabited localities, especially on the banks of rivers.

Later, when he was taken prisoner, General von Erdmannsdorf, commandant of the Mogilev Fortified Area, testified that the orders were to hold such areas at all costs, even though completely surrounded. A Fortified Area could be abandoned only with Hitler's personal permission at the request of an Army Group Command. In April all the commandants of Fortified Areas in Belorussia were summoned to Army Group headquarters and there they gave written pledges that they would hold their fortresses to the last man and to the last round of ammunition.

In April 1944 Stalin and Zhukov had in general terms discussed the plan for the summer campaign for that year.

'You have come straight from the front,' Stalin said to Zhukov at that time. 'What is your fresh impression of the German troops?'

Zhukov replied:

'They have everything they need for putting up a stubborn defence on our front. In so far as High Command and Army Group Command strategy is concerned, I would say that after the disaster at Stalingrad and especially at Kursk its quality has sharply declined.'

Zhukov went on to remark that, as distinct from the early period of the war, the German Command had become rather 'thick-skulled' and had lost its ingenuity, especially in difficult situations. Marshal Zhukov knew exactly what specifically interested Stalin then. So he laid special emphasis on points of primary importance for the forthcoming operation.

'We have analysed some of the recent decisions of top German generals,' said Zhukov. 'They clearly reveal the lack of a true appraisal of the potentialities of the German forces and of the enemy, that is to say, our potentialities. For instance, they are always late in withdrawing groupings threatened by flank attacks and encirclement. So their forces are caught in hopeless situations.'

Decades after the war some German generals who survived would place the entire blame for defeat on Adolf Hitler, accusing him of incompetence, blunders and refusing to heed their opinions. While there appears to be some truth in this, the view of Zhukov and Vasilevsky – that the major operational and strategic concepts of German (and Prussian) military thinking had been elaborated without Hitler's participation – also rings true.

Zhukov confirmed the views of the Supreme Commander-in-Chief and the General Staff to the effect that the main attack in Belorussia in the summer campaign of 1944 would come as a complete surprise to the enemy. Zhukov said confidently that he was sure of its success. First of all, he believed that the operational dispositions of Army Group Centre, which formed a bulge pointing eastward, created favourable conditions for deep pincer thrusts at the base of the bulge. Second, he was sure that it would be possible to build up the necessary superiority in manpower and equipment in the direction of the main thrust.

Zhukov also maintained that, as a preliminary step, it would be necessary to strike a number of major blows in other directions to make the enemy withdraw from Belorussia as many units as possible of his strategic reserve. These attacks later materialized in relatively big offensive operations on the Leningrad and Karelian Fronts.

In his summing up, Zhukov set out his views on the difficulties the

Nazi armies would face on the Soviet–German front in the summer of 1944.

At this point Stalin, with a slight movement of his hand, stopped him and for the first time mentioned the Second Front being prepared on British soil:

'There will be others too. In June the Allies intend to land a big force in France after all. Our allies are in a hurry,' Stalin said. (Zhukov says Stalin said this with an ironical smile.) 'They are afraid we may complete the defeat of Nazi Germany without their participation. Of course, we want the Germans to start fighting on two fronts at long last. This will put them in an even worse position with which they will no longer be able to cope.'

At this time, to preserve maximum secrecy the top Soviet leaders were given new pseudonyms on the eve of Operation Bagration. Stalin was known as Semyonov till the end of the year, Zhukov became Zharov and Vasilevsky – Vladimirov.

In mid-May 1944 the Soviet General Staff was completing draft documents for Operation Bagration, the code name for the huge action in Belorussia (White Russia). Stalin himself had named the operation after Prince Pyotr Bagration, a general who came from a noble Georgian family and died a heroic death while fighting against Napoleon's army in 1812. By the end of this titanic engagement, German losses on the entire Eastern front amounted to almost one-third of their original strength. These losses sharply aggravated Hitler's manpower problem. No longer could they be replaced by total mobilization.

On 20 May Stalin called in Zhukov, Vasilevsky and A.I. Antonov, Chief of the General Staff, to finalize the Supreme Command decision on the plans for the summer campaign. An offensive was to be launched first in the Karelian Isthmus; another was to begin later, in the latter half of June, in Belorussia. Zhukov and Vasilevsky were ordered to supervise the coordination of the actions of various fronts. Vasilevsky was responsible for the 1st Baltic and 3rd Belorussian Fronts while Zhukov was responsible for the 1st and 2nd Belorussian Fronts. On 4 June Vasilevsky left for the front to prepare for Operation Bagration.

Marshal Zhukov begins his account of the leviathan Belorussian Operation with a few words about the nightmarish German occupation of that republic, now known as Belarus. Hitler's armies, he records, destroyed 7,000 schools, burned 1,200,000 buildings and killed 2,200,000 civilians. These bare facts are made more stark by official figures. Thus, one out of every four citizens perished. In one city, Vitebsk, the death toll was higher, one in three. Moreover, the occupiers razed 9,000 villages to the ground. It is doubtless true to say that no other European territory in the Second World War suffered more.

In July 1944 most of Germany's combat troops remained on the Nazi–Soviet front. Zhukov's armies faced almost 180 full-strength divisions and 5 brigades, as well as 49 divisions and 12 brigades of Hitler's allies: Italy, Romania, Hungary and Finland. Hitler's armies numbered almost 4.5 million men armed with 59,000 artillery pieces and mortars, 7,800 tanks and assault guns and nearly 3,200 aircraft.

Zhukov's armies totalled nearly 6.6 million men with 98,000 guns and mortars, 7,000 tanks and self-propelled artillery, and almost 13,000 combat aircraft.

Before each commander left for his respective post, they met to discuss in minute detail all the strong and weak points of the enemy defence and the measures to be carried out at the various headquarters and among the troops. 'I reached agreement with General Antonov on the ways to control the concentration of troops, material supplies and the Supreme Command reserves, as well as the question of communications and information on the actions of the Supreme Command on other sectors.'

Zhukov mentions the vast quantities of matériel and equipment needed for the fronts. According to the General Staff's estimates the troops taking part in Bagration needed nearly 400,000 tons of ammunition, 300,000 tons of fuel and lubrication, up to 500,000 tons of food and fodder. Five combined armies, 2 armoured, 1 air army and the units of the 1st Polish Army had to be concentrated. Other substantial units were also allocated by the Supreme High Command.

Zhukov stresses the caution that had to be employed to prevent the enemy from detecting preparations for the offensive.

This was especially important since our reconnaissance reports showed that the German High Command expected us to strike the first blow of the summer campaign in the Ukraine, not Belorussia. It evidently believed that the wooded and boggy terrain [in Belorussia] would not allow us to move freely in that republic and employ to best advantage our four tank armies now located in the Ukraine.

Early on the morning of 5 June Zhukov was at the command post of the 1st Belorussian Front and met Rokossovsky, and also Member of the Military Council Bulganin, and Chief of Staff Malinin. They had detailed discussions on the actions then going on, especially on the flanks of the armies. Also present was the commander of the air army, General Sergei Rudenko. Special attention was given to a meticulous study of the terrain in the battle area and to the reconnaissance of the enemy defence system as well as additional preparation of the troops and logistic support for the operation.

Zhukov knew the area well. 'I had served in Belorussia for more than six years and had walked the length and breadth of the country,' he says. 'I had done quite a bit of duck shooting in the swamps . . . which abounded in water and forest game.'

Not everything was going smoothly. Zhukov had to phone Stalin and point out that the schedule of troops and cargo transportation was not being met. He asked Stalin to instruct the proper officials to look into the matter; otherwise the operation would have to be put off.

In the middle of June rehearsals of Bagration were held by several armies. Generals from the Supreme Command were in attendance with Zhukov and his staff. Three armies were to lead the troops to rout the Wehrmacht's Army Group Centre – the major enemy grouping that was holding onto a strategic position. Theirs, says Zhukov was a 'great responsibility' since the defeat of the Army Group Centre spelled the complete expulsion of the Nazi armies from Belarus and Eastern Poland.

To give an idea of the physical extent of Bagration, the armies under Zhukov and Vasilevsky were spread out for more than 1,200 kilometres and had a depth of 600 kilometers. 'In fierce battles our troops would have to engage 200,000 enemy soldiers armed with 9,599 artillery pieces and mortars, 900 tanks and assault guns and over 1,300 combat planes.' He adds that the prearranged defences, 250–270 kilometres deep, also had to be overcome.

This was the third anniversary of the war, an event Zhukov underlines, of world historic importance. Zhukov pauses here to pay tribute to the Second Front that was opened when on 6 June the Allies under General Eisenhower's command invaded France across the English Channel. Soviet soldiers enthusiastically welcomed the Second Front, said Zhukov, which brought the downfall of Hitlerism and the end of the war closer.

On 27 June two 'pockets' were made in the Bobruisk area; trapped in them were the German 35th Army Corps and the 41st Panzer

Corps, in all nearly 40,000 men. Zhukov says he did not witness the 'liquidation of the enemy' but did see the rout of the Germans south-east of the city of Bobruisk. Also, hundreds of bombers of Rudenko's air army struck blow after blow at the enemy group. Zhukov recounts:

> Scores of trucks, cars and tanks, fuel and lubricants were burning all over the battlefield. More and more bombers took their bearings from the blazing fires, and kept dropping bombs of various weights. The terror-stricken German soldiers scattered in every direction; those who did not surrender were killed. Thousands of Germans who had been taken in by Hitler who had promised them a victorious Blitzkrieg against the Soviet Union were dying in the fields of Belorussia.

The Belorussian partisans operating in the Minsk area informed Zhukov's headquarters that the city's main buildings, including Government House and the Officers' House were being hastily mined for demolition before retreat. 'To save the city's biggest buildings we decided to accelerate the advance of our armoured troops and send along engineers for de-mining. Their task was to fight their way into the city – avoiding engagement with the enemy on the approaches – and seize the government buildings.'

The action was performed successfully, and the important buildings were cleared of mines and saved.

By the evening of 3 July all of Minsk was liberated. At the same time a major group of Wehrmacht formations was cut off from withdrawal routes and encircled east of Minsk. It included the 12th, 27th and 35th Field Corps and the 39th and 41st Tank Corps – more than 100,000 officers and men in all.

Zhukov, who knew Minsk well, got a shock when he saw the city.

> The capital of Belorussia was barely recognizable. I had commanded a regiment there for seven years and knew well every street and all the main buildings, bridges, parks, stadiums and theatres. Now everything was in ruins; where whole apartment buildings had stood, there was nothing but heaps of rubble. The people of Minsk were a pitiful sight, exhausted and haggard, many of them in tears.

According to officials in Minsk, before the enemy left that city it destroyed 300 factories. The Wehrmacht also set the torch to 78 schools, the State Art Gallery, the Ballet and Opera House, and all of the city's cultural centres and libraries.

By 11 July the surrounded German troops, in spite of their resistance, were killed or taken prisoner. Among the 35,000 prisoners were

12 generals, including 3 corps commanders and 9 division commanders. Zhukov's men spent several days tracking down groups of
German officers and men trying to join their troops, but the enemy
was rolling back so rapidly that this was not easy. The local population
and the partisans – Zhukov calls them 'the real masters of the
Belorussian forces' – helped the Soviet soldiers immensely in clearing
the territory of the enemy.

Five days earlier Stalin summoned Zhukov to Supreme Command
Headquarters. On that day he flew to Moscow, 'put myself in order,
and went to the General Staff'. Before meeting the Supreme
Commander he wanted to study the latest developments in greater
detail.

Zhukov, who had once been Chief of the General Staff, says he was
pleased to note that the leadership of the General Staff had greatly
improved their strategic and operational skills.

At 2 p.m. Zhukov and Antonov arrived at Stalin's summer house.
He noted that 'the Boss' was in good humour and joked. One reason
was that Vasilevsky had called over the radiotelephone and reported
good news about the 1st Baltic and 3rd Belorussian Fronts.

'I haven't had breakfast yet,' he said. 'Let's go to the dining room
and talk.'

Zhukov and Antonov had already had breakfast but, says Zhukov,
'we did not decline the invitation'. During breakfast they talked about
Germany's capacity to wage war on two fronts, against the USSR and
the Allied Expeditionary Forces which had landed in Normandy, and
about the role and tasks of the troops at this concluding phase of the
war.

From the precise manner in which Stalin expressed his ideas,
Zhukov guessed that Stalin had already thought about these matters
very carefully. He recalls: 'Although Stalin believed that Russia was
strong enough to finish off Nazi Germany single-handed, he sincerely
welcomed the opening of the Second Front in Europe, which brought
closer the end of the war, so much desired by the Soviet people who
were extremely exhausted by war and its privations.'

No one, adds the marshal, had any doubt that Germany had definitely lost the war. 'This was settled on the Soviet–German front in
1943 and the beginning of 1944. The discussion now centred on how
soon and with what political and military results the war would end.'
At this point, says Zhukov, Molotov and other members of the State
Committee for Defence joined them.

The question was asked what Hitler's military leaders could hope for in the given situation. Stalin's answer was:

> They are like a gambler betting his last coin. All their hopes were pinned on the British and Americans. In deciding to wage war on the Soviet Union, Hitler took into account the imperialist circles in Britain and the USA, who totally shared his thinking. And not without reason: they did everything they could to direct the military actions of the Wehrmacht against us.

Molotov added that Hitler would probably attempt at any cost to make a separate agreement with the US and British government circles.

'That is true,' said Stalin, 'but Roosevelt and Churchill will not agree to a deal with Hitler. They will try to attain their political aims in Germany by setting up an obedient government, not through collusion with the Nazis, who have lost all the trust of the people.'

Then Stalin asked Zhukov: 'Can our troops begin liberating Poland, reach the Vistula without a stop, and in which sector can we commit the 1st Polish Army which has now become an effective fighting force?' This army was commanded by General Zygmunt Berling and, says General Beloborodov, 'fought courageously' in Belorussia and Poland.

'Not only can our troops reach the Vistula,' replied Zhukov , 'but they have to secure good bridgeheads beyond it which are essential for further offensive operations in the strategic direction of Berlin. As for the 1st Polish Army, it should be directed towards Warsaw.'

Antonov completely agreed with Zhukov. He also mentioned to Stalin that the enemy's strength in the sector of the 1st Ukrainian Front had been weakened.

Stalin then turned to Zhukov, saying:

> You will now have to undertake the coordination of the 1st Ukrainian Front. Give special attention to the left flank of the two Fronts, the 1st Belorussian and the 1st Ukrainian. You know the general plan and the tasks. No changes have been made in the Supreme Command's plan, and you can acquaint yourself with the details at the General Staff.

Next they discussed the capacities of the troops being coordinated by Vasilevsky at which time Zhukov said it was advisable to greatly strengthen Vasilevsky's group of fronts and ask him to cut off the German Army Group North and occupy East Prussia.

'Are you in cahoots with Vasilevsky?' asked Stalin, 'because he also asks for his Fronts to be reinforced.'

'We are not,' Zhukov replied, 'but if that is his opinion, he is correct.'

'The Germans will fight for East Prussia till the very end,' Stalin said, 'and we may get stuck there. We should first of all liberate the Lvov Region and the eastern part of Poland. Tomorrow you will meet some Poles, Bierut, Rola-Zimerski and Osubko-Morawski at my place.'

Two weeks later Zhukov submitted a plan asking for reinforcements and strengthening of the Fronts that would advance towards East Prussia and Poland. He called East Prussia 'a very serious obstacle'. However Stalin refused to accept his plan, causing Zhukov to think he had made a 'really serious mistake here, as what was involved was the very complex and bloody East Prussian operation'.

In the latter part of July the German High Command found itself in a difficult position which was further complicated by the offensive begun by the 2nd and 3rd Baltic Fronts and the pressure of the Allied Expeditionary Force in the West. The German General Buttlar wrote in this connection: 'The rout of the Army Group Centre by the Russians put an end to the organized resistance of the Germans in the East.'

In smashing the Army Group Centre the Wehrmacht lost more than 30 divisions in various pockets. Belorussia and most of Lithuania were cleared of the enemy. On forcing the Niemen, the Red Army reached the German frontier. The offensive proceeded along a front of nearly 1,300 kilometres at a depth of 550–600 kilometres.

By the beginning of the fourth summer of the war the Russians had driven the Nazi invaders and their satellites off vast territories of Russia. In the course of operations in the winter and spring of 1944 Red Army troops, taking the offensive along a 2,500-kilometre front, had advanced up to 450 kilometres in some directions and had routed over 150 German divisions. Hitler's armies had suffered extremely heavy losses. The Nazi High Command was compelled to move 40 more divisions to the Eastern front. In addition to losses of manpower, the Wehrmacht had lost thousands of guns, mortars, tanks and aircraft. The might of Hitler's armies had been very much sapped. Though the German forces were still in a position to put up, and did put up, a ferocious resistance, they had irrevocably lost their superiority in manpower and equipment.

But it was clear that the Nazi forces would fight to the very end, carrying out Hitler's orders: all Germany was right behind them.

In August 1944 with the Red Army bogged down in Eastern Poland, there was an unexpected uprising in Warsaw when some 40,000 courageous Poles rose in arms against the German occupiers. The insurgents wanted to liberate their country before the Russians did. Therefore, they did not inform Moscow in advance of their uprising but received all of their instructions from the Polish Government in exile in London which, in fact, was as much anti-Stalin as it was anti-Hitler. The Soviet armies were engaged in bitter fighting, having entered Polish territory, and the Poles received no aid from them. Moscow has often been accused of holding back on purpose, of lacking humanity by failing to supply the fighters of the Polish Home Army that was organizing the revolt.

When Zhukov arrived at the Warsaw front in early September he messaged Stalin that the powerful German forces made it impossible to cross the Vistula at that time.

To help the Poles who were in distress, a limited number of air drops by American and British heavy bombers began in early August but the amount was negligible and it seems that at least part of the supplies fell into German hands. Hitler's troops put down the uprising and took revenge on the population.

But as Richard Overy says the truth of the matter is complicated. The uprising in Warsaw was not a move to help the Russians in their drive towards Berlin. Militarily, the city was at that time beyond the grasp of Zhukov's armies in the month of August. Fighting alongside the Russians at this time was the 1st Polish Army under General Berling. This army attacked Warsaw in September but due to stubborn German defences was forced to withdraw. That the Warsaw Poles made a suicidal mistake can hardly be in doubt.

B.H. Liddell Hart, a British historian, viewing the tragic events, says it was natural that the Polish underground forces felt that the Russians had deliberately held off. But he points out that military factors rather than political ones were what kept Moscow from storming the city.[2]

A measure of the strength of Hitler's armies inside Poland in the summer of 1944 is shown by the enormity of Russian casualties in the Polish campaign: 500,000.

Notes

1. With the break-up of the USSR the Republic of Belorussia changed its name to Belarus. Except for wartime names of army groups, and a few other cases

where the former name is more appropriate, the new name is used throughout this book.

2. In the 1980s, declassification of British documents added to the evidence that Moscow was not notified in advance of the uprising in Warsaw. A commission appointed by the British General Staff reported on 31 July 1944, on the eve of the uprising: 'It would be politically and militarily unacceptable to undertake any such measures without the approval and cooperation of the Russians.' German General Kurt von Tippelskirch wrote after the war: 'The Warsaw uprising broke out on August 1, when the force of the Russian advance had already spent itself.' (His *A History of the Second World War*, Berlin, 1956. In German.)

12

BERLIN: DEFEAT AND REVIVAL

The Berlin Operation crowned Zhukov's achievements as a military leader.
Sputnik, December 1996

When the final mammoth offensive of the war began on 12 January 1945 few people in Germany, and also in America and Britain, realized the extent of Hitler's predicament. Although Germany would soon become a theatre of operations, the Wehrmacht was still very strong, and German war production still significant – yet in a little over 100 days Hitler's Reich collapsed.

The final lunge to the west was carried out jointly with Polish, Czechoslovakian, Bulgarian and Romanian troops. During the offensive in Poland the Red Army encountered the world's biggest cemetery – the Nazi extermination camp of Auschwitz – and a number of sinister facts, concealed by Hitler's minions, came to light. In the camp's stockrooms Russian soldiers found 7,000 kilograms of hair clipped from the heads of 140,000 executed women, cases of powdered human bone, heaps of children's shoes, babies' vests and even dolls, which the children played with until the last minute.

Details of the liberation of the camp were released by Moscow on 7 May 1945. Richard Overy points out in his book, *Russia's War* (1998), that the Soviet report makes no mention of Jews who comprised a large number of the estimated 3 million or more victims at Auschwitz. Did Zhukov have opinions on Nazi anti-Semitism? It is known that he detested the Hitler regime. Zhukov's daughters Ella and Era are emphatic: Zhukov was never an anti-Semite; he judged people only by their ability to carry out tasks promptly, to the best of their ability. They note that one of the generals highly praised by Zhukov in December 1941 was cavalryman Lev Dovator, a Jew by origin who died a hero's death.[1]

Here is what Georgi Zhukov says about his last great battle:

During the entire war I took a direct part in many large and important offensive operations but the coming battle for Berlin was a special, unprecedented operation. The forces of the Front were to break through a zone of strong solid defensive lines organized in depth beginning from the Oder river and ending with strongly fortified Berlin. At the approaches to Berlin we would have to smash an enormous group of Nazi troops and capture the capital of Nazi Germany for which the enemy would undoubtedly wage a deadly struggle.

Zhukov's expectations were correct. Nazi Germany was getting ready for the decisive battle on the Eastern front. In so doing the German High Command turned the country's eastern region into a so-called Dead Zone. Every region abandoned by German troops, says German historian Walter Gorlitz, was to become a desert. Industrial plants, food supplies, bridges, railway facilities, dams, the telegraph, radio stations and mines were to be destroyed. Field Marshal Wilhelm Keitel and Reichsleiter Martin Bormann, respectively Chief of the High Command and Chief of the Party Chancellery, issued a strict order whereby every town was to be defended to the last man. Army tribunals had a field day trying commanders who failed to do so. The hangman reaped a bumper harvest as people who hoisted white flags as the enemy troops approached were killed. Soldiers who lost their units were hanged in the streets. Death roamed the land in many disguises.[2]

The Berlin operation had basically been drawn up by the Soviet Supreme High Command in November 1944 when account was being taken of actions by General Eisenhower's Allied Expeditionary Force which had reached the Rhine on a wide front in late March and early April 1945 and had begun to launch an offensive into the heart of Germany.

Powerful Nazi forces in East Prussia, which had been cut off from the rest of Germany in late January, held out until April when the remnants of Hitler's units in Königsberg were defeated. Meanwhile, the Wehrmacht prepared for a last stand in front of their capital, enlisting the Hitler Youth and other raw recruits. In late March, Eisenhower had decided to make his main thrust through central Germany to the Leipzig–Dresden area, with the object of cutting the country into two and linking up with the Russians on the Elbe. He reasoned that Berlin was still hundreds of kilometres away but only tens of kilometres from the Russian lines where Marshal Zhukov now had a bridgehead across the Oder and a million men under his command. US General Omar

Bradley estimated that rushing towards Berlin would cost 100,000 casualties – possibly an exaggerated figure – and not be worth whatever political advantage accrued from the capture of that city. More important, he felt, was the quick destruction of Hitler's armies on his own front (Omar Bradley, *A Soldier's Story*, 1951). In any case, Stalin was determined to be first inside Berlin. His armies had already supplied the bulk of the blood required to crush Hitler's forces and his generals were not to be deterred by the probability of additional heavy casualties in reaching the heart of Berlin.

Meanwhile, on 21 April, Hitler ordered a major assault on the Russians who were now besieging Berlin. Any commander who held back his troops, Hitler fumed, would immediately 'forfeit his life'.

Eisenhower it should be noted was not bound by any 'stopping line' in pursuing the Germans. No such line had been agreed upon at the Yalta Summit in February 1945. Ike believed that a thrust towards Berlin would leave most of his other army units immobilized which he thought was 'more than unwise; it was stupid' (Eisenhower, *Crusade in Europe*, 1948). Meanwhile the Americans had stopped at the Elbe, allowing Soviet forces to capture territories within reach of their armies. (After the Cold War began, Eisenhower's decision concerning Berlin was much criticized, especially after the Berlin blockade in 1948.) On 30 March 1945 Eisenhower sent a message to Churchill saying: 'I propose driving eastward to join hands with Russians or to attain the general line of Elbe. [The drive] will not involve us in crossing the Elbe.' The next day Churchill replied to Eisenhower saying: 'I do not know why it would be an advantage not to cross the Elbe.' And, turning to Berlin, Churchill said: 'If we deliberately leave Berlin to them [the Russians], even if it should be in our grasp, the double event may strengthen their conviction, already apparent, that they have done everything.' Ike promptly answered on 1 April, mentioning Berlin: 'if at any moment [the enemy's] collapse should suddenly come about everywhere along the front we would rush forward, and ... Berlin would be included in our important targets.' Churchill's motive was apparent the following day in his message to Eisenhower: 'I deem it highly important that we should shake hands with the Russians as far to the east as possible.'

But the Russians forged ahead, wishing to end the war as quickly as possible, routing the enemy, remembering the mass killings and wanton destruction that the Wehrmacht had committed on the territory of the USSR. In a Gallup-type poll taken among 5,848 Russian soldiers of the 2nd Guards Tank Army towards the end of the war, it was learned that 4,447 of their relatives had been killed, 1,169 maimed, and 908 deported to Germany as slave labour. The enemy had also burnt down 2,430 villages, towns and cities where the servicemen had lived before the war. Almost every soldier had a horror tale to tell.

But there was no question of reverting to Old Testament vengeance, of 'an eye for an eye' retaliation – of doing to the German people what their armies did to Russia. Most historians credit the Russians with making a sharp distinction between Nazi henchmen and the German population. It is difficult to take exception to the following remarks by Russian General Vasili Shatilov, whose division had raised the Victory flag over the Reichstag:

> Berliners looked at our people with ever greater attention. Of course their gaze expressed different emotions – humility, ingratiation, ill-concealed hatred. But more and more often we saw in their eyes genuine surprise. The victors' conduct was incomprehensible to people whose outlook had been moulded by persistent Nazi propaganda. The Russians did not engage in massacring and plunder; they did not take vengeance for the atrocities the German army had committed on our territory. On the contrary, they fed those whom, it seemed, they ought to have regarded as their mortal enemies.

Antony Beevor's controversial book on Berlin has been cited earlier. Despite the author's wealth of detail, the book contains some obvious lacunae.[3]

On 29 March Zhukov arrived in Moscow, summoned by the Stavka, with the plan of the First Belorussian Front for the Berlin operation. (Not for the first time in the war, Zhukov had been appointed a Front commander.) Late that evening Stalin called him to his Kremlin office. Stalin was alone following a conference with members of the State Defence Committee.

Offering his hand in silence, Stalin began to speak, as if, says Zhukov, he were continuing a conversation that had been interrupted:

'The German front in the west has collapsed completely and, apparently, the Hitlerites do not want to take measures to stop the advance of Allied troops. At the same time they are strengthening their groups on all the most important sectors against us. Here is the map, take a look at the latest data on German troops.'

Stalin lit his pipe and said: 'I think it's going to be quite a fight.'

Then he asked Zhukov his opinion of the enemy on the Berlin

sector. Producing his front map, Zhukov laid it on the table for the Supreme Commander who began to examine the details of the operational–strategic group of German troops in the vicinity of Berlin with close attention. According to Zhukov's data, the Germans had four armies in place with no less than 90 divisions, including 14 panzer and motorized divisions, 37 separate regiments and 98 separate battalions. Later, it was learned that on the Berlin sector there were at least a million men, 10,000 artillery pieces and mortars, 1,500 tanks and assault guns, and 3,500 combat planes. Behind them was a 200,000-strong garrison being formed inside Berlin.

'When will our troops be ready to attack?' asked Stalin.

Zhukov reported:

'The First Belorussian Front can begin the offensive not later than in two weeks. The First Ukrainian Front will apparently also be ready by that time. The Second Belorussian Front by all appearances will be delayed because of the fighting in the Danzig and Gdynia area until mid-April and will be unable to begin the offensive from the Oder simultaneously with the First Belorussian and First Ukrainian Fronts.'

'In that case,' said Stalin, 'we will have to begin the operation without waiting for Rokossovsky's Front to act. If he is a few days late, it's no tragedy.'

Then the Supreme Commander came up to his desk, leafed through some papers and picked up a letter.

'Here, read this.'

The letter was from a 'well-wisher' in Europe, presumably someone on the Soviet payroll, who told about secret talks between Nazi agents and official representatives of the Allies, and indicated that the Germans were proposing to the Allies to stop fighting against them if they would agree to a separate peace. But the letter also indicated that the Allies had rejected the German overtures. Nevertheless, the Kremlin believed it was not to be excluded that the Germans would make it easier for the Anglo-American troops to advance towards Berlin.

'Well, what do you make of it?' asked Stalin; and not waiting for an answer, remarked: 'I think Roosevelt won't violate the Yalta accords, but as for Churchill, he wouldn't flinch at anything.'

Of his two major wartime partners, Stalin thought more highly of Roosevelt than of Churchill. But the feeling was mutual. According to Churchill's doctor Lord Moran (*Churchill, Taken from the Diaries of Lord Moran*, Boston, 1966), Churchill, believing he had been insulted when he met Stalin in Moscow in August 1942, privately cursed Stalin as a 'brigand'.

Two days later, Marshal Konev, commander of the First Ukrainian Front joined in the preparation of the general plan for the Berlin operation. Zhukov says that, as far as he can remember, 'We were unanimous at the time on all questions of principle.'

However, the Supreme Commander refused to agree with the entire boundary line between the troops of the two Fronts and erased part of it. He told Konev: 'In case the enemy puts up stiff resistance on the eastern approaches to Berlin, which will undoubtedly happen, and [Zhukov's] Front is delayed, your First Ukrainian Front is to be ready to attack Berlin from the south with your tank armies.'

While making preparations for the storming of Berlin, Zhukov's thoughts often turned to the Battle of Moscow when strong enemy forces at the approaches to the capital inflicted powerful blows on the defenders. He says: 'I reconsidered separate episodes again and again, analysing the mistakes of the two sides. It was my desire to take into account the experience of that most involved battle to utilize the best in the coming operation to the most minute details, and try not to make any mistakes.'

Zhukov says his men were eager to finish off the enemy as soon as possible and end the war; that the storming of Berlin would be the final act along the 3,000-kilometre route of continuous fighting that these soldiers had travelled.

On the evening of 1 April Zhukov, who was still in Moscow, called his Chief of Staff, M.S. Malinin, who was at the front, and told him: 'Everything has been approved without any special changes. We have very little time. Begin to take measures. I fly out tomorrow.'

These curt instructions were all that was needed for Malinin to begin immediately implementing the plan for the coming assault on Berlin.

Deeply reflecting on the coming operation, Zhukov realized the difficulties ahead for his troops. 'During the war we had not had any occasions to take cities as large and strongly fortified as Berlin. Its total area was nearly 900 square kilometres. A ramified network of undergound communications enabled the enemy troops to carry out concealed manoeuvres.' The defences on the approaches to Berlin would also present difficulties. An unbroken system of defensive works consisting of a number of uninterrupted zones of several trenches each existed from the Oder river to Berlin. The main defensive line had up to five continuous trenches. The enemy, says Zhukov, took advantage of natural obstacles: lakes, rivers, canals and ravines. All towns and villages were 'prepared for all-round defence'. Meanwhile, his engineering units had made a scale model of the city with its suburbs which was used in studying questions concerned with preparing the general assault on Berlin and the inevitable fighting in the city centre.

Unforeseen problems arose during the offensive. For instance, there were moments when the 2nd Guards Tank Army was up to 70 kilometres ahead of the field armies. This, says Zhukov, was not envisaged in the operation, because the distance to Berlin along a straight line was not more than 60 to 70 kilometres. In addition, it was harder than expected to take the strongly fortified Seelow Heights which were 12 kilometres from the forward line of the German defences. It seems Zhukov had underestimated the strength of the Seelow Heights, a Nazi strongpoint, with its steep gradient.

Hitler, in an attempt to rally his troops, wrote an appeal on 14 April, two days before the Berlin operation commenced:

'We have foreseen this attack and countered it with a strong front. Our infantry losses are being replenished by innumerable new formations, combined elements and units of the Volkssturm reinforcing the front. Berlin will remain German.' The Volkssturm were volunteer militia made up mainly of elderly men. But there were also many conscripts of 15 and 16 year-olds, members of the Hitlerjugend, the Nazi youth organization, many of whom were armed with the *Panzerfaust* (bazooka-type anti-tank weapons).

At first Heinrich Himmler, chief of the SS, headed the defence of the immediate approaches to Berlin, and all the top posts were given to SS generals. Nine divisions had been transferred to the Berlin sector from others in March and April 1945. (Himmler would later commit suicide rather than stand trial at the end of the war. There is some evidence that before he took his own life, he and his generals hoped in vain for an alliance with Britain and the USA against the Russian Bolsheviki.) Himmler thought of the 'postwar period' as being a short breathing space between the Second and a Third World War. In April 1945 Himmler had several talks with a visitor from Sweden, Count Folke Bernadotte, in which he sought to pass word to Washington and London that Germany was willing to surrender on the Western Front but never on the Eastern.[4]

Colonel-General Alfred Jodl, Operations Chief of Staff of the Nazi High Command, during interrogations at the end of the war said:

In order to provide the necessary reinforcements for the Eastern Front by the beginning of the decisive Russian offensive, we had to disband our entire reserve army, that is, all the infantry, panzer, artillery and special reserve units, military schools and colleges, and send their personnel to reinforce the troops.

Taking all this into consideration, Zhukov says the main plan was to attack enemy troops in the defensive area with such force that they would be stunned immediately and then crushed by using masses of aircraft, tanks, artillery and other equipment. 'But,' he adds, 'to muster secretly all the arms and military hardware on the theatre of military operations in so short a period of time required titanic – and I would say – highly skilful work.'

Now, hundreds of trains with artillery, mortars and tanks moved westerly through Poland. From a distance they did not look like military trains but flatcars transporting timber and hay. But as soon as the trains arrived at their destination the camouflage was quickly removed and tanks, artillery pieces and tractors came off the flatcars and were immediately sent off to hidden shelters. As an idea of the huge quantity of the supplies, only in terms of ordnance it was necessary to have 7,147,000 shells available by the beginning of the Berlin operation.

'We were absolutely sure that the troops would have no shortage of ammunition, fuel and food,' says Zhukov.

Late at night on 15 April, a few hours before the artillery and air strikes were to begin, Zhukov set out for the observation post of the 8th Guards Army commanded by General Vasili Chiukov. (He is described by American writer Edgar Snow who was on a visit to the Russian front as having a big body, big hands, big face with all-gold teeth 'and a big heart'.) The hands of the clock, says Zhukov, moved slowly as never before. 'In order to fill the remaining minutes before the artillery barrage we decided to have some hot strong tea which was made for us in the dugout by a girl. I remember that she had a non-Russian name: Margot. We sipped tea in silence, each deep in his thoughts.'

Zhukov looked at his watch. It was exactly 3 o'clock in the morning. At this moment thousands of guns, mortars and rockets lit up the sky followed by a tremendous din from the explosions of shells and aircraft bombs. The continuous roar of bombers was steadily growing louder. It was time for the general offensive. At this moment thousands of flares flew into the air. 'This was the signal for 140 searchlights placed at intervals of 200 metres to flash spotlights to blind the

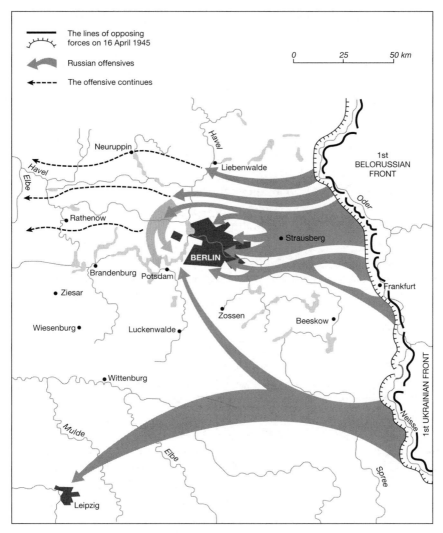

The Berlin Operation

enemy and light up targets for our tanks and infantry in the darkness,'
says the marshal. By dawn Zhukov's troops had taken the first position
and begun to attack the second. Russian bombers made 6,550 sorties
dropping bombs on targets too far for the artillery to reach. Other
bombers cooperated with the infantry in the morning.

The closer Zhukov's men approached the Seelow Heights the
stronger became enemy resistance. Berlin lay behind the heights. By
one o'clock in the afternoon Zhukov realized that the guns of the
enemy defence were largely intact on the Seelow Heights. He and his
commanders decided to commit two tank armies to reinforce the
attacking troops and break through the defence by all means.

Zhukov called the Stavka and spoke to Stalin telling him of the stiff
resistance by the Germans. Stalin ordered:

'Support the attack of your tank armies with bombers. Report in the
evening how things are going.'

In the evening Zhukov called again, repeating the difficulties of
taking the heights but saying they would be captured on the evening
of the next day.

'This time, Stalin spoke to me not as calmly as he had earlier,' says
Zhukov.

'You should not have committed the 1st Guards Tank Army to
battle on the sector of the 8th Guards Army instead of where the
Supreme Command had instructed.' Then he added: 'Are you sure
you'll take the Seelow line tomorow?'

Zhukov says he tried to appear calm as he told Stalin that by the end
of the day, on 17 April the heights would be breached. He told Stalin:
'I believe that the more of his troops the enemy hurls at our forces
here, the quicker we will later take Berlin because it is easier to defeat
the enemy in the open field than in a city.'

On 20 April, the fifth day of the operation, long-range artillery of
Zhukov's 3rd Shock Army opened fire on Berlin. It was the beginning
of the historic storming of the Nazi capital.

In order to crush the enemy defence in Berlin as swiftly as possible
it was decided to commit two tank armies to assist the 8th Guards, 5th
Shock, 3rd Shock and 47th armies in the fighting in the city. But as
these armies approached the city centre enemy resistance stiffened
sharply. The Germans used all the advantages offered to that side
which is on the defensive inside a city: multi-storey buildings, thick
walls, bomb shelters and bunkers connected with each other through
underground passages. The Germans could move from one block to

another along these passages or even appear in the rear of Zhukov's men. But the most heavy fighting in the central part of Berlin fell to the lot of assault groups and assault detachments consisting of all the arms of the service.

The Battle of Berlin was reaching its peak. Although in agony the defenders continued to fight for every house, every cellar, for every storey and roof.

German General Jodl revealed some details later to Allied interrogators:

> On 22 April Goebbels asked me if it was possible to avert the fall of Berlin by military means. I answered that it was possible only provided we withdrew all the forces on the Elbe and sent them to defend Berlin. On Goebbels' advice I reported my thoughts to the Fuehrer. He agreed and instructed Keitel and me together with Headquarters to be outside Berlin and personally command the counterattack.

The commander of the Berlin garrison, General Helmuth Weidling said at an interrogation after the surrender:

> On 25 April Hitler told me: 'The situation will improve[!]. Our 9th Army will approach Berlin and hit the enemy together with the 12th Army. This attack will be inflicted along the Russian southern front. Another army will advance from the north and hit the enemy's northern wing.'

Needless to say, these were the fantasies of a man who had lost the capacity of thinking rationally.

Meanwhile, Zhukov noted that the medical orderly of the 832nd Artillery Regiment was writing on the battery's shells destined for Berlin: 'For Stalingrad, for the Ukraine, for the orphans and widows . . . For mothers' tears!'

On 30 April stubborn fighting was going on in the Reichstag which was defended by crack SS units, almost 6,000 strong, equipped with tanks, assault guns and artillery. Meanwhile Zhukov reported that one of his divisions had captured the Moabit Prison freeing thousands of POWs, including political prisoners. His soldiers found guillotines and other instruments of death and torture which they also found at Pletzensee Prison.

A week after his last conversation with Hitler, General Weidling was facing General Chuikov who was giving him the terms of surrender. Weidling had offered to surrender the armoured corps he commanded, the 56th, but was reluctant to order the Berlin Garrison to do likewise. A Russian poet with the rank of major, Evgeny Dolmatovsky, was present and says Chuikov was blunt in his remarks. (A large photograph exists showing at least 200 Russian soldiers sitting on the ground in front of Berlin's Brandenburg Gate just after the surrender, listening to Dolmatovsky, who is standing on a T-34 tank, reading poetry.)

'Your cause is lost,' said Chuikov. 'Further sacrifice is futile. With every minute that goes by the death toll is mounting.'

Weidling was shaking his head, objecting.

'I am no longer in command. I am your prisoner. Which means I have no right to issue orders. The troops will not obey me since I'm a prisoner.'[5]

Dolmatovsky says he expected to see General Chuikov lose his towering temper. ('The object of Chuikov's wrath was not to be envied,' he recalls.) But Chuikov remained cool and told Weidling it was essential to save the lives of thousands of German soldiers, that the cellars and the underground railway were packed with peaceful citizens. He urged Weidling to show wisdom and humaneness.

At long last, Weidling bowed his head and, on a scrap of paper, pencilled an order stating that further resistance by the Berlin Garrison was senseless.

But the Reichstag had to be stormed once more on 30 April by units from two rifle divisions who cleared storey after storey of the enemy. Three hours later two sergeants hoisted the Victory Flag on the main cupola of the building. (The last group of Reichstag defenders surrendered on the following day.)

1 May – a holiday on the socialist calendar – was a busy time for Zhukov. He learned about Hitler's suicide. German General Krebs – who would himself commit suicide – had told Soviet General Chuikov that Hitler's body had been burnt. Zhukov put through a call to Stalin. A duty officer answered that 'Comrade Stalin has just gone to bed.'

'Please wake him up. The matter is urgent and can't wait till morning.'

In a little while Stalin was on the line. Zhukov told him about the suicide. Stalin answered: 'Now he's done it, the bastard. Too bad he could not have been taken alive. Where is Hitler's body?'

'According to [German] General Krebs Hitler's body was burned.'

'Tell [General Vasily] Sokolovsky that there can be no talks – either with Krebs or any other Hitlerites – only unconditional surrender,' said the Supreme Commander. 'If nothing special happens, don't call me till morning. I want to have a little rest before the May Day parade.'

About one hour later Sokolovsky phoned Zhukov to report on his lengthy conversation with Krebs.

'The Germans have something up their sleeve,' he said. 'Krebs says he is not authorized to decide on unconditional surrender. According to him, that can be done only by the new German government headed by Doenitz. Krebs maintains that he seeks to arrange a cease-fire in order to assemble the members of the Doenitz government in Berlin. I think we should tell them to go to hell if they don't consent to unconditional surrender.'

'Just so, Vasily Danilovich,' Zhukov answered. 'Tell Krebs that if Goebbels and Bormann don't agree to unconditional surrender before ten o'clock, the blow we shall strike will knock all ideas of resistance out of their heads. They had better think of the senseless sacrifices made by the German people and of their own personal responsibility for courting disaster.'

But no reply came from Goebbels and Bormann at the appointed time.

And at 10:40 a.m. Russian guns opened fire on the remnants of the special defence sector in the centre of the Nazi capital. Eight hours later Sokolovsky reported to Zhukov that the German leaders had sent a truce envoy with the message saying that Goebbels and Bormann had rejected the demand for unconditional surrender.

In less than thirty minutes, the Russians gave their reply. The final assault on the central part of Berlin, where the Imperial Chancellery was situated and where the last of the Nazi leadership had dug in, began with what Zhukov calls 'incredible force'.

Zhukov says in his memoirs that the men who conquered Berlin had come from 'hero cities' like Moscow, Leningrad and Stalingrad; from the Ukraine, Belorussia, from the republics on the Caucasus and else-where. 'Many had wounds from previous fighting which had not healed yet. The wounded did not leave the ranks. Everyone was intent on surging forward ... Morale had risen, spirits were high, so it was easier to carry out the great undertaking, to hoist the victory flag in Berlin.'

But the cost in life was dear: the Berlin Operation alone cost the Soviet Army some 100,000 killed and 200,000 wounded.

Signing the surrender documents in a Berlin suburb (a preliminary surrender ceremony had taken place earlier at Rheims) were, for the Allies, Zhukov, British Air Marshal Arthur Tedder, representing the

Allied Command; General Carl Spaatz, Commander of the US Strategic Air Forces; and French General Jean de Lattre de Tassigny, Commander-in-Chief of the French Army. Signing for Nazi Germany were Field Marshal Wilhelm Keitel, Admiral of the Fleet Hans Georg von Friedeburg (he took his own life two weeks later), and Colonel-General of the Luftwaffe P.F. Stumpf.

Zhukov sized up Keitel. 'Before us was another man, no longer that arrogant Keitel who accepted the surrender from defeated France. Although he tried to maintain some kind of pose [he had held up his Field Marshal's baton in greeting the Allied officers] he now had a beaten look.' When Zhukov asked Keitel to approach his table and sign the instrument of Germany's unconditional surrender, the German quickly rose 'shooting a malign glance at us'.

As Keitel put his signature on the surrender document, Zhukov noted that his hand was shaking. Another observer, Russian poet and journalist, Konstantin Simonov, described the scene: 'Keitel's face had darkened and he became rigid. He tossed his head back as though to contain the tears about to roll from under his lids ... His eyes kept shifting from the table to Marshal Zhukov.'

After the signing, Keitel saluted with his baton, pivoted and marched from the room. As the door closed behind Keitel and his fellow German officers, the tension broke, and there were collective sighs of relief among the Allies and mutual congratulations. At a banquet that lasted till six in the morning, Zhukov gave this tribute to Eisenhower: 'His great strides in the West helped me in the East.' One of those present, America's General John Deane, who was the US liaison officer in Moscow, said 'the banquet was one never to be forgotten'.

Notes

1. George Bernard Shaw said that suffering is not cumulative; that the suffering of 1,000 women is not greater than the suffering of ten. Ella and Era say Zhukov had friends and well-wishers among Jews and other minority peoples.
2. Walter Görlitz, *Der Zweite Weltkrieg*, 1955.
3. The following are some of the lacunae:
   General Nikolai Antipenko. This popular general who helped in the postwar administration of Berlin (his sister was brutally tortured by the Nazis) says in his reminiscences: 'It's a fact that the Soviet Command issued orders that the death penalty be used in any case of looting or gratuitous violence committed on German territory.' Antipenko provides information about the steps his unit

took to help ensure a normal life in Berlin. But his name, like the others, does not appear in the book.

Air Marshal Sergei Rudenko, who fought under Marshal Zhukov, was in Berlin in May 1945 and he questioned Berliners about their lives, alluding to their fears of rape and pillaging. He tried to calm the citizens.

Colonel David Dragunsky. Of Jewish origin, this tank officer lost his whole family, including his mother and two sisters, to the invading Nazis but he arrived in Berlin with no outward malice towards the German people. He described his impressions of Berlin and meetings with German inhabitants in a memoir. Like Rudenko, he assured citizens that no reprisals would be taken against them. (Beevor lists Dragunsky's memoirs in his bibliography but does not report on his talks with Berliners.)

Anastas Mikoyan, a chief lieutenant of Stalin, visited Berlin only hours after the surrender, checking on food supplies for the population. (He gave orders to Antipenko that real, not ersatz, coffee be distributed to Berliners.)

Marshal Zhukov makes several references in his memoirs to instructions to his troops about non-violence and fairness in dealing with the civil population.

Dmitry Shcheglov, an officer and playwright, was in Berlin in May 1945, spoke German, and talked to the people on the subject of revenge. 'There is no revenge and there will be no revenge,' the political officer tells Germans he meets. (Although Beevor omits this and other reasonable statements by the playwright he selects one angry, impulsive thought by Shcheglov, who, upon seeing a full larder in a German home, and thinking of the thousands of Russian homes destroyed by the Wehrmacht, says he would like to smash the tins and bottles. But it is just a thought.)

Antony Beevor, in his book finds fault with a Russian general for his apt description of a notorious Berlin prison. The general is V.M. Shatilov, who is quoted above, on the subject of vengeance and how German people viewed the men of his division. Shatilov at war's end sees the Moabit Prison from the outside and calls it 'menacing'. Beevor wonders why 'all' of Berlin's buildings look menacing to the Russians. But he makes no mention of the thousands of prisoners who were tortured and killed inside the gloomy grey building that was Moabit. But Shatilov knew what was inside: that one of the best known Soviet inmates of Moabit was the Tatar poet, Mussa Jalil, author of a remarkable book of poems, *The Moabit Notebooks*. Mussa Jalil had joined the army, was captured and died in Moabit in August 1943 after – according to fellow inmates – the Gestapo broke his left arm, injured his kidneys and beat him to death with a rubber hose. A few days before his death Mussa Jalil wrote a poem that ends with these lines:

> Victorious force of life!
> I knew life is sweet.
> And I die in prison.
> This song is my last.

4. Documents of the International Military Tribunal.
5. Dolmatovsky's recollections appeared in the journal *New Times*, no. 19, 1985.

13

HITLER'S MARRIAGE AND DEATH

The bodies found in the pit near [Hitler's] bunker were those of Hitler and Eva Braun. Both died of poisoning by cyanide compounds.
From a statement by DR FAUST SHKARAVSKY and NIKOLAI KOTLYAR, medical and forensic investigators in Berlin, May 1945

Hitler's funeral pyre, with the din of the Russian guns growing ever louder, made a lurid end to the Third Reich.
WINSTON CHURCHILL, *History of the Second World War*, vol. 2, 1949

When Red Army officers entered Berlin early in May 1945 they found what appeared to be the authentic diary of a leading Nazi, Martin Bormann, who was Hitler's secretary, adviser and chief of the party chancellery. He kept this diary from December 1944 until April 1945. It mentions the marriage of Hitler and Eva Braun.

A brief extract:

Wednesday, 25 April: First full-scale air raid on Obersaltzburg. Berlin is surrounded!

Thursday, 26 April: Himmler and Jodl have delayed the arrival of divisions coming to our aid. [Heinrich Himmler, chief of the SS, committed suicide. Alfred Jodl, Operations Chief of Staff of the Nazi High Command, was sentenced to death by hanging.)

Friday, 27 April: We stand by the Fuehrer and die with him.

Saturday, 28 April: Our Imperial Chancellery is a heap of rubble. The world is on the brink of destruction . . . For the second time the day starts with a hurricane of fire.

Sunday, 29 April: Last night the foreign press announced that Himmler offered to accept unconditional surrender. Adolf Hitler and Eva Braun had a marriage ceremony. The Fuehrer had his political, and then personal, will written down . . . A hurricane of fire again!

Monday, 30 April: Adolf Hitler is dead. Eva Hitler is dead.

Georgi Zhukov created a furore when he told a press conference in Berlin in June 1945 that Adolf Hitler might have escaped from Berlin by air. This was 'feasible', he said, adding that he didn't think Adolf Hitler's body had been found. But he did say he had evidence that Hitler had married Eva Braun two days before the fall of Berlin. Possibly it was a 'death-bed marriage' to Eva Braun, whom Zhukov described as a film actress. Hitler's fate, concluded the marshal, was 'very mysterious'. (But it seems even high-placed Americans had lingering doubts about Hitler's end. *The Times* reported on 8 and 13 October 1945 that General Eisenhower told journalists when he visited Holland that although he initially believed Hitler was dead, 'there are now reasons to assume he is still alive'. But a few days later in Frankfurt, Ike modified his statement, saying it was hardly likely that Hitler was still alive. But he said his 'Russian friends' – this was five months after Victory Day – still maintained uncertainties about the Fuehrer's death.)

In any case, given the talent for earlier subterfuge by Goebbels' Propaganda Ministry, it was understandable that Zhukov was sceptical. Many other stories were then making the rounds: that Hitler and other Nazi bigwigs had escaped in a Tiger tank, that Hitler and Eva Braun were last seen boarding a submarine. Martin Bormann had indeed fled. Not making life easier for investigators – or photographers – was the repeated claim that there existed some fifty Hitler doubles.

Not long afterwards, Zhukov received more information about Hitler which helped put his mind at rest. He says: 'Some time later, after an inquiry and the questioning of Hitler's personal medical staff, etc., we started to receive additional, more concrete evidence confirming Hitler's suicide. I became convinced that there were no grounds for doubting Hitler's suicide.' He adds that 'most of the Nazi ringleaders, among them Goering, Himmler, Keitel and Jodl, fled from Berlin in different directions in good time'.[1]

Some writers assert that Stalin hid all or part of the evidence about Hitler from Zhukov; that the marshal had to wait 10 or 15 years to get the facts. Given that Stalin was an artist of skulduggery, he was certainly capable of such tricks. However, it appears that, after 5 or 6 weeks Zhukov had enough new information of his own to convince him of Hitler's suicide. For example, forensic experts attached to one of his armies had made tests and provided proof about the deaths of Hitler and Braun. But as to other dimensions of the story – for example that Beria's secret police had spirited away to Moscow

Hitler's skull or jawbone – such a secret could well have been kept from Zhukov's knowledge for years.

In his memoirs, the marshal says that after the seizure of the Imperial Chancellery in early May, he and some of his generals went there in order to make certain of the suicide of Hitler, Goebbels and other Nazi leaders. He adds: 'We looked for the place where the bodies of Hitler and Goebbels were burned, but could not find it. Admittedly, we saw the ashes of some fires but they were obviously too small. Most likely German soldiers had used them to boil water.'

What raised additional suspicion were the results of Zhukov's own interrogation of Hans Fritzsche, a close associate of Hitler, Goebbels and Bormann, who was the Deputy Minister of Propaganda under Goebbels. Thus he was conversing with one of the practitioners of Nazi dissimulation. (He was tried by the Nuremberg International Tribunal and acquitted.) Fritzsche, in a reply to a question by Zhukov on Hitler's last plans, said he had heard that some Nazi leaders had gone to Berchtesgaden (Hitler's 'Magic Mountain') and Southern Tyrol taking some crates with them. It was there, Fritzsche said, that the High Command headed by Hitler were supposed to fly. At the last minute there was talk of evacuation to Schleswig-Holstein, a Nazi stronghold close to the Danish border. Planes were kept ready near the Chancellery but were soon destroyed by Air Marshal Rudenko's planes.[2]

On the fate of Goebbels, Zhukov has this to say:

When we had almost finished inspecting the Imperial Chancellery, it was reported to us that the bodies of Goebbels' six children had been found in an underground room. I must admit I had not the heart to go down and look at the children killed by their own mother and father. Shortly afterwards the bodies of Goebbels and his wife were found close to the bunker. Dr Fritzsche, who was brought to identify the bodies, testified that they were those of Goebbels and his wife.

At this time, Zhukov thought Hitler might have escaped because investigators were unable to find his accomplice Martin Bormann who was tried *in absentia* in accordance with Article 12 of the Nuremberg International Tribunal Charter.

Among Bormann's papers a puzzling telegram was found:

22.4.45
To Hummel. Obersalzberg.
I agree to the proposed move south across the ocean.

Reichsleiter Bormann

Bormann, apparently, was preparing a hideout for himself outside Germany. Had he in fact succeeded in escaping from Berlin?

It is probable that Zhukov based his opinion on the fate of Hitler on the detective work of Lieutenant-Colonel Faust Shkaravsky and procurator Nikolai Kotlyar. Shkaravsky, an expert in forensic medicine, was a member of the Medical Corps that belonged to Zhukov's First Belorussian Front which led the way into Berlin. What follows is a report on their investigations.

Nikolai Kotlyar was appointed military procurator of the Berlin garrison while street battles were still continuing. He also remained the military procurator of the 5th Strike Army. Earlier, during military operations in Poland, when he learned that the 5th Strike Army would take part in the storming of Berlin, Kotlyar daydreamed: 'What if we capture Hitler? What kind of interrogation shall I give him!'

On 2 May at a few minutes past six on the morning, Kotlyar and a group of officers and machine gunners headed for the observation post of one of the regiments of the 301st Infantry Division. The liaison officer appointed by the commander took them to a plain barracks-like building.

'This is the Hitler bunker,' the officer said. 'We are still fighting inside it.'

At 10 a.m. the group was allowed to enter the Imperial Chancellery and go down to the cellar. Kotlyar was repelled by an overpowering smell of blood, gunpowder and what seemed to be chloroform. The stairs were dark and shooting was heard somewhere in the darkness. The group climbed back into the offices and halls of the Chancellery where soldiers sat or lay in nearly all the rooms, worn out by combat. He noticed that many of them were wounded. Everywhere were heaps of reichmarks, scraps of papers, pieces of furniture and glass, and official orders and other documents. A huge chandelier stood at an angle on the floor of an office. Those who entered it first said: 'Hitler's room.'

The group searched the yard and closely inspected the empty swimming pool: It was claimed to have previously been 'filled to capacity' with the bodies of Hitler's doubles.

There was, in fact, much discussion revolving around the subject of Hitler's doubles. Kotlyar believes that if so many of them existed, then those who searched for Hitler would likely have found some of them. (The body of at least one double was actually photographed and widely circulated later.) The question was: why would Hitler, in his final moments, keep so many doubles in the Chancellery, especially when his fate was sealed?

In the afternoon of 2 May, search parties set up by the Soviet Command in the Chancellery discovered the bodies of Goebbels and his wife Magda, who had committed suicide, in addition to the bodies of Colonel-General Hans Krebs, chief of the Army General Staff, and one of Hitler's personal aides.

Some time later, Kotlyar attempted once more to 'find' Hitler. Already he heard several stories – legends, really, and there were even 'witnesses' who said they saw Hitler escape to Spain or South America. It was also said that Hitler underwent plastic surgery. There were others who said they saw him and Eva Braun board a submarine.

The next day, 3 May, Kotlyar learned that the Smersh section of military counter-intelligence (Smersh, or *Smert Shpionam* – death to spies) had got hold of Otto Gunsche, Hitler's bodyguard, and another guard, for interrogation. The men revealed details of Hitler's and Eva Braun's deaths, saying they were present when the bodies were cremated.

Nevertheless, Kotlyar continued his search for Adolf Hitler, questioning a number of officers and functionaries. He reconstructed the situation in Hitler's bunker just before the suicide. Much later he learned more details as he read documents as well as the testimonies of witnesses, some of which were recorded in the minutes of the Nuremberg War Crimes Trials. But what struck Kotlyar most forcefully was his recollection of 'the sinking Nazi ship', where those who had once slavishly kowtowed to Hitler, calling him a genius, now dashed about like rats and betrayed him when their time came.

On 4 May the group was told that the charred bodies of Hitler and Eva Braun had been found by the intelligence body of the 3rd Strike Army and that they were being identified. Kotlyar learned that a special unit was set up to make certain of the identities of the bodies. The remains were so charred that outer indentification was impossible. Therefore, other means had to be used: teeth and jaws.[3] The group interrogated dozens of witnesses and learned that Hitler's and Eva Braun's dentist was a professor who had fled to the West. But they were able to locate his assistant who had helped make false teeth for the Fuehrer.

Dr Faust Shkaravsky said he asked the assistant to inspect the false teeth and she affirmed that they belonged to Hitler. But the main proof was a comparison of the teeth and the plaster casts found in the dentist's clinic.

The investigations thus found proof that the bodies discovered in a pit outside the Chancellery were those of Hitler and Eva Braun. The report said conclusively that both died of poisoning by cyanide compounds.[4]

Notes

1. Himmler committed suicide. Goering, Keitel and Jodl were sentenced to death by the International Military Tribunal, but Goering committed suicide before execution.

2. Hans Fritzsche, Dr Goebbels' Deputy Minister of Propaganda, in a postwar book, *Sword in the Balance*, said Hitler's Reich never had in mind the extermination of 30 million Russian citizens. However, at the Nuremberg Tribunal it was learned that Field Marshal Walter von Reichenau said in an order that 'supplying civilians and war prisoners with food is needless squeamishness'. The Tribunal also heard evidence that the mass killing of Russian prisoners of war was decided on beforehand. A War Prisoners Department was set up under General Reinecke at the headquarters of the High Command. He issued secret instructions in March 1941 'on how to treat war prisoners'. The Russian POWs were to be kept in the open and not fed.

3. Adolf Hitler's autopsy is cited in Lev Bezymenski, *Death of Adolf Hitler*, 1968; Yelena Rzhevskaya, *Berlin, May 1945* (in *How Wars End*, Moscow, 1969); and Ron Rosenbaum, *Explaining Hitler*, 1998.

4. There is still disagreement on the circumstances of Hitler's death. Some writers say a gun was used in the suicide. There are reports that another person who was close to Hitler administered the *coup de grâce* after the Fuehrer swallowed poison.

14

'BASTARDS AND PLOTTERS'

Beria's web had ensnared him.

VIKTOR ANFILOV, *Stalin's Generals*

Stalin was jealous.

From official reports

Zhukov is guilty of 'Bonapartism'.

KHRUSHCHEV, *Khrushchev Remembers*

Zhukov's resurrection.

From *The Russian Mirror*

Georgi Zhukov was able to enjoy the fruits of victory for little more than a year. In the spring of 1946 Eisenhower and Montgomery were recalled from Berlin by their governments. General Lucius Clay replaced Eisenhower. He said in a memoir that Ike had felt strongly about his friendship with Zhukov and he even went so far as to say that US–Soviet relations might well have remained on track if only Eisenhower and Zhukov had continued to work together. But perhaps Clay was putting too much emphasis on relations between individuals. In any case, Zhukov received a phone call from Stalin, telling him about the recall of Ike and Monty.

'Perhaps you should return to Moscow as well,' said Stalin.

Zhukov agreed and recommended his deputy, General of the Army V.D. Sokolovsky, to replace him as Commander-in-Chief of the Soviet occupation zone. 'He is better acquainted with the work of the Control Council than anyone else and knows the troops well.'

Despite the seeming reasonableness of the change it was the first step in the marshal's reversal of fortunes.

Almost immediately, a second phone call came from Stalin: the Politburo had agreed to appoint Sokolovsky in his place and suggested that Zhukov leave for Moscow after the next Control Council meeting in Berlin. In Moscow they had decided to do away with the post of first deputy of the people's commissar of defence. Instead, Bulganin, who had submitted a project for restructuring the armed forces after the war, was appointed as a deputy to deal with general questions.

Stalin said: 'Vasilevsky is being appointed chief of the general staff. We're considering appointing Kuznetsov commander-in-chief of the Navy. You are not on the list of the higher command echelon of the armed forces. This is, I believe, wrong. What post would you like to have?'

Zhukov answered like he always did, showing not a trace of ambition, like the professional soldier he remained: he would take any post the Central Committee considered most appropriate for him.

'I think you should be in charge of the ground forces,' said Stalin. 'It's our strongest branch. We think that a Commander-in-Chief should be at the head of them.' He instructed Zhukov to come back to Moscow and work out with Bulganin and Vasilevsky the duties of the leading figures of the Defence Commissariat.

On May Day in 1946 Zhukov appeared together with Stalin atop Lenin's Mausoleum with other ranking political and military officials. Then, in less than 90 days, a brief article appeared in *Pravda*, the Party paper, imparting astonishing news: Zhukov had a new job, one observer called it a 'singularly lowly one'. He had been appointed Commander of the Odessa Military District. In addition he had been expelled from the Communist Party's Central Committee of which he was a prominent member. It looked to some observers that Zhukov had fallen victim to Stalin's 'purge of the heroes'. Clearly, Zhukov's Achilles heel was his independence of mind; and perhaps it was inevitable that he would sooner or later run foul of the secret police, as well as the high priests of the Party. He had been far removed from the sycophants around Stalin and his goon squads led by Lavrenti Beria and V.S. Abakumov. As it was, arrests of generals on the spurious charge of anti-Soviet agitation began to take place between 1947 and 1949, the officers being confined to Lefortovo Prison. Zhukov's fall from grace was an additional warning sign to the military not to stray far from Party control.

Since the war, 'unfriendly information' had begun circulating about Zhukov; that he was taking too much credit for wartime victories and slighting the role of other members of the Supreme High Command; that well-known generals seemed to pay more homage to Zhukov than to Stalin who many citizens still hailed as the Military Genius responsible for the victory over Nazi Germany; that Zhukov was secretly plotting against Stalin. And was not Zhukov becoming too cozy with the capitalist American general, Eisenhower? (Within Beria's secret police there was a handy accusation that could be used at any time to snare the innocent: 'too much association with the West'.) Not least, Zhukov had spoken out often against undue Party influence in the armed forces.

While Stalin seems still to have retained a high regard for Zhukov's generalship during the war, his huge popularity was bound to rankle a jealous leader. The secret police were also getting in their innings. At the end of 1945 Abakumov landed in Berlin and straightaway began arresting some officers who worked under Zhukov. What he was after was evidence of Zhukov's disloyalty. It was well known that once somebody landed in Beria's torture chambers that person after a 24-hour 'workout' would admit to anything that was asked for. Beria is supposed to have told a colleague: 'Give me a man for one night and I'll make him say he's the King of England!' When Zhukov found out what Abakumov was doing he told him in no uncertain terms to turn around and head back to Moscow or he would send him there under military guard.

But witnesses had already made confessions that were damaging to Zhukov. One of those who was arrested was General A.A. Novikov, who was forced into saying that Zhukov was overly ambitious and that he, Novikov, had frequently passed information to Zhukov about what was going on inside the Kremlin. Another general who was tortured into giving information about Zhukov, and imprisoned, was K.F. Telegin, who had been the head of the Front political department under the marshal. It wasn't long before Zhukov was summoned to a meeting to confront his accusers who included the intelligence officer F.I. Golikov, a man Zhukov found beneath contempt.

After several speakers censured Zhukov, he was asked to defend himself. Zhukov was a convincing speaker, and he explained that all accusations against him were baseless, that he had only one aim and that was to be a faithful servant of the party and the motherland. He also asked that some of those persons who had submitted written denunciations of him be questioned because he was convinced they had been tortured and would only put pen to paper under duress.

Understandably, such accusations were painful. Zhukov's daughters have said that their father did his best to weather the storm. He would not, he told them, be broken by those who plotted against him.

But in the end the accusations, suspicions, the searches conducted at his home in an attempt to find 'incriminating evidence', the bugging of his premises – all this impacted on his health. In 1948 he had his first heart attack and was hospitalized.

After another meeting in the Kremlin at the end of 1945, Admiral of the Fleet Nikolai Kuznetsov gave Zhukov more bad news: that everyone was critical of what they had been told about Zhukov – about the marshal's boasting of his victories and almost shutting out the role of the Supreme High Command – and all those present approved of a censure motion. At the meeting, a number of well-known marshals, including Ivan Konev, K.K. Rokossovsky, and Alexander Vasilevsky and V.D. Sokolovsky, pointed out shortcomings in Zhukov's character, but denied that he was or could be involved in any coup attempt. (It was, incidentally at the Twentieth Party Congress in February 1956 that Party leader Nikita Khrushchev promoted the view that Stalin was highly jealous of Zhukov. Some writers claim that it was Stalin himself who invented far-fetched stories to damage Zhukov in the eyes of the public.)

The most serious charge – one that had apparently been wrung from Novikov at his police interrogation – was that Zhukov stood at the head of a conspiracy to stage a military putsch. Marshal of Tank Troops Pavel Rybalko boldly declared that the time had come to stop giving credence to 'testimony extracted by force in the prisons'. He concluded by saying: 'Comrade Stalin! Members of the Politburo! It is not true that Zhukov is a conspirator. He has his faults, as everyone does, but he is a patriot, which he proved during the Great Patriotic War.'

Then Stalin asked: 'And what do you, Comrade Zhukov, have to say to us?'

The marshal replied: 'Comrade Stalin, such accusations are without foundation. Ever since I joined the Party I have served it and the Motherland honourably. I have never been connected with any conspiracy. I ask that you investigate how the testimony of Telegin and Novikov was obtained. I know these men well, having worked with them in the war and so I am certain that they told these lies under torture.'

Stalin listened, studying Zhukov's face with care. 'However, Comrade Zhukov, you need to leave Moscow for a while.'

Zhukov the soldier replied that he would serve wherever Party and government determined. The place decided upon was the relatively unimportant Odessa Military District. He stayed there until December 1947.

Meanwhile there were other maddening investigations. At a certain customs house scores of boxes were found containing items belonging to Zhukov that he had obtained in Germany, including furniture, household equipment, carpets, mink pelts, artificial seal pelts, flannel material to use as furniture covers and curtains, gifts and mementos, etc. A detailed inventory was attached and, it was clear, everything had been obtained legally. Beria's stooges were again on the lookout for incriminating evidence against Zhukov.

Even the smallest suspected infractions by Zhukov were investigated. For instance, in June 1947 the Party Central Committee reprimanded him for rewarding artists in his district. The only body that had the right to reward artists in peacetime was the Supreme Soviet of the USSR.

There was more to come. In 1948 the authorities were breathing down Zhukov's neck. He had written to the Party's Central Committee in reply to a critical letter from his former adjutant, a Colonel Semochkin, which he said was full of slander. It contained a number of complaints against Zhukov, the most serious of which was that Zhukov allegedly was 'hostile' towards Stalin. Zhukov had addressed America's famed 82nd Airborne Division at a reception in Frankfurt in 1945 and, it was said, had not larded it with praise of Stalin. But, said Zhukov, he had checked with his political adviser, Andrei Vyshinsky, who was alongside him to see that everything he said was sufficiently patriotic.

Zhukov's adjutant apparently reported that his boss was greedy and had no right to keep many of the trophies in his possession. Zhukov admitted that he made some mistakes in purchasing a large quantity of material for his family and relatives with his own money. But he said that by and large the jewellery and watches were gifts from different organizations. As to the rings and costume jewellery, they were acquired by the family over many years.

Zhukov pointed out that his silverware set was a gift from Poland on the occasion of the liberation of Warsaw. This was verified by an inscription on the set. But Zhukov said he regretted that he had not donated some of the items to a museum and given others to friends, but he had left Germany with too little time and had forgotten about it. Yet another criticism was that Zhukov had purchased five or six hunting rifles in Germany although he already owned six Russian rifles. He confessed that like any true hunter he was unable to part with a good weapon.

As an illustration of the extent to which the police spies were used, they discovered that at a banquet held in Zhukov's dacha on the evening of the Victory Parade in 1945 (participants included Chuikov, Sokolovsky, Kuznetsov, Gorbatov, Fedyuninsky and Minyuk), in violation of Party conduct, the first toast at the banquet was not to Stalin but to Chuikov 'our old army commander'.

As a final humiliation, Zhukov was pilloried for having had two, perhaps three, amorous attachments during the war outside of his marriage. On the subject of sex and the family the Communist Party of the Soviet Union was then probably evenly divided between hypocrites and puritans. Zhukov admitted to one long-term affair with a female member of his security team.

Zhukov was disposed to prostrate himself, saying he never had any evil intent in his work and always did his best to serve Party and Motherland loyally.

At about this time Foreign Minister V.M. Molotov sent a short letter to the Party to confirm that his daughter gave one of Zhukov's daughters a gold ring costing 4,200 roubles for her birthday. Other gifts were inexpensive trinkets.

Some years later, after Beria's arrest and execution in 1953, a Military Collegium examined the cases of generals who were released from detention, and restored their awards and decorations. When Beria's deputy, Abakumov, was later arrested, it was learned that he had deliberately concocted these cases, just as he had done during the prewar period of the Great Purges. He was sentenced to be shot.

But things began to look up for Zhukov when, at the Nineteenth Party Congress in 1952, he was chosen as candidate member of the Party's Central Committee. Following a period of convalescence after his first heart attack, Zhukov was appointed commander of the Ural Military District, and in February 1948, he and his wife Alexandra left Moscow for Sverdlovsk in a special military train.

But there were consequences from Zhukov's fall from grace. His role in the war now received minimal attention. Often the only recognition he received was that his name appeared in a list of prominent wartime commanders. In the *Great Soviet Encylopedia*, published after his problems with the Party were exposed, he was allotted just one short paragraph. However, as was his custom, he remained active. All his energies went into his job, including the training of his men. Often he could be seen at sports events or attending the theatre with his wife. He also kept up with current writing on the war by Soviet and foreign authors.

In February 1953 Zhukov gave up command of the Ural district and was summoned to Moscow. Little is known of the reason why Stalin brought him back to Moscow. Some reports say that Party leaders, due to the Korean War, were seeking more dynamic leadership over the armed forces. In any case, Stalin's health had deteriorated. In Moscow at the end of the month Zhukov saw reports about the Korean hostilities and read about the 'the Doctors' Plot'. ('Nothing more shocking was known in Russia since Ivan the Terrible,' wrote John Gunther.)[1] Nine prominent doctors, many of them Jews, all eminent specialists, were arrested in January 1953, charged with attempting to poison members of the Party. There was unconfirmed speculation that Stalin contemplated deporting all Jews to Siberia.

Death came to Stalin at 9:50 a.m. on 5 March 1953.

Following Beria's removal a new government was formed and Zhukov became Deputy Minister of Defence, under Nikolai Bulganin. (Four years later Zhukov would be named Defence Minister.) But even as Deputy Minister, Zhukov put all his energies into his new job. He saw that great advances in science and technology were having a major impact on military hardware and that nuclear weapons had become a decisive factor in the military field. Even prior to the Second World War, Zhukov had backed the speedy development of heavy industry; now he spread the word that first-class nuclear missiles could not be produced without a powerful scientific and economic base.

But Zhukov spearheaded other changes, for example sweeping aside old Stalinist ideas. Zhukov upheld the primacy of army commanders, and urged political officers to be ideologists second and soldiers first. He was therefore trying to lessen the influence of the Main Political Administration within the armed forces. He was also strongly against army commanders coming under criticism at party meetings. Some of these positions taken by Zhukov would later boomerang against him.

An incident concerning an army exercise using a live nuclear weapon took place in Sepember 1954. Zhukov was in a protected observation post, the troops were dug in far enough away not to be affected by the blast. Close to the epicentre, obsolete tanks and other vehicles were hurled into the air while others were melted down.

Shock waves from the blast shattered glass a mile away. Zhukov's cap blew off.[2]

In the spring of 1955 President Eisenhower created a stir when he said he had written to Marshal Zhukov for the first time in nine years. Ike wouldn't say who began the correspondence. But he told the media that it could lead to an improvement in the world situation; that when he had worked with Zhukov in Berlin at the end of the war he believed Zhukov was sincere in striving for Russian–American friendship. At about the same time, in reply to a question, Zhukov sent a message to the Overseas Press Club of America, in support of peaceful coexistence.

The stage was set for a summit conference in Geneva in July 1955 after Moscow had signed the Austrian State Treaty and was soon to pull its troops out of Austria, which was pleasing news to Washington. The Soviet delegation included Khrushchev, Zhukov, Bulganin, Molotov and Gromyko. (The interpreter was Oleg Troyanovsky, later ambassdor to Japan and the United Nations.) The Big Four meeting at Geneva – the USA, Russia, Britain and France – was pronounced a success; the four foreign ministers would pursue the question of European security in the near future. If there was one bombshell at the summit it came when, after the Western delegates called the North Atlantic Treaty Organization (NATO) a force for peace, the Soviet delegation said in that case they would like to join NATO. Silence reigned in the meeting hall. One report said that Eisenhower's vote-winning smile suddenly vanished. Later in the corridor, Secretary of State Foster Dulles asked Gromyko if Moscow was serious about joining. Gromyko, difficult to catch off guard, said Moscow does not make unserious proposals, and certainly not at such an important forum.

Later the *New York Times*, reporting on a private Eisenhower–Zhukov meeting in Geneva, claimed that Eisenhower had got from Zhukov 'a first-hand account' of what was going on behind the Iron Curtain, including the stresses of collective leadership. The US President also said that in his two and a half hour talk with Zhukov he learned something about the marshal's personal misfortunes. Although Ike did not go into details, it seemed as if Ike felt sympathy for his former comrade.[3]

Nikita Khrushchev made his famous 'secret speech' exposing Stalin's crimes at the Twentieth Party Congress in February 1956. Much less known is Zhukov's speech, giving details on Soviet disarmament, including reductions in military expenditures and the closing of 2 or 3 bases on foreign soil. Zhukov also spoke out against American overseas bases. Speaking of the nation's economic capabilities, Zhukov said that the success of heavy industry made it possible to provide the armed forces with state-of-the-art equipment.

According to some sources, Khrushchev's 'volcanic speech' against Stalin helped escalate dissatisfaction in Poland and Hungary, adding to a spirit of independence in Eastern Europe. Significant uprisings occurred in Poland and Hungary in the autumn of 1956. As Defence Minister, Georgi Zhukov was instrumental in putting down the uprisings. In Poland there was a riot by workers in Poznan that was bloodily suppressed by Polish forces. An end to the Polish discontent came when a new leadership won concessions from the Russians. Zhukov, it appears, alerted the border military districts of the USSR and sent a naval squadron from Leningrad towards Gdansk. In the Hungarian events police fired on student demonstrators and Soviet tanks rolled into Budapest along with ten thousand troops. (Later, it was reported that Marshal Tito of Yugoslavia called the use of Russian troops in Hungary a 'fatal' mistake.) Students were demanding such things as the right to strike for workers, freedom of speech and press, and the evacuation of Soviet troops from the country. Hungarian patriots were finally beaten down. Marshal Zhukov followed the line that if Hungarians were allowed complete freedom from Moscow's control, the whole Soviet position in Eastern Europe would be lost. It was said at the time that millions of Poles hoped – vainly as it turned out – that the 'Hungarian Revolution' would be successful.[4]

That same year (1956) the 'Suez Crisis' broke out when Israel, France and Britain defied the United States and attacked Egypt. When Washington strongly objected, the Anglo-French forces withdrew from the Suez Canal. One report said Eisenhower gave British Prime Minister Anthony Eden 'absolute hell' over the telephone. That year found the two blocs, the Soviet and the American, racked with revolt, although the convulsions were much more serious in the Soviet camp (especially the Hungarian Revolt). Speaking of the Suez Crisis a few months after it ended, Georgi Zhukov had this to say:

> You know how events unfolded. The Egyptian people showed stubborn armed resistance to the aggressors ... The Soviet government came out resolutely in defence of Egypt and issued a serious warning to Britain, France and Israel. Hundreds of thousands of volunteers from various countries, especially from the USSR, China and other [people's] democracies,

expressed the desire to fight against the marauders. Our firm stand played a decisive role in bridling the aggressors.' Zhukov added: 'Anglo-French troops were duly repulsed by the Egyptian army and the Egyptian people' [*sic!*].[5]

It is noteworthy that the curmudgeon–maverick philosopher, Bertrand Russell, spoke of the 'two misfortunes' of that year: the Hungarian Revolt and its suppression, and the Suez crisis. On Suez, he had, he said, fulminated against the British government's 'machinations, military and other'. On the former, he said most of the Western World had voiced criticism of the Russians. Russell regretted that on the Suez crisis 'only some people spoke out strongly against [it], but most people were acquiescent'.[6]

On Zhukov's sixtieth birthday in 1956, he was eulogized and his photograph appeared in every major newspaper in Moscow not to mention other large and small cities. The Soviet parliament announced that Zhukov was awarded another Gold Star Hero medal, his fourth. Robust and young for his years, on his chest now reposed eight solid rows of decorations. Above them were three red-and-gold Victory medals, the nation's supreme badge of distinction. At that time only he enjoyed so many. Speaking to journalists, a foreign diplomat told why the marshal was 'unique': 'Zhukov is the only man high up who tells the truth. He may evade a question, but he will not lie.'

The following year Zhukov became the first professional military man to be elevated to the highest ruling body in the country, the party Presidium. The move confirmed the prestige of the marshal which was clearly higher than that of anyone else. Millions of citizens who fought against the Wehrmacht could identify with Zhukov. The fact was apparent that most citizens put more trust in the army – and Zhukov as the symbol of the nation's victory – than in either the Party or the police and security bodies. This situation could not but arouse anxiety, if not intense jealousy within the leadership.

At this time Zhukov became the father of another daughter, Maria, born to Galina. However, he was still unable to get an official divorce from his first wife, Alexandra. His family life was being discussed at the highest levels of government. It would be a few more years for his divorce to be granted.

But glitter as war hero was one thing; Zhukov's reformist tendencies were another. The marshal was desirous of change. For instance, he wanted to see an official denunciation of Stalin's purges of military officers. And his efforts gained momentum in the case of Mikhail

Tukhachevsky and Vasili Blyukher. In addition he wanted the main political body within the armed services, known as the Main Political Administration, to report to him (at that time the Minister of Defence) and not directly to the Party.

What had helped Zhukov's rise was his full backing of Khrushchev in his bid for power over members of the Old Guard like Molotov, Kaganovich and Malenkov. Thus when a vote was to be taken in the Central Committee of the party, Zhukov reportedly gave orders to use military planes to fly members to Moscow. The marshal also made a stirring speech on Khrushchev's behalf. It was reported that Zhukov compared the tactics of the Old Guard to those of the departed Beria. He even hinted at documents that might prove the guilt of some of the Old Guard in the prewar repressions of military men and civilians.

At the same time, the government of India invited Zhukov to visit New Delhi and other cities in January 1957. The visit was extensively covered and a colour documentary film was produced, *The Friendship Visit of Marshal of the Soviet Union, G.K. Zhukov to India and Burma.*

Another overseas visit, early in October 1957, on board a Soviet cruiser to Yugoslavia (and later Albania), would not produce a film and would end in the marshal's downfall. But during his voyage Zhukov gave speeches, concentrating on the launching of the world's first artificial satellite, Sputnik 1, which he called a great success for the Party and Russian science.

Suddenly, without warning after his return home, Zhukov was deposed as Defence Minister and dropped from the party Presidium and the Central Committee. Although he retained a party card, he was back to being an ordinary citizen, not an easy life for the energetic marshal to contemplate.

Khrushchev's main accusation against Zhukov was 'Bonapartism', or the intention to seize power; that is, an actual military putsch. The proof Khrushchev offered was the formation of a special body of troops to be used for 'surgical strikes', roughly similar to America's 'special forces'. That was the main charge, but there were also disciplinary 'faults'; such as coarseness, abusiveness, unfairness, even 'excessive exactingness'. By the latter was meant Zhukov's insistence on the highest levels of performance in all military activities.

Vladimir Karpov, a high party official and veteran of the Stalingrad battle, discusses the actions taken against Zhukov in a series of pungent articles for various newspapers, but the most important of them appeared in August 1991. Karpov wrote that although 'the executioners' pistols were aimed at him', Zhukov could have explained the truth to his accusers. Instead, he said that at least his military colleagues were treating him fairly. None of them said he had the slightest thought of taking over the reins of power. As to the charges of rudeness, unfairness and abusiveness towards other officers, Zhukov admitted his faults and promised to rectify his errors.

Arrayed against Zhukov was the chief of the Main Political Administration General A.S. Zheltov who was gnashing his teeth over Zhukov's continual chopping away of the authority of the MPA within the armed services. Speaking at a meeting of the Party's Central Committee, Zheltov sought to portray the marshal as an apostate from Party orthodoxy. Among those others who spoke against Zhukov was Admiral Sergei Gorshkov, cynically described by some as an 'old sworn friend' of the marshal.[7]

But the most hostile attack came from an old comrade, Marshal Ivan Konev. The son of a peasant and bald as a billiard ball, Konev had been head of the tribunal that sentenced Lavrenti Beria to death. Some observers said Konev was still seething because Zhukov and not himself had been allowed to capture the symbol of Nazi power, the Berlin Reichstag. Konev aimed a whole string of criticisms at his former partner in the assault on Hitler's capital: Zhukov was conceited, lacked respect for the opinions of others, undermined the role of the Party, was politically naive and guilty of 'adventurism'. This was the same charge advanced by Nikita Khrushchev after Zhukov's dismissal. Was it Zhukov's handling of the Hungarian crisis that had displeased Khrushchev? In any event, he had used the ambiguous expression 'adventurism in foreign policy' in attacking Zhukov. (When US journalist Bob Considine asked Khrushchev in Moscow in November 1957 what was meant by the phrase, he replied: 'The pursuance of an unrealistic foreign and home policy – this is adventurism.' Was Hungary, for example, involved? No, said Khrushchev.)

Konev, who held many high posts after the war, including Deputy Minister of Defence, also accused Zhukov of committing blunders on the eve of Hitler's invasion and criticized his role in various military campaigns. Some historians are doubtless correct when they say that Khrushchev, in going after Zhukov, was clever to exploit the rivalries and ambitions of ranking officers such as Konev and Zhukov. But Konev was not the only famed commander who took issue with Zhukov. Another was Marshal Vasily Chuikov who later claimed that Berlin could have been captured earlier.[8]

Zhukov's fall had a harmful affect on his daily routine.

What helped me? . . . Having gone home I took a sleeping pill. I slept several hours. I got up. I had something to eat. I took another sleeping pill.
Again I fell asleep. I woke up, again took a sleeping pill and again fell asleep
. . . This continued for 15 days when I slept with short breaks. In a way I
relived everything that I had been thinking, all that I had been internally
disputing, what I had gone through awake, all of this I relived, obviously,
in my dreams. I disputed. I proved my point. I grieved – all in my sleep.
Later, when these 15 days had passed, I went off fishing.[9]

Zhukov was almost completely out of grace from late 1957 until
May 1965. During this time the aging marshal began work on his
memoirs. His name popped up when Khrushchev visited America in
September 1959 and, in a chat with Eisenhower, the visitor said:
'Don't worry about your old friend Zhukov. He's down in the
Ukraine fishing, and like all generals he is probably writing his
memoirs.'

Ironically, Khrushchev himself was deposed in October 1964. He'd
been on a holiday on the Georgian coast of the Black Sea when his colleagues decided to dethrone him.

Zhukov's rebirth as a national hero was not long in coming. In
1965 his name began to appear again in public. On 8 May when
Leonid Brezhnev, the party first secretary, in a keynote speech at the
Kremlin Palace of Congresses, mentioned Zhukov's name, there was
loud and prolonged applause. On the following day, Victory in
Europe Day, in Moscow, Zhukov was among other high-ranking officers invited to stand atop Lenin's Tomb in Red Square to review a
military parade.

From North America, Zhukov's old comrade-in-arms, Dwight
Eisenhower, learning about his friend's reappearance in public,
commented:

'I think it's time he was rehabilitated. He was a very good soldier
and he tried his best to make things work in Berlin [after the war as a
member of the Allied Control Council].'

Zhukov kept working away at his memoirs, the work made more
onerous because he was asked to submit each chapter for Party
review.[10]

Among those who felt deeply about the way Zhukov had been
treated by the party flunkies was the Indian scholar–diplomat Krishna
Menon, who was New Delhi's ambassador to Moscow during the time

of the marshal's ascent and fall. Menon, who knew Zhukov personally, wrote sympathetically about Zhukov in his diary in November 1957:

> No star shone in the Russian firmament after Stalin's death with greater lustre than Zhukov's. The attempts that are now being made to blot it out can only be called pitiful. The Party may succeed in keeping Zhukov's figure out of the public eye, but it will not succeed in keeping his memory out of the hearts of men … Ultimately truth will triumph, and Clio will place Zhukov by the side of such favourites as Alexander Suvorov, Mikhail Kutuzov and Alexander Nevsky … And the grateful Russian land will always hold his memory in esteem and affection.[11]

Notes

1. John Gunther, *Inside Russia Today*, London, 1957. Ivan the Terrible, the six-teenth century Russian autocrat, founded the distant cousin of the KGB, the Oprichniki, a legion of 6,000 men dressed in black, riding on black horses, their mission: to sniff out and eliminate treason. Incidentally, Ivan the Terrible sometimes pretended to be dying to see how his courtiers reacted.
2. A number of speculative articles have appeared in the West alleging Zhukov's involvement in one or more nuclear weapons exercises, or possible accidents.
3. The *New York Times*, 29 July 1955. For more details of the Eisenhower–Zhukov meetings at Geneva, see chapter 18.
4. A bitter Warsaw joke at the time was: 'The Hungarians behaved like Poles, the Poles behaved like Czechs, and as usual the Czechs behaved like cads.'
5. *Current Digest of the Soviet Press*, 17 March 1957.
6. Bertrand Russell, *Autobiography*, London, 1971.
7. The author had an opportunity to speak to two of Zhukov's critics, Admiral of the Fleet Gorshkov and chief of the Main Political Administration, General Zheltov, in the 1980s. When he mentioned to Gorshkov that many people in the West felt Stalin was responsible for huge mistakes at the beginning of the war, the admiral said: 'And Zhukov bears responsibility for some mistakes that he made.' Zheltov was upset by a question the author posed, whether the general would have wanted to change Stalin for another C-in-C. Zheltov: 'That's a question that comes from the imagination. As C-in-C, Stalin led this country to victory. We did not think of finding a substitute for Stalin. Not at the time, and not now. This question is very tricky.'
8. After the war, Marshal Chuikov claimed that Berlin could have been captured in February, and the war ended that same month, not in May. But Chuikov was possibly blinkered. His 8th Guards Army in February consisted of 9 div-isions while the entire Soviet force closing in on Hitler's Germany amounted to almost 200 divisions. Zhukov is convincing in his reply: 'There was more to the Berlin offensive that Marshal Chuikov appears to see.' Zhukov says that before Berlin could be tackled, a powerful Wehrmacht force in Pomerania,

northeast of Berlin, had to be crushed. German General Guderian backs him up (*Memoirs of a Soldier*), saying Nazi forces in Pomerania were preparing to deliver a shattering counterblow to the Russians who were aiming for Berlin. Apparently Chuikov had a lapse of memory because until the last week of February 1945 his men were still fighting a strong Germany army 250 kilometres east of Berlin, at Poznan.

9. Reminiscences of Zhukov's daughters; a talk with journalist K. Simonov.
10. See chapter 12.
11. K.P.S. Menon, *Memoirs*.

15

STALIN AND ZHUKOV

Zhukov: Where would you order me to go?
Stalin: Where would you want to go?
Zhukov: I can do any work. I can command a division, a corps, an army, a Front.
Stalin: Don't get excited, don't get excited! You spoke earlier about organizing an operation at Yelnya. Well, take it into your hands.

Few people knew Stalin better than Georgi Zhukov during the war years. He met the Supreme Commander-in-Chief at all hours, hundreds of times, sometimes twice daily, more than enough for him to size up the dictator, know his style, identify his moods. When they met they sometimes argued, on occasion it ended in a shouting match. But the arguments had to do with war, with strategies, the date of an offensive – matters concerning the life and death of thousands, sometimes scores of thousands of men. The two often dined together at Stalin's dacha (simple meals: kasha, boiled meat, fruit, Georgian wines), sometimes they walked in the garden ('to limber up', said The Boss). When Zhukov was on assignment outside Moscow, in the thick of battles, there were endless conversations between the two by telephone or telegraph.

Zhukov paints a portrait of Stalin that is not unfamiliar to the West: a man who was impetuous, secretive, often irritable; a dictator who when angry 'stopped being objective, changed abruptly before one's eyes, grew paler still, his gaze becoming heavy and hard'. Zhukov knew well this side of Stalin and doesn't hold back regarding their wartime quarrels. Since both men had short tempers, it is no wonder that at times they were unable to restrain themselves. But Stalin needed Zhukov and, as the war progressed, he gained increasing respect for the man he appointed as his deputy. According to Zhukov, 'Not many were the brave men who stood up to Stalin's anger and parried his attacks.' Zhukov was one who could.

Zhukov's grief over Stalin's repressions of the 1930s is evident in his writings about the war. (Like most citizens he didn't learn the full extent of the horrors committed by Stalin and his henchmen until Stalin's death in 1953.) When Zhukov refers to the blood purge of the army before the war including the loss of irreplaceable marshals like Mikhail Tukhachevsky – among thousands of officers – it is understood he is saying that the Red Army missed sorely their competence during the war with Hitler. It is also implicit that had they been alive during 1941–45 the war casualties would have been less. As it was, the shortage of skilled commanders and specialists at the start of the Blitzkrieg was keenly felt. In his memoirs Zhukov gives a brief roll-call of top-ranked officers who disappeared under Stalin, some of whom he knew personally. These men included Mikhail Tukhachevsky and I.P. Uborevich, both of whom he admired.

As for Stalin's military capability or lack of it, Zhukov sums it up in three sentences: 'I can say that Stalin was conversant with the basic principles of organizing operations of Fronts and groups of Fronts, and that he supervised them knowledgeably. Certainly, he was familiar with major strategic principles. Stalin's ability as Supreme Commander was especially marked after the Battle of Stalingrad.' What he means is that Stalin went through a learning process in the year and a half leading up to the victory on the Volga.

The view, expressed by some writers that Stalin only committed blunders and interfered with his generals during the war is difficult to sustain if one accepts Zhukov's opinion (which is also that of other well-known Soviet marshals and generals including Vasilevsky, Rokossovsky, Meretskov, Bagramyan and Shtemenko). Meretskov probably speaks for many generals when he says that the Supreme Commander imparted political and military knowledge to his officers but was also, in turn, taught by them.

To read Zhukov's voluminous memoirs is also to understand much about Stalin for Zhukov cites hundreds of his wartime meetings and conversations with his Commander-in-Chief. What follows is a selection of some of the more striking Zhukov–Stalin encounters.[1]

Early in 1941 shortly before the war, Marshal Timoshenko called Zhukov, then Chief of the General Staff, and said Stalin wanted to see him in a few days. The shaven-headed Timoshenko was one of the luminaries in the Red Army who had risen to the position of Commissar of Defence.

'What is he liable to ask me about?'

'Everything,' said Timoshenko. 'But remember that he won't listen to long reports. What it takes you several hours to tell me, you must tell him in ten minutes.'

Zhukov was shocked.

'What can I tell him in ten minutes? They're serious questions and call for serious consideration. Their importance has got to be understood and the necessary measures taken.'

'He knows for the most part what you want to tell him,' Timoshenko said, 'so try to concentrate on the key problems.'

On Saturday night Zhukov visited Stalin at his dacha outside Moscow, taking along a list of the questions he wanted to raise. He found Timoshenko and a few others already there. After greeting him, Stalin asked if he knew about the Katyusha rocket launchers. Zhukov hadn't seen them and Stalin asked Timoshenko to take him to the testing grounds in the next few days and see them fired off. Stalin then asked Zhukov how things were at the General Staff. Zhukov mentioned that in view of the gravity of the political and military situation urgent measures needed to be taken to eliminate flaws in the fortifications on the western border and within the armed forces.

V.M. Molotov, the Foreign Minister, who was present interrupted: 'So you think we'll have to fight the Germans soon?'

Stalin motioned to Mototov to keep quiet.

After listening to what Zhukov had to say, Stalin invited everyone to the dinner table. There the conversation continued, with Stalin asking Zhukov what he thought of the German air force. Zhukov had words of praise for it but said that the main problem for the Soviet Air Force was that it had too few of the new fighters and bombers.

Dinner was simple as usual, says Zhukov, with thick Ukrainian borsch, followed by well-cooked kasha and boiled meat, then stewed and finally fresh fruit. Stalin, recalls Zhukov, was in high spirits and given to joking. He drank light Georgian Khvanchkara wine and pressed it on the others, but most of them preferred brandy.

Zhukov says that when he returned to the General Staff he jotted down everything Stalin had said and picked out the questions that would have to be tackled first.

Late in July (the month after Hitler's invasion) Stalin again summoned Zhukov and Timoshenko to his dasha. Zhukov thought Stalin wanted to consult them on what further action should be taken concerning the different armies. But Stalin's summons had a totally different purpose. Entering the room, Zhukov and Timoshenko saw all the Politburo members seated around the table. Stalin, wearing an old jacket, was standing in the middle of the room, holding an unlit pipe in his hands, a sure sign (as Zhukov had learned) of displeasure. Zhukov knew that there had been some accusations made about Timoshenko's allegedly poor performance.

'Now then,' said Stalin, 'the Politburo has discussed Timoshenko's activities as Commander of the Western Front and decided to relieve him of his post. It proposes that Zhukov take over.' Stalin turned to Timoshenko and Zhukov and asked what they thought of this.

Timoshenko was silent.

'Comrade Stalin,' Zhukov said, 'frequent replacement of Front Commanders is having a bad effect on operations. Without hardly any time to become familiar with the situation, the new commanders are compelled to conduct exceedingly hard battles. Marshal Timoshenko has been in command of the Front for less than four weeks. During the battle of Smolensk he has come to know the troops and what they are capable of. He has done all that could be done and has held up the enemy at Smolensk for almost a month. I don't think anyone else could have achieved more. The troops have trust in Timoshenko and that is most important. I feel it would be unjust and inexpedient to remove him from the Front at this time.'

Mikhail Kalinin, the bewhiskered, elderly President, who had been listening attentively, said:

'I think he's right.'

Stalin unhurriedly lit his pipe, then eyed the others and said:

'Suppose we agree with Zhukov?'

'You're right, Comrade Stalin,' several Politburo members said. 'Timoshenko may rectify things yet.'

Zhukov and Timoshenko were given permission to leave. Timoshenko was ordered to return to his Front immediately.

Zhukov's judgement: 'Plainly the accusations had seriously offended Timoshenko. But then, all sorts of things happen in war and there isn't always a chance to consider people's feelings as there are often major, intricate problems to be dealt with.'

Zhukov says that Stalin displayed a complete absence of formality. Everything he did in the framework of the Supreme Command or the State Defence Committee (Stalin headed both) led to the immediate fulfillment of the decisions these bodies may have taken.

In July occurred one of the famous blow-ups between Zhukov and Stalin. It was a long meeting at the Kremlin. Zhukov gave a lengthy report and suggested ways to beef up the Central Front which appeared to be the most dangerous place in the nation's defence. He recommended bringing up not less than 8 combat-ready divisions from the Far East, including 1 tank division.

L.Z. Mekhlis, a member of the Supreme Command, cut in with what Zhukov took as a caustic remark:

'And you want to give the Soviet Far East up to the Japanese?'

Zhukov did not answer. Mekhlis, a Stavka representative at the front line, had the unfortunate reputation of often leaping to conclusions. During times of crisis he would straightway recommend dismissal of a commander, often, many felt, unjustly.

Zhukov continued, suggesting that the South-Western Front be withdrawn right away behind the Dnieper river.

It was obvious to all that Stalin was clearly worried about Kiev, the capital of the Ukraine.

Zhukov knew beforehand what the sound of the words 'to surrender Kiev' mean for Stalin and for all Russian people. But, he pulled himself together thinking: 'I should not be carried away by emotion, and I as Chief of the General Staff have to suggest the only possible and correct strategic decision in the existing situation.' Zhukov also knew that the entire General Staff supported him.

'We shall have to leave Kiev,' he said firmly.

There was a long silence. Zhukov continued, trying to remain calm. He now recommended that counterblows be immediately organized on the western sector with the aim of eliminating the Yelnya Salient, west of Moscow, at the enemy front. 'The Nazis may later use the Yelnya bulge as a springboard for an offensive on Moscow.'

Stalin flew into a rage.

'What counterblows? It's nonsense!' he said and suddenly asked in a high voice:

'How could you hit upon the idea of surrendering Kiev to the enemy?'

Zhukov admits in hindsight that he could not restrain himself. He retorted:

'If you think that as Chief of the General Staff I am only capable of talking nonsense, I've got nothing more to do here. I request that I be relieved of the duties of Chief of the General Staff and sent to the front. Apparently I'll be of better use to my country there.'

There was an acutely painful pause in the conversation.

'No need to get excited!' said Stalin finally. 'However, if that's the way you put it, we'll be able to do without you.'

'I'm a military man and ready to carry out any orders, but I have a firm idea of the situation and ways of waging the war. I believe that my idea is correct and have reported what I think myself and what the General Staff thinks.'

Stalin no longer interrupted, but listened to Zhukov without anger and said in a calmer tone:

'Go and do your work. We'll send for you.'

Collecting his maps, Zhukov went out of the office with a heavy heart. But in half an hour he was invited to return to see the Supreme Commander-in-Chief.

'You know what,' Stalin said. 'We've sought each other's advice and decided to relieve you of the duties of Chief of the General Staff. We'll appoint Shaposhnikov to the post. It's true, his health is rather poor, but we'll help him all right.' Then Stalin added: 'We'll use you in practical work. You have extensive experience in commanding troops in field conditions. You will be of undoubted use for the army in the field. Of course, you will remain Deputy People's Commissar for Defence and member of the Stavka.'

'Where would you order me to go?'

'Where would you want to go?'

'I can do any work. I can command a division, a corps, an army, a Front.'

'Don't get excited, don't get excited! You spoke earlier about organizing an operation at Yelnya. Well, take it into your hands.'

Then, pausing a moment, Stalin added:

'The operations of the reserve armies of the Rzhev–Vyazma defence line [west of Moscow] must be unified. We'll appoint you Commander of the Reserve Front. When can you leave?'

'In an hour.'

'Shaposhnikov will arrive soon in the General Staff. Turn over your duties to him and set out.'

'Do I have your permission to leave?'

'Sit down and have some tea with us, we'd like to talk about some other matters,' said Stalin, who was now smiling.

Zhukov recalls:

'We sat at the table and began to drink tea, but the conversation did not shape up.'

A month later, Zhukov, at the front line, received a telegraph message from an aide to Stalin at the Kremlin, asking him if he could leave for Moscow directly. He replied immediately, asking if his arrival in Moscow could be put off a little because he needed to 'restore order' in a 'complicated situation' involving the 149th Rifle Division that was facing the enemy. He telegraphed:

Zhukov: Things are developing quite well at Yelnya. We have reached the Yelnya–Smolensk railway line. If I am ordered to leave, I will leave Bogdanov as deputy and order him to pass the command of the group on the Roslavl sector to Sobnennikov. I await Comrade Stalin's orders.

After a minute, Stalin himself telegraphed:

Stalin: How do you do, Comrade Zhukov! In that case, put off your trip to Moscow and travel to the front line.

Zhukov: How do you do, Comrade Stalin! Should I still be ready to go to General Headquarters in a couple of days or can I work according to my plan?

Stalin: You can work according to your plan.

Zhukov: Fine. Best wishes!

The German Yelnya group and the Yelnya Salient was eliminated on 6 September and the successful operation heightened morale among the troops. But not everything was developing smoothly. Zhukov describes an 'unfortunate occurrence' involving a rifle division of the 43rd Army which didn't secure its left flank after forcing the river Stryna and moving quickly ahead. He says:

> Having failed to take the required measures to provide for combat security, the young and inexperienced commander committed a serious mistake. The enemy immediately took advantage of that mistake. A tank counter-attack disrupted the divisions's battle formation. The Soviet soldiers fought stubbornly, skilfully repelling enemy attacks and inflicting considerable losses on the Germans. Their panzers sustained particularly telling losses due to our anti-tank and division artillery.

But Zhukov says that it was difficult to say which side suffered more losses. The German counter-attacks were repulsed 'but we were also compelled to halt our offensive on this sector. Such was the price of unconsidered action by the division commander. I was forced to remain with the commander at his observation post almost till night on 9 September to correct the mistakes that had been committed.'

Unexpectedly a telephone message arrived for Zhukov from the Supreme Commander-in-Chief who summoned him to his headquarters in the Kremlin at 8 p.m.

There was nothing more in the message and it was difficult to understand the reason why I was being summoned. I had to go but the situation required my presence here until order had been restored on the Army's left flank. Certain other combat orders had to be issued to the Army commander. In addition, Moscow was a long distance away. An estimate showed that I would be late for the appointed time. Stalin was extremely intolerant of late arrivals when he summoned anyone. But what could I do? Situations in war do not take into account the character traits of the commanders. It was necessary to decide correctly what was more important: to complete the mission on the field of battle or to arrive at the prescribed time before one's senior commander in response to his call and thus ignore the urgency at the front?

Zhukov got off the following message to the Supreme Commander-in-Chief: 'In view of situation here I will arrive one hour late.'

Despite his high position Zhukov was nervous on his return to Moscow. ('I wondered how to explain the situation on the left flank of the 24th Army in a more convincing way so that Stalin would correctly understand the reason for my delay.')

He arrived at the Kremlin in pitch darkness. Suddenly he was blinded by a flashlight. The car stopped. He recognized an approaching officer as chief of the security department.

'The Supreme Commander-in-Chief has ordered me to meet you and take you to his flat,' the officer, a general, said.

I came out of the car and followed the general. It was no use asking him anything, because I would not get the answers to the questions which interested me. As I climbed the stairway to the second storey where Stalin's flat was I had still not decided what I would say as an excuse for my delay. Entering the dining room where Stalin, Molotov and other high officials were seated around a table, I said:

'Comrade Stalin, I am an hour late in arriving.'

Stalin looked at his watch and said:

'An hour and five minutes,' and added, 'sit down and have something to eat if you're hungry.'

The Supreme Commander-in-Chief was examining the map of the situation in Leningrad. Those who were present sat in silence. I did not have anything to eat and also remained silent. Finally, Stalin broke away from the map and addressing me, said:

'We have discussed the situation with Leningrad once again. The enemy has taken Schlusselburg and bombed the Badayev food stores on 8 September. Large supplies of food have perished. We have no communications with Leningrad by land. The population is in a difficult situation. The Finnish troops are advancing from the north on the Karelian Ishmus, while the Nazi troops of Army Group North reinforced by the 4th Panzer Group are driving towards the city from the south.'

Stalin fell silent and turned to the map again.

A dangerous situation was facing the country's second biggest city, the second biggest industrial city, a major shipping port, the city known as 'Peter's city' (built by Peter the Great) and 'Cradle of the Revolution'.

Stalin suddenly asked Zhukov to appraise the situation on the Moscow sector. Zhukov said that Moscow must be readied for steadfast defensive actions, that the Nazi High Command would hardly begin an offensive in the Moscow sector without completing the operation at Leningrad and in meeting up with Finnish troops.

Then Stalin announced:

'You will have to fly to Leningrad and take over command of the Front and the Baltic Fleet from Voroshilov.'

This was completely unexpected but Zhukov said he was ready to depart immediately.

'You must be aware,' said Stalin, 'that in Leningrad you will have to fly over the front line or over Lake Ladoga which is controlled by the German air force.' He added: 'The Supreme Command order on your appointment will be issued when you arrive in Leningrad.'

'I realized that these words reflected concern that my flight might end badly.'

Before leaving Zhukov asked Stalin to permit him to take along two or three generals who would be useful on the spot.

'Take anyone you want,' answered Stalin.

At Moscow's Central Airfield the clouds were densely packed. 'Couldn't be better for crossing enemy lines,' the pilot said.

But the flight could easily have ended in disaster. From Moscow to Lake Ladoga the plane had suitably cloudy weather. Enemy fighters, thwarted by rain and low clouds stayed on the ground and all went well without an escort. But as soon as Zhukov's plane came to Lake Ladoga the weather improved and fighter escort was ordered. The plane flew low over the water but was suddenly pursued by two Messerschmitt fighters. After a short while Zhukov's plane landed safely on the city's army airfield. As he was in a hurry there was no time to find out why his supposed air cover had not driven off the enemy planes.

Early in January 1942 a general offensive by the Red Army was to be launched in the shortest time possible. Major gains had already been achieved in front of Moscow, driving the enemy back in some cases up to 200 kilometres. Zhukov had been called back to Moscow to help discuss the new draft plan for an overall offensive. The Russians had retaken the city of Klin and Zhukov notes that he read in the party paper *Pravda* a statement by British Foreign Secretary Anthony Eden who had gone to Klin for a visit. Zhukov quotes Eden as saying: 'I was happy to see the feats of the Russian armies, feats that were truly magnificent.'

At the Supreme High Command, Stalin asked Zhukov for his opinion on the draft plan.

'We must go on with the offensive in the western theatre of operations where the situation is more favourable for us and where the enemy hasn't had time to restore his fighting efficiency,' Zhukov said. However, he said the offensive would fail unless the forces were replenished with men and weapons. Reserves and tank units had to be built up.

Zhukov continued, this time addressing the issue of casualties. (The subject of casualties is an important one as Zhukov is often accused, mainly in the West, of having no regard for soldiers' lives. Here is an occasion where, inside the Kremlin, he showed his opposition to unnecessary loss of life.)

'As for the Leningrad and southwestern offensive operations, I must say that our troops are up against strong enemy defences. Without powerful artillery means they will not be able to pierce the defence line but will only unjustifiably sustain great casualties and wear themselves out. I'm for strengthening the western theatre and stepping up the offensive there.'

Someone from the Stavka spoke up, saying the means were not available to ensure simultaneous offensive operations on all the fronts. Stalin then said that Timoshenko backed the offensive in the south-western direction.

As they all left the conference room, Shaposhnikov, the Chief of the General Staff told Zhukov: 'You shouldn't have argued, the Supreme Command had the question of the offensive already settled.'

'Why then was our opinion asked?'

'That, my dear fellow, I do not know,' said Shaposhnikov.

Two weeks later the order came from the Supreme Command to withdraw the 1st Shock Army from action and assign it to the Supreme Command Reserve. Zhukov and General Sokolovsky, Chief of Staff of the Wesern Front, asked for permission to keep the 1st Shock Army.

> We got the same reply [says Zhukov.] It was the Supreme Commander's order.
>
> I called up Stalin. I insisted that pulling the army out would weaken our attack forces. The answer I got was: 'Enough of this stupid talk. You have a lot of troops. Count your armies.'
>
> I tried to continue: 'Comrade Stalin, we are fighting on a very wide front, fierce battles are being fought all along the line, and that rules out regrouping. I ask you not to withdraw the 1st Shock Army from the Western Front's right flank so as not to lessen the pressure on the enemy.'

Stalin hung up without a reply. Zhukov says his talks with Shaposhnikov were also to no avail.

'My dear fellow, there is nothing I can do,' Shaposhnikov said. 'It is the Supreme Commander's own decision.'

Some years later, when discussing the German defeat at Kursk, Zhukov denies that Stalin made the big decisions himself.

> After Stalin's death, the idea became current that he alone took decisions on questions of a military and strategic nature. I cannot agree with this. I have already mentioned that when someone who had a good knowledge of the matter made a report to him, he would take notice of it. I even know of cases when he changed his mind with respect to decisions previously taken. This was the case now.

The case Zhukov refers to was Stalin's order for two Fronts, Voronezh and Steppe, to begin an immediate counter-offensive (before the end of July 1943). But Zhukov says the men needed fresh supplies of fuel and ammunition, careful reconnaissance, more coordination of units, and some regrouping of troops. 'After repeated talks, the Supreme Commander reluctantly approved our decision to wait at least eight days, since this was the only way.'

After the huge victory at Kursk, the Wehrmacht was steadily pushed back in a number of mammoth operations. Disagreements now between Zhukov and Stalin were rare. From then on until Nazi

Germany's surrender, there was one triumph after another, with constant nightly salutes in Moscow from many guns to mark each major victory with the radio announcement of the commander's name who led the troops to victory.

A month after victory day, Stalin asked Zhukov whether he had forgotten how to ride a horse.

'No, I haven't,' he said.

'Good,' said Stalin. 'You will have to take the salute at the Victory Parade. Rokossovsky will command it.'

Zhukov at first protested.

'Thank you for the great honour, but wouldn't it be better for you to take the salute? You are the Supreme Commander in Chief and by right and duty you are supposed to take the salute.'

Stalin replied:

'I am too old to review parades. You do it, you are younger.'[2]

At 3 minutes to 10 a.m. on 24 June 1945, Zhukov was in the saddle on a white horse (chosen by famed Civil War cavalryman Semyon Budenny) at the Kremlin's Spassky Gate. 'I heard the clear command: "Parade shun!" A thunder of applause followed.'

The clock struck 10 o'clock.

'Honestly speaking,' says Zhukov, 'I felt my heart beating faster . . . I sent my horse forward and headed for Red Square. The powerful and solemn sounds of Glinka's "Glory", dear to the Russian heart, sang out. Then abruptly, silence fell on the square. I heard the clear report of the parade commander, Marshal Rokossovsky, who was, to be sure, as nervous as I. But his report riveted my attention and I became absolutely calm.'

Zhukov mentions the 'war-scorched gallant faces' of the soldiers, their sparkling eyes, the new uniforms ablaze with orders and medals – all this created an unforgettable impression.

The incomparable moment for Zhukov came when, to the sound of drums, 200 war veterans flung 200 Nazi banners at the foot of the Mausoleum.

Zhukov was in a reflective mood. How sad, he thought, that so many sons of Russia had fallen in battle against a satanic foe and not lived to see this happy day.

When Zhukov returned to Berlin to take up his duties as Commander-in-Chief of Soviet forces in Germany, and Russia's representative on the Allied Control Council in Berlin, he suggested to the Americans, British and French that a victory parade be held in Berlin to celebrate the victory over Hitler's Germany. The salute would be taken by the Commanders-in-Chief of the Soviet, US, British and French forces. But on the eve of the parade he was informed that these men would not be coming to Berlin for the parade but were sending their deputies instead.

Zhukov immediately put through a call to Stalin who heard Zhukov's report and said:

'They want to belittle the political importance of the parade of troops of the anti-Hitler coalition ... Ignore the refusal of the Allies and take the salute yourself, all the more so, as we have more rights to do it than they.'

If he was referring to the shedding of blood, it was true. Approximately three out of every five persons killed in the Second World War were Russian.

After reviewing the troops in the march past in Berlin on 7 September, Zhukov made a speech in which he paid tribute to Russians, Americans, British, French and all others who contributed to the common victory.[3]

Notes

1. This chapter is based on Zhukov's *Reminiscences and Reflections.*
2. See Introduction for a story about Stalin and the white horse from an unreliable witness.
3. For more on Zhukov–Stalin relations, especially between 1945 and 1953, when Stalin died, see chapter 14.

16

BERIA: ARREST AND DEATH

'Silence!' Zhukov snapped. 'You are not in command here.'
Moscow News, no. 23, 1990

Death came to Stalin at 9:50 a.m. on 5 March 1953. There are various versions of Stalin's death scene, some of them grotesque. One of them, as believable as the others, says that Beria, who was present when Stalin collapsed, danced a jig around the prostrate form, crying out: 'We are free, we are free!' Suddenly, Stalin opened one eye but could not speak. Fearing that Stalin might recover, Beria dropped to his knees in hysterics and began to plant kisses on the dictator's hands. When Stalin's death was finally confirmed, Beria began rubbing his hands, no doubt reckoning his chances were excellent to move into the dictator's job. After all, he had the allegiance of several thousand internal security troops, including a garrison right inside the Kremlin.

Lavrenti Pavlovich Beria had come a long way from his university days in Georgia where he had reportedly studied architecture. But he had taken up police work in Georgia and in 1938 was appointed by Stalin as secret police chief in Moscow. Short of stature, often wearing a plain dark suit and fedora, it was said that with his pince-nez he looked like a bookkeeper. But to many of those who knew him he was a hangman and sadist.

His vindictive character was well known. Colonel-General of Artillery N.N. Voronov remembers an incident when Beria handed him in the presence of Stalin an order for 50,000 rifles. Stalin agreed with Voronov that 25,000 would be enough but Beria kept insisting on more. Irritated, Stalin finally approved only 10,000 rifles for the secret police. On leaving Stalin's office, Beria caught up with Voronov and said angrily: 'Just wait, I'll fix your guts!'

Another time Beria, who was put in charge of the Soviet nuclear weapons development, wanted to inform Stalin about the results of a special test, but someone else had already informed Stalin. Like a child having a tantrum, Beria exploded in front of those around him, saying: 'Even here you put spokes in my wheels, you traitors! I'll grind you into powder!'[1]

In the event, Beria who was head of the MVD (Ministry of Internal Affairs), moved quickly in an attempt to grab power. But people had had enough of witch hunts and torture chambers, and feared and loathed Beria, as they had his predecessors, Yagoda and Yezhov. The terror that had been part of the air the people breathed had to be stopped, and there were enough people with the backbone to take on the grisly job.

And so Beria, with his reputation as Stalin's mass executioner, was doomed.

Nikita Khrushchev, the Party First Secretary, was convinced that Russia faced disaster if they failed to stop Beria in his tracks. But first a consensus was needed on how to go about removing Beria. This was soon obtained. To stop a take-over by Beria and his stooges it was necessary to act fast and with absolute secrecy. Above all, they needed the backing of the army. In an ironic twist, it fell to Georgi Zhukov, who had been exiled by Stalin to the provinces, and who had been on Beria's hit list for years, to be one of the arresting officers. Those involved in the plot (some called it a post-Stalin purge against Beria) included, in addition to Zhukov and Khrushchev, the Minister of Defence, Nikolai Bulganin; Georgi Malenkov, the Deputy Chairman of the Soviet Council of Ministers; and war hero General K.S. Moskalenko. Zhukov's presence was a guarantee of the support of the armed forces, and he quickly moved into the capital a tank division and a motor rifle division. These units would, if necessary, be able to outgun Beria's internal security units, who packed only small arms.

Zhukov had already learned to be on his guard against Beria. Early in the war Beria showed his hostility when Zhukov was an army general and Chief of the General Staff. In mid-July 1941 someone was spreading information, which proved false, about enemy paratroops landing near the right flank of Moscow's 24th Army. Zhukov telephoned the commanding officer who told him he knew nothing about it. But the officer was punished, being relieved of his command the next day even though the rumour had no basis in fact. Beria, it turned out, was piqued because his own (faulty) intelligence was not confirmed. When he asked Zhukov what sort of man the commanding officer of the 24th Army was, and Zhukov replied that he hardly knew him, Beria's reply was menacing: 'If you hardly know him, why did you agree to his appointment as commander?' He left Zhukov's office without waiting for an answer and the commander's fate was sealed.

Zhukov had other unpleasant brushes with Beria during the war. Both Beria and Stalin were said to be jealous of Zhukov's popularity which rose sharply after victories in the Battles of Moscow and Leningrad. Beria, as was his custom, took it upon himself to gather compromising materials about high officers, so as to undercut their authority. In the spring of 1942 Beria had Zhukov's Chief of Operations, Major General V.S. Golushkevish, arrested in order to get testimony from him that would be harmful to Zhukov. But the general did not cave in. Eventually, however, Beria's intrigues against Zhukov would have their intended effect.

Now, with Stalin's death, Beria's removal would put an end to such wrongdoing.

Before any action was taken, however, a special meeting of the Party Presidium, with Beria present, would discuss Beria's misconduct. The meeting was fixed for 26 June.

On that day Zhukov was to enter the Kremlin through the Borovitsky Gate with the other officers and wait outside the reception room where the session of the Presidium would take place.

Khrushchev is said to have arrived at the 26 June meeting with a gun in his pocket.[2] Beria was summoned and was in attendance, but curious as to why this meeting had been called so hastily. He apparently did not suspect the plot against himself. When the session opened, Malenkov proposed that 'we discuss the matter of Beria'. Khrushchev said a couple of words in agreement. Beria, sitting next to Khrushchev, turned pale and asked, 'What's this, Nikita? What did you say?'

'Pay attention,' Khrushchev snapped. 'You'll find out.' Khrushchev said there was one urgent item on the agenda: the anti-Party, divisive activity of Beria, whom he branded 'an imperialist agent'. Being 'anti-Party' in the old Soviet Union was the sin of sins, justifying severe punishment. He then listed Beria's unlawful activities and his attempts 'to legalize arbitrary rule'. Khrushchev therefore put forward a proposal to drop Beria from the Presidium and the Central Committee, expel him from the Party and bring him before a military court. Bulganin followed with similar accusations against Beria and his cohorts. Among the other crimes they were accused of was snatching pretty girls off the street, taking them home, and raping them.

One of the accusations against Beria was that he had worked for British intelligence. An official report said Beria 'continued and widened his secret connections with Foreign Intelligence until the moment of his arrest'. This meant that Beria would become the third secret police chief to be executed for crimes that included alleged service as a British secret agent. This was perhaps the weakest of the charges against Beria. It seems that the only evidence of his link with British intelligence presented at Beria's trial was a document stating that Beria had worked for a counter-intelligence service in Baku in 1919, during the civil war, when the region (including Baku) was under partial British control.

The meeting was also told that Beria considered the police to be his private domain, superior to both party and government. (In fact, some of the gulag camps in the early 1950s had Beria's name attached to them. There were reportedly ten such special camps, at least one of them located in the Kola Peninsula in the Arctic, that were called 'Beria Camps for Enemies of the People'. The unfortunates sent there were said to be prisoners who were 'unspeakably contaminated'.)[3]

Apparently, Malenkov was supposed to summarize the charges against Beria, but he lost his nerve at the last minute.

One of the officers involved in Beria's arrest, Colonel I.G. Zub, was chief of the political section of the Moscow Air Defence District. In late June he was summoned to the Ministry of Defence and told he would take part in a special armed mission. Soon a half dozen other officers came to the ministry building. While waiting for orders they saw Marshal Zhukov enter the Minister's office. Zub thought Zhukov looked a bit anxious. However, the presence of Zhukov also gave Zub confidence that the job he was about to undertake would be successful even if he still was in the dark as to exactly what it was. Before long, Zub was ordered to draw up a list of 50 reliable officers who were to be used to replace the Kremlin guard at the end of their watch. Later he was told that when these men had been replaced with reliable officers, the prisoner Beria would be led out of the Kremlin by military men loyal to Zhukov.

The group of officers was then driven to the Kremlin in two automobiles, Bulganin's and Zhukov's, each of which had darkened windows. They entered under the guise of attending a meeting, and were ushered into a waiting room. Except for Zhukov they were still unaware of their assignment. Eventually Bulganin and Khrushchev came out of the meeting room and explained that the officers were there to arrest Beria. Khrushchev issued instructions: on a signal from Malenkov from inside the meeting room, they were to enter in pairs from the three doors, block any attempt by Beria to escape, and arrest him.

They would wait until the coast was clear and then hand over the prisoner to a loyal army officer. Other precautions were taken. For example, Zhukov and the other officers were allowed to bring their sidearms with them into the Kremlin on the day of the meeting. Also, an hour before Beria's arrival, the guard at the Kremlin was replaced with regular soldiers. Everyone involved was told that if something went wrong, if their mission failed, they would probably be arrested and accused of being 'enemies of the people', a very grave crime. As the men checked their weapons, one man's automatic pistol temporarily jammed when being loaded with a magazine. Even this small hitch added to the nervousness of the group.

Zhukov and the other officers were, meanwhile, waiting outside the meeting room. He later recalled: 'We waited. There was no signal an hour later. I imagined that it was Beria who had arrested the others and might be looking for me. The situation was cause for alarm. Then, in another fifteen minutes, we heard the buzzer.'

Malenkov remained in a state of nervousness and didn't even put Khrushchev's motion to arrest Beria to a vote. But he remembered to press a secret button which gave the signal to the officers in the adjacent room. Zhukov appeared first. Moskalenko was behind him along with the others. Now Malenkov addressed Zhukov, saying:

'As the Chairman of the Council of Ministers, I request that you take Beria into custody pending investigation of the charges against him.'

At this moment the arresting officers opened the flaps on their holsters in case Beria made an attempt to escape. Zhukov, the professional, barked a couple of commands and that was all that was needed to cow the already frightened police chief.

'Hands up! Follow us,' Zhukov commanded.

Beria, now surrounded by six officers, asked to use the restroom and, regaining his composure, told the officers, 'Let's sit down, comrades.' Until the last minute Beria apparently hoped for an opportunity to summon help from his own Ministry of Internal Affairs troops. But to prevent this happening, Zhukov's tank and rifle divisions were standing by.

'Silence!' Zhukov ordered. 'You are not in command here.'

Zhukov next turned to the other officers and in a firm voice told them to shoot the prisoner if he tried to escape. Some reports say that to make sure Beria would not run off, they broke his glasses and cut off the buttons from his trousers so he would have to use his hands to keep them up.

Five of the escorts put their prisoner in a large government limousine and drove him out of Spassky Gate during the change of the guards at 3:00 a.m. Zhukov remained behind. The first stop for Beria was Lefortovo prison, where he was kept secretly for one week before being transferred to an underground bunker of the Moscow Military District headquarters.

Beria's arrest was announced on 10 July. A short while later, Zhukov was raised to full membership in the Party's Central Committee and appointed a Deputy Minister of Defence. Zhukov was temporarily back in the limelight.

A Special Judicial Body of the USSR Supreme Court tried Beria – sometimes called 'the Kremlin monster' – and six of his lieutenants behind closed doors, beginning on 18 December 1953. The only outsiders allowed to attend were the arresting officers. The trial, conducted in the Moscow Military District headquarters, was headed by Marshal Ivan Konev. On 23 December the verdict was announced: Beria and his accomplices were sentenced to the supreme punishment – to be shot, with confiscation of their personal property and deprivation of military titles and awards. The sentence was final and not subject to appeal. That same day the sentence was carried out.

A recent article by Colonel Y. Klimchuk describes Beria's last moments:

The attorney general said to Moskalenko, the senior officer, 'Please have the sentence carried out.'

Some minutes later at the site of execution, Moskalenko turned to his aide, Lieutenant-Colonel V.P. Yuferev, and said quietly: 'You're the youngest of us. Will you do it?' Yuferev resolutely stepped forward and took a pistol from his holster.

Klimchuk continues:

'But when he saw Beria's wildly bulging eyes he turned in disgust. The miserable and horrible look of the man made him sick.'

At that moment Lieutenant-General P.F. Batitsky, one of the men who had arrested Beria, stepped forward.

'Pardon me,' he said to Moskalenko and unsheathed his weapon.

The general tried to speak calmly, but his voice betrayed hatred and anger. The faces of many of his battlefield comrades who had been killed or tortured at Beria's will appeared in his mind's eye. He himself had escaped their lot by a sheer miracle in 1940.

A younger officer paled, seeing the kneeling man on the floor pleading for his life. Granted permission to finish off Beria, Batitsky took aim and fired. The officers went across to the wall to make sure Beria was dead.

As the American author John Gunther put it, Beria now joined Genrikh Yagoda and Nikolai Yezhov in the community of ex-Soviet police chiefs who did not die natural deaths.

Winston Churchill, in a little known comment on the dismissal of Beria said: 'Beria – Siberia. Strange things are happening there.'

Marshal Zhukov was quoted as saying after the country was rid of Stalin's henchman: 'I regarded it as my duty to make my small contribution to the affair.'

Marshal Konev looked down at the corpse and said: 'Cursed be the day this man was born.'

Notes

1. *Moscow News*, no. 41, 1989.
2. General K.S. Moskalenko, 'Beria's Arrest', *Moscow News*, no. 23, 1990.
3. After the war, tens of thousands of Cossacks, who had been held prisoner by the Germans, were returned by British forces – a certain proportion of them against their will – to the Soviet Union, where an undetermined number landed in Stalin's gulag or suffered a worse fate. There were individual tragedies among many Cossack families. Some historians have questioned the wisdom of British compliance with the Kremlin demands for their return.

17

BIG BROTHER AND ZHUKOV

Big Brother had a super aim in mind by calling lies the truth, by rewriting pages of history, by censoring all books – to hold back for at least several millennia the march of history.

The author's paraphrase of GEORGE ORWELL'S novel, *1984*

Zhukov's truthful memoirs were censored for the first nine editions.

From Russian press reports

One can only serve one's country properly with the truth and the struggle for the truth.

G.K. ZHUKOV

In 1989 the Russian public learned for the first time details about Marshal Zhukov's doctored memoirs. Whole pages, paragraphs and sentences had been cut from the original edition of his popular memoirs published 20 years earlier. Because Zhukov had given his approval for publication of his memoirs with the cuts – this was during the era of Soviet leader Nikita Khrushchev who first exposed Stalin's cult of personality – some wits called it 'the first capitulation of the undefeated marshal'. But it appeared that Zhukov had little choice in the matter. As his wife, Galina Aleksandrovna, explained to him, if he had not agreed to a compromise with Party censors, the book would not have come out at all.

Zhukov began working on his wartime memoirs in 1958 after retirement, not knowing if they would ever be published. The memoirs, *Reminiscences and Reflections*, were published in 1969 in an issue of 600,000 copies and became an instant bestseller. Twenty years later as many as seven million copies of the book had been printed. Meanwhile the 11th unexpurgated edition of Zhukov's memoirs, published in 1992, had an edition of 100,000 copies. Many foreign translations also appeared.

Maria Zhukova, Zhukov's youngest daughter, has written that her father could leave in his book only what coincided with the views of the oligarchs at that time. She said that some materials, including almost the entire chapter about Stalin's decapitation of the prewar Army, 'were cut out of my father's book'.

The censored parts of Zhukov's memoirs, in addition to the purge of the army in 1937–39, deal with such matters as Stalin's alleged infallibility, and Zhukov's criticisms on the eve of Hitler's invasion of Russia. This passage, for example, was excised from the original edition:

> I will not conceal that it appeared to us then [before the war] that Stalin knew no less but even more than we did about matters of war and defence and had a deeper understanding and foresight. When we had to encounter difficulties in the war, however, we understood that our views about Stalin being extraordinarily well-informed and possessing all the qualities of a military leader had been erroneous.

It must be borne in mind that even high-ranking military leaders like Zhukov were themselves gaining self-confidence and understanding; that while they innocently assumed that Stalin was some kind of 'military god' prior to the invasion-blitzkrieg by Nazi legions, they saw that the principle of trial and error applied even to 'the Boss'. What is not mentioned by Zhukov is that the High Command Headquarters in Moscow had no alternative at the outset but to depend on the incapacities and errors of some front-line generals.

The following selection also was censored out of the original memoirs:

> At the end of May 1941 Marshal Timoshenko and I were urgently summoned to the Politburo. We thought that at last we would probably be permitted to put the border military districts on high alert. So one can imagine our amazement when Stalin told us: 'The German Ambassador von Schulenburg has passed on to us a request of the German Government to allow them to search for the graves of soldiers and officers killed during the First World War in battles against the old Russian Army. For this search the Germans have formed several groups which will arrive at the border points according to our map.'

Here of course intruded Stalin's paranoia. He feared the provocations that might be created by his armies more than an actual invasion by the Wehrmacht. In any case, Russian historians continue to debate the complex events between August 1939 and June 1941, including the notorious Non-aggression Pact signed by Russia and Germany in the summer of 1939.

Similarly omitted from the first editions was part of the dialogue in which Stalin was first told that Hitler's armies had thundered across the Soviet border.

Stalin's reaction was: 'Isn't that a provocation by German generals?'

Marshal Timoshenko, who was present, replied: 'The Germans are bombing our cities in the Ukraine, Belorussia and the Baltic area – and land forces have launched operations on the border. It certainly cannot be called a provocation.'

Stalin commented: 'If a provocation needs to be staged, than the German generals would bomb even their own cities.'

Further, he said that 'Hitler knows nothing about it for sure. What is needed is to urgently contact Berlin.'

With the invasion underway, Zhukov met Stalin and raised the question of counter-strikes against the German armies. The following exchange appeared in the original and newer version but an additional sentence about Lenin was excised:

Stalin (irritated): What counter-strikes? Don't give me that rubbish.

Zhukov: If you think that as Chief of the General Staff I am only giving you rubbish, there is nothing for me do here. So I ask you to relieve me of my duties and send me to the front. There I will apparently be of greater use to our Motherland.

Stalin: Don't get excited! But then, if you put the matter that way, we will manage to do without you.

Then Stalin, according to Zhukov, added the following stinging words which were eliminated from the original:

'We have managed to do without Lenin, so we will certainly manage to do without you.'

Since the author of *Reminiscences and Reflections* was the nation's most popular marshal and war hero, the political leadership had immediately asked to see the manuscript before the book could be published. Mikhail Suslov, the party's ideologist-in-chief, is reported to have concluded after reading the manuscript that no mere cuts would change the essence of the memoirs; that it would be better if they were not published at all. But Brezhnev disagreed and allowed publication, incorporating the changes, to proceed. According to Vladimir Karpov, an authority on Zhukov's life, 'before this happened, two groups of subcontractors (from the main political administration of the Soviet Army and Navy and the Military-Scientific department of the General Staff) went to work on the book'. One of those involved admitted that a main task of his group was to 'eliminate the under-evaluation of the Party and its political work in Zhukov's memoirs'.

Not surprisingly, the doctoring of his manuscript by a platoon of Party flunkies and advisers was extremely painful for Zhukov who had already spent more than three years in writing his book, which is still considered by many historians to be the best of the postwar memoirs on the Russian front.

After he completed his book, Zhukov had to spend months on end arguing with the censors. Often when he sent pages back to the editors showing their deletions, he would note in the margins, 'Leave this in the revised edition!' or 'This all took place; how can you exclude such important data?' But in those years of stagnation these requests were consistently ignored. Some researchers say that upwards of 150 pages were blue-pencilled out of the original manuscript of 1,430 typed pages. When someone asked the publisher who was responsible for the many changes, the reply was that 'Georgi Konstantinovich's book was monitored at the very highest level'. This meant the manuscript had been distributed among Politburo members and that presumably Mikhail Suslov had especially occupied himself with it. It was therefore impossible to tell which sentence or paragraph was distasteful to which Politburo member.

There is little doubt, though, that on the military campaigns, and in his dealings with his commanders, the book is all Zhukov with no outside additions. No one has come forth with evidence to the contrary. Except for the invasion day blow-up with Stalin (when Stalin brought up the name of the departed Lenin), the 200 or so other Zhukov–Stalin wartime exchanges appear to be as they were, verbatim, in the original typescript.

On the insertion of political officer Brezhnev's name: this is by far the best-known addition to Zhukov's original text. 'Father,' says Maria Zhukova, 'wanted very much to see his book in print as he was afraid he might die before the book was published.' Brezhnev was now (in the late 1960s) the head of the party and Zhukov was persuaded to write in his text that he had desired in the spring of 1943 on a visit to the North Caucasian Front to 'consult' this political officer – at that time L.I. Brezhnev was head of the political department of the Eighteenth Army – about operations at a time when he was a colonel and Zhukov a marshal. As a small price for publication, the marshal wrote only of his 'desire'. But the two didn't meet during the war (although they were as close as two or three hundred miles) and

Zhukov never said they did. His daughter, Maria, says this interference in his accurate recording of his experiences led to sleepless nights and terrible migraines at a time when he was already seriously ill. Maria recalls: 'It was my mother, Galina Aleksandrovna, who convinced my father that no one would believe that he had written these lines himself.' She was able to convince him that he needed to sacrifice a small percentage of the book to save the whole.[1]

Wearied and discouraged by the obligatory changes and differences over what to remove from the book, and by the irritating delays in the publication of his memoirs, Zhukov suffered a second severe stroke in late December 1967 while he was resting at a sanitarium outside Moscow. He spent six months in hospital and at another sanitarium. At home he continued his rehabilitation under the care of his wife, Galina Aleksandrovna, who was a physician.

The new uncensored edition of Zhukov's memoirs although it now included the previously expurgated criticisms of Stalin, also retained positive images of the Supreme Commander-in-Chief. But other marshals who were never sycophants, also wrote memoirs praising Stalin's wartime merits, writing about him long after his death. (They include Marshals Rokossovsky, Vasilevsky and Meretskov.) A sample of Zhukov's remarks: 'With strictness and exactitude Stalin achieved the near-impossible.' Also: 'He had a tremendous capacity for work, a tenacious memory.' And: 'Stalin's merit lies in the fact that he correctly appraised the advice offered by the military experts and then in summarized form – in instructions, directives and regulations – immediately circulated them among the troops for practical guidance.'

Zhukov said that Stalin's military knowledge was insufficient throughout the war but in a majority of cases he displayed common sense and an understanding of the situation. Most of Stalin's orders and requests were 'correct and fair'. Zhukov added: 'Stalin knew strategy well because it was close to his customary sphere: politics. But he had a poor understanding of operational art and tactics.'

At last, at the end of 1968 it was learned that the Kremlin had given its approval to the manuscript; now the memoirs could be published. The first books reached the shops in the spring of 1969. Within a few months Zhukov received 10,000 letters from readers, congratulating him and offering corrections and comments. The first edition was quickly sold out. Citizens could now remember the 'marshal of victory'. Zhukov had risen from oblivion. He was even elected a delegate to the Twenty-fourth Party Congress which was to be held in Moscow in March 1971.[2]

Notes

1. Maria Zhukova, *Literaturnaya Rossiya*, 17 June 1994.
2. But Zhukov was discouraged from attending. Doctors advised against his attendance. Brezhnev himself told Galina that it would be too much for Zhukov to be sitting and standing at the Congress for at least four hours. And to make sure there was non-attendance a pass was refused to Galina. They got the message. Brezhnev did not want the most popular war hero at his Congress. One witness saw tears in Zhukov's eyes for the first time.

18

THE EISENHOWER–ZHUKOV FRIENDSHIP

Zhukov said that his daughter was being married that day but that he had passed up the ceremony because of this opportunity to see his 'old friend' General [now President] Eisenhower.

JOHN EISENHOWER, *Strictly Personal*, 1969

When we flew into Russia, in 1945, I did not see a house standing between the western borders of the country and the area around Moscow. Through this overrun region, Marshal Zhukov told me, such numbers of women, children, and old men had been killed that the Russian Government would never be able to estimate the total.

GENERAL DWIGHT EISENHOWER, *Crusade in Europe*, 1948

The universally admired Yank and the renowned Russian 'marshal of victory' met for the first time in June 1945 in a simple manner as befits old soldiers. The heady war record of Georgi Konstantinovich Zhukov (the victories at Moscow, Stalingrad, Kursk and Berlin, to name a few) was well known to Dwight David ('Ike') Eisenhower. Gripping him by the arms, the American visitor regarded Zhukov for fully five seconds, uttering finally:

'So that's what you are like!'

Although the two men came from different worlds they got on well, as old soldiers usually do, but it also seemed to augur well for the future relations of the two giant powers. There was an inspired moment when each soldier presented the other with a high government decoration. Their friendship deepened when General Eisenhower, accompanied by his deputy, General Lucius Clay, and his son John, an army lieutenant, visited Russia as Zhukov's guests in August 1945. The Americans received full red-carpet treatment; upon their arrival Zhukov said they could visit any place they wanted in Russia, including Vladivostok, which was seven times zones away to the east. Ike, however, preferred to see Moscow, including the Kremlin Museum (banned to rank-and-file visitors during Stalin's time), with its accumulated treasures of the Tsars; and the city that Peter the Great built (the wartime Leningrad, today once more St Petersburg). During a mammoth sports parade on Red Square, Stalin invited Ike to stand on the reviewing platform atop the Lenin Mausoleum, a first for any foreign official.[1]

Incidentally, Ike's warm relations with Zhukov were not unique. For example, General Clay expressed the same feelings. He wrote later: 'I liked the marshal instinctively and never had reason to feel otherwise.' (In his research the author discovered that one flamboyant Russian general, who distinguished himself against Hitler's armies, actually fought side by side with the Americans in the First World War. Rodion Malinovsky, who became a marshal and replaced Zhukov as Defence Minister in 1957, was fighting as a youth in France in July 1916. Moscow had sent two infantry brigades to France by ship to reinforce the Allies. 'I had the pleasure of fighting next to an American division,' said Malinovsky. 'In spirit I got on better with the Americans than with the others,' he told US journalists in 1943.)

But the very first Ike–Zhukov meeting could have ended badly but for Ike's diplomatic talent. Recalling that meeting in Berlin, Zhukov says the two began by talking about some of the major events of the war that had just ended. Eisenhower told him about the great problems he had in conducting the landing operation in France in 1944, and then the difficulties later during Hitler's surprise counter-offensive in the Ardennes forest. Then they passed on to serious business: how to organize a four-power administration of Germany.

Only a minute after this formal part of the conversation opened, there was a very awkward moment. Eisenhower had mentioned access to Berlin:

'We'll have to agree on a number of questions bearing on the organization of the Control Council [for the Allied Administration of Germany] and the provision of land communication routes across the Soviet zone to Berlin for the US, British and French personnel.'

Zhukov then pointed out the need for setting up air corridors.

'It seems to me,' he said, 'we'll have to agree not only on land communications, but also address the problem of flights to Berlin by the American and British air forces over the Soviet zone.'

Upon hearing this, General Carl Spaatz, a member of Eisenhower's entourage, and Chief of the US Strategic Air Command, leaned back in his chair and remarked in an offhand way:

'The US air force has always flown and flies anywhere without restrictions.'

When these words were translated into Russian, Zhukov shot back his reply:

'Your air force is not going to fly over the Soviet zone without any restrictions. You shall fly only along established air corridors.'

Eisenhower quickly broke in, telling Spaatz:

'I did not authorize you to pose the question of air force flights in such a manner!'

Then, turning to Zhukov, he said:

'Today I have come here to meet you personally, Mr Marshal. As for our business matters, we'll settle them after we have organized the Control Council.'

To this, Zhukov said:

'I believe that we, as old soldiers, will be able to find a common language and work as a team. Right now I would like to make only one request: please pull the US troops out of Thuringia as soon as you can, for, according to the Yalta Agreement between the heads of the Allied governments, Thuringia is supposed to be occupied only by Soviet troops.'

'I agree with you, and will insist on it,' said Eisenhower.

Hearing these words, Zhukov did not feel like asking Eisenhower to whom he was going to insist. For Zhukov this was a matter of high government policy that mainly concerned President Truman and Prime Minister Churchill.

After the formalities were over, Zhukov asked Eisenhower and his staff to have lunch right there in his office before the guests flew off to their headquarters in Frankfurt-am-Main.

Summing up that first meeting, Zhukov says simply:

'Eisenhower's outward appearance impressed me favourably.'

Zhukov became a familiar figure at Allied banquets and parades marking various national holidays as well as the days commemorating victory in the war in Europe and the Far East. On these special occasions Zhukov wore a blue tunic that fairly dripped with a glittering display of medals, crosses and ribbons. One writer described this display as 'MacArthuresque'.

But not every Allied military man approved. One US general –

known for his flamboyance and indiscretions – found the display on Zhukov's expansive chest too garish. On meeting Zhukov at an inter-Allied review in September 1945 celebrating VJ Day, General George ('Blood and Guts') Patton wrote to his wife that the marshal's full-dress uniform was 'much like comic opera – all covered with medals'. (When Patton himself received a Russian award, the Order of Kutuzov, from the headquarters of Marshal Fyodor Tolbukhin, he jotted in his diary: 'He is a very inferior man and sweats profusely at all times.') Although he was a brilliant commander of armoured forces, Patton's political statements and anti-Russian and anti-British feelings would often get him into hot water.

It appears that Zhukov once had a specific complaint against Patton, although the latter gave it his characteristic brush off: 'Why do we care what those God-damn Russians think?' What happened was that a complaint was issued from Zhukov's office in Berlin saying that Patton was too slow in disbanding and confining some Wehrmacht units in his sector of military government.

Since Patton also mouthed the opinion that 'Sooner or later we'll have to fight those bastards', his immediate superior told him to 'Shut up, Georgie, you fool!' and he was eventually reprimanded by Eisenhower.

At the beginning, Zhukov had a dispute with British Field Marshal Montgomery over the detention of German soldiers when he also took up the question of British occupation troops. But because in Russian eyes the issue of the Germans was a matter of urgency Zhukov sent a memorandum to the Control Council, the contents of which Montgomery regarded as a personal attack. (Monty in his memoirs uses such phrases as 'he accused me', 'a direct attack upon us', 'suspicious of [our] intentions', and 'a direct challenge'.) In November 1945, says Monty, just when all affairs in the British Zone seemed to be going well, Zhukov made his complaint to the Control Council about the British allegedly retaining tens of thousands of organized former German Army troops in the British sector. Zhukov had circulated a memorandum 'in which he accused me', says Monty, of lacking good faith. The memorandum, he goes on, demanded a 'heavy counter-attack'. Monty went ahead and prepared his paper counter-attack. But the issue was eventually settled amicably and Monty says that when he next met Zhukov the meeting was 'throughout very friendly', that his relations with the Russian marshal remained 'excellent' despite the deeply suspicious attitude of the Russians on such a subject as the German units.[2]

But, on the whole, Eisenhower and other ranking Western military men did not withhold their praise of Zhukov as warrior – his hard-driving leadership under fire, his near-fanatic inspiration, his courage and self-control. Sometimes, however, they were appalled by Zhukov's seeming ruthlessness, which made it appear that he did not take into account the cost of life in an operation if the desired military advantage were obtained. To be fair, however, there was for the most part a different order of magnitude in the ferocity of the fighting between the Eastern and Western fronts. Added to this, the enormity of the tragedy created by Hitler's armies on Russian soil goaded the defenders to do all they could to drive out the enemy as soon as possible or send him to an early grave.

Eisenhower says that the more he learned about the Russian front the more he understood the bitter resentment toward Hitler's armies. It would, says Ike, have been 'completely astonishing' if the Russians had not had a 'more direct and personal vindictiveness' towards the Germans and 'a sterner attitude' toward the realities of war than was the case in countries far removed from the scene of hostilities. Even in their successful offensives, he adds, Zhukov's armies paid a terrible price for victory.[3]

During the Potsdam Conference in July 1945 Stalin and Zhukov talked about inviting Eisenhower to Moscow. Zhukov suggested to Ike that he visit Moscow during a grand sports festival scheduled for 12 August. Eisenhower accepted and Stalin ordered an official invitation sent to Washington which specified that during his stay in Moscow the US general would be Zhukov's personal guest. This implied that the American visitor was being invited to Moscow not as a statesman, or political figure, but as a famous general of the Second World War.

'Since Eisenhower was to be my official guest,' says Zhukov, 'I would travel to Moscow with him and then accompany him on his visit to Leningrad and, finally, on the return flight to Berlin.' Ike and Zhukov would find ample time to exchange opinions on different aspects of the war. When the two war heroes attended a football game one evening in Moscow, the Russian fans spotting Eisenhower gave him a standing ovation.

About their long conversations, Zhukov says he felt that Eisenhower was 'quite frank in all he said to me'. Zhukov adds that what he himself was interested in most were the war strategies employed by the Supreme Command of the Allied Expeditionary Force in Europe.

As remembered by Zhukov this is what Eisenhower told him about the fateful year 1941:

> In the summer of 1941, when Nazi Germany attacked the Soviet Union and Japan was manifesting its aggressive intentions in the Pacific, US Armed Forces were brought up to one and a half million men. For most of the War Department and in the US Administration, Japan's attack on Pearl Harbor in December 1941 came as a surprise ... When following Russia's unfolding battle against Germany, we were at a loss to guess how long Russia could hold out and whether she could at all resist the onslaught of the German Army. American business circles, together with the British, were at that time greatly concerned over India's raw material resources, the Middle East oil, the Persian Gulf and the Middle East in general.

Zhukov is critical of this and Eisenhower's remarks about the year 1942, since as is widely known Moscow ardently wished that the Allies open a Second Front in France during that year:

> From what he [Ike] said it was obvious that the principal concern of the United States in 1942 was securing its military and economic positions rather than opening a Second Front in Europe. Theoretically, the United States and Britain began to give thought to plans for a Second Front in Europe from the end of 1941, but took no practical decisions until 1944.

'We,' Eisenhower told Zhukov, 'had rejected Britain's demand to launch an invasion of Germany across the Mediterranean for purely military reasons and no other.'

Zhukov was fully aware of the difficulties involved in an invasion of Normandy.

The Allies, he says in his memoirs, were obviously highly apprehensive of German resistance along the French coast of the English Channel and deeply worried about the widely publicized 'Atlantic Wall' that Hitler had allegedly built in France to withstand an Allied invasion in force. The plan for an assault across the Channel was finally agreed upon with the British in April 1942, but even after that Churchill repeatedly attempted to persuade Roosevelt to undertake a landing across the Mediterranean. According to Eisenhower, a Second Front in 1942–43 could not be opened because the Allies were not ready for a major combined strategic operation. But Zhukov echoes the disbelief of Kremlin officials, saying that Ike's statement appeared to be 'far from the truth'. Zhukov claims that the Allies 'could have opened a second front in 1943, but they wittingly did not hurry to do so, waiting for our troops to inflict greater damage on Germany's armed forces and, consequently, to become more exhausted'.

During their talks, Zhukov put this question to Eisenhower: 'And what in fact was the Atlantic Wall like?'

'There was actually no "Wall" at all,' Ike replied. 'There were the usual trenches, and those did not run in a continuous line. There were no more than 3,000 guns of different calibre along the entire length of the "Wall". On the average this was a little over one gun per kilometre. There were only a few ferro-concrete fortifications equipped with artillery and they could not serve as an obstacle for our troops.'

It appears that the Germans themselves did not think very highly of their defences in France against a major Allied invasion from Britain. Colonel-General Franz Halder, the wartime Chief of the General Staff of the German Army acknowledges the 'unreliability' of the Wall. In his memoirs Halder writes: 'Germany had no defences against the landing force of the Allies which attacked under cover of aviation which was fully and entirely dominant in the air.'[4]

According to Eisenhower, the main difficulties in the invasion of France lay in landing the troops across the Channel with their material supply. As for the German resistance, it was relatively light.

Musing on these events after the war, Zhukov says he was puzzled when in 1965 he saw the Hollywood film, *The Longest Day*, based on the historical fact of the invasion of Normandy in June 1944. In his view the film shows the Nazi enemy to be far stronger than it actually was. Zhukov, obviously disappointed, says: 'The political lining of the film is easily understandable – but after all there has got to be a limit somewhere.' However, the marshal was genuinely thrilled when he first heard about the cross-Channel invasion: 'The Normandy landing was truly an operation on a grand scale and requires no false gloss. To give it the objective credit it merits, it was ably prepared and conducted.'

In Zhukov's opinion the Wehrmacht did not put up any major resistance to the Allied armies until July 1944 when they transferred their forces from the coast of France. The marshal mentions a book, *The Supreme Command* by F.C. Pogue, which says that the 1st US Army commanded by General George Patton lost only three men on 23 April 1945, while on the same day it captured 9,000 German officers and men. What, asks Zhukov rhetorically, were the losses suffered by the 3 million-strong American army while moving out in all directions from the Rhine? He says the Americans suffered less than 10,000 casualties, while the number of German prisoners of war were in the hundreds of thousands.

On the Ardennes thrust by Hitler's armies, Zhukov has this to say: 'I was very interested in the German counter-offensive in the Ardennes in late 1944 and in the Allied defensive action there.' He claims that Eisenhower and his companions were 'always reluctant to talk about that'. From what they did say, however, it appears that the German counter-offensive in the Ardennes came as a complete surprise for the Allied Supreme Command HQ and for the Command of the 12th Army Group under General Omar Bradley. The German operational plan boiled down to repeating the breakthrough Hitler had accomplished in the direction of Dunkirk in May 1940. Once more it was planned to move rapidly to the coast and cut off and destroy the Allied forces, this time, American and British troops. On Christmas Eve a German vanguard reached the bank of the river west of Liège. In their retreat, Anglo-American forces abandoned stocks of armaments, munitions and fuel. The German troops were poised to inflict a second Dunkirk. At this point, Churchill appealed to Stalin to relieve the Anglo-American forces with a new offensive on the Soviet–German front. The reply received the next day said the Russians would begin offensive operations on 12 January, much earlier than planned, all along the Eastern Front from the Baltic to the Carpathians. This helped relieve pressure on the Allied forces. At the same time, General Patton's 3rd Army moved at breathtaking speed to help General Bradley's troops during the German Ardennes offensive – the so-called 'battle of the Bulge'.

In his memoirs Zhukov raises the subject of Lend–Lease deliveries. He says that Russia received supplies that its economy needed badly: mainly machinery and equipment, fuel and foodstuffs. He acknowledges receiving 400,000 jeeps and trucks, many locomotives and communications systems brought from the United States and Britain. But he stresses, as all of his colleagues and Foreign Ministry officials have also said consistently, that these items could not have played a decisive role in the Russian victory over Germany. To prove his point he says Russia received under Lend–Lease from America and Britain about 18,000 airplanes and over 11,000 tanks. That, he says, made up less than 10 per cent of the total amount of armaments that Soviet Russia herself produced for the armed forces during the war. Thus Lend–Lease, he argues, could not have played a decisive role on the Nazi–Soviet front.

Zhukov says that Eisenhower on his visit to Russia was greatly interested in how the blockade of Leningrad was overcome; and also in the battles of Moscow, Stalingrad and Berlin. When Ike asked how hard the situation was physically for Zhukov as the Front commander during the Battle of Moscow, Zhukov gave this answer:

> The Battle of Moscow was equally trying both for the soldier and the army group commander. During the fiercest fighting – from 18 November to 8 December – I managed to get no more than two hours of sleep a day. To keep going somehow and be able to work, I resorted to brief but frequent physical exercise, drank strong coffee and once in a while permitted myself a 15- to 20-minute workout on skis. When a turning point in the battle was achieved, I fell so fast asleep nobody could wake me. Stalin phoned twice and was told 'Zhukov is sleeping and we can't wake him'.[5]

When Eisenhower and his party arrived in Moscow from Berlin, Stalin ordered the Chief of the Army General Staff A.I. Antonov to familiarize Ike with all the exact campaign plans for Russian armies in the Manchurian area which had been initiated a few days earlier. Ike was taken into the War Room and treated with great cordiality. Stalin, says Zhukov, talked much with Eisenhower about the war, giving his view that the Second World War was the outcome of short-sighted politicians who had connived at Hitler's aggression.

In flying back to Berlin on Ike's official aircraft, the two men had more long talks together. Zhukov became completely at ease on the plane. Before taking his seat, he'd shed his uniform, exposing a blue silk undershirt. When Ike offered the marshal a berth for sleeping, Zhukov turned him down, thinking there was only one bed on the plane, but also not wanting to appear fatigued. But another berth had been made up for Ike and, therefore, both were able to stretch out. Just before the plane landed in Berlin, Zhukov asked Ike for some magazines for his daughter. Both Eisenhower and his son, John, leafed through a number of racks, taking care to choose magazines that had no embarrassing anti-Russian articles in them.

The last Eisenhower–Zhukov meeting took place in 1955 at the Geneva summit conference of America, Britain, France and Russia. At that time Eisenhower was President, Zhukov the Minister of Defence. Many US observers felt that Zhukov was included in the Soviet delegation to Geneva (Bulganin, Khrushchev, Molotov, Zhukov and Gromyko), mainly as 'window dressing'; but also because of his past friendship with the President.

At Geneva, Ike and Zhukov met privately several times and talked not only about the war years and the administration of Germany by the Allied Control Council but also about topical problems such as co-existence and the need to strengthen peace between peoples.[6]

John Eisenhower was quick to notice a more subdued marshal than he and his father had known previously, a man who now spoke slowly and softly, who seemed rather inhibited. This was not, says John, the 'same cocky little rooster' they had known in Germany shortly after the war.

Zhukov also noted that a different Ike had replaced the man he had closely worked with in Germany. 'What he said now differed from what he used to say in 1945.' (Two years after the Geneva Summit, Zhukov, on a visit to New Delhi, was asked by Indian journalists his opinion of Eisenhower. The marshal replied frankly: 'Eisenhower is my old friend – as a soldier. I do not know what is left of him . . . whether he is the same man.')[7]

No doubt it is true that Zhukov and Eisenhower were both changed men. But in the decade since the war there had been a sea change in the political atmosphere: the growth of the Cold War, the quest by each superpower for more nuclear arms, the recent war in Korea.

A witness at Geneva, the then Foreign Minister Andrei Gromyko, has given a detail or two on the Conference. Zhukov, according to Gromyko, said that at their private talks Eisenhower was not forth-coming, that he was 'merely mouthing a few platitudes'. The upshot was that Zhukov told Gromyko that Russia should 'keep its powder dry' in the future. This view, Gromyko says in his memoirs, was shared by other members of the Soviet delegation.

Gromyko also reveals an anecdote a few years later about Eisenhower's wife, Mamie, which reflected American opinion about the Soviet empire. It happened when Premier Khrushchev, on a visit to the US capital in 1959, invited Eisenhower to a farewell dinner at the Soviet Embassy in Washington. Gromyko's neighbour at the table was the President's wife who appeared to be sympathetic to the Russians for the losses they suffered in the war. However, she quickly took the offensive: 'But now it looks like the Russians want to impose their system on others . . . There is much being written about this over here . . . Is it true?'

Gromyko said: 'Don't believe everything you read or hear.' He added that Moscow 'strictly adhered to the principle of non-interference in the affairs of other nations'.

In reply, the President's wife said: 'They don't say that over here, and I have never read about it in the Bible ... The Bible is my handbook.'

Gromyko, although atheist to the core, records that he chose not to argue with Ike's wife, saying yes there was nothing on the subject in the Bible.

Zhukov had wartime meetings with several other Americans, including Harry Hopkins, a close aide to President Franklin Roosevelt, and Eddie Rickenbacker, a pilot who was also a friend of the President.

With the war in Europe over but the war with Japan still underway, Hopkins visited Berlin and met the marshal. Both men agreed that the new US President, Harry Truman, was not the 'friend of Moscow' that Roosevelt had been. Zhukov, who had been appointed head of the Soviet Administration in Germany, says in his memoirs that in May 1945 Stalin told him: 'Now that President Roosevelt is dead [he died in April 1945], Churchill will quickly come to terms with Truman.'

US Captain Eddie Rickenbacker, a First World War ace, arrived in Moscow in June 1943. He has written: 'Our War Department could not be positive of any action the Russians might take. If they collapsed, as in 1917 ... several German armies would be released to resist us in the west. Or did the Russians have the capability and the determination to carry on the war with Germany?' Rickenbacker met Zhukov and asked him about the possibility of a renewed German offensive. Zhukov told him that Hitler's armies were now concentrated some 320 kilometres south of Moscow; that the Russians had already stopped two frontal attacks on Moscow and that the attacking German armies were thinking of going around and 'coming in the back door'.

If Hitler's troops attacked, said Zhukov, the Russians would defend; if they did not attack until winter, the Russians would – and 'we will tear them to shreds'.

'Zhukov's eyes bored into mine,' says Rickenbacker. 'I believed him completely.'

The American reported to Washington his confidence that Russia's armies would hold, that the Kremlin would never make peace with Hitler.[8]

On the testing of the atomic bomb, it is Zhukov's belief that Churchill suggested informing the Russian delegation about the new super weapon so as to take advantage of it at the Potsdam summit in July

1945. Truman wrote in his memoirs: 'On July 24, I casually mentioned to Stalin that we had a new weapon of unusual destructive force. The Russian Premier showed no special interest.' Truman and Churchill thought the Soviet leader had failed to realize the significance of what had been told to him.

Marshal Zhukov recalls:

'In actual fact, on returning to his quarters after this meeting, Stalin, in my presence, told Molotov about his conversation with Truman. Molotov reacted immediately: 'Overbidding his hand?'

Stalin replied: 'Let them. We'll have to talk it over with Kurchatov and get him to speed things up.' (Igor Kurchatov was a well-known atomic physicist. He led the development of the world's first hydrogen bomb.)

Zhukov: 'I understood they were talking about research on the atom bomb.' (See Note 10 for Prof. Sir Joseph Rotblat's insight on Stalin's atom project.)

At Potsdam, where Zhukov attended some of the Big Power meetings (17 July–2 August 1945), Zhukov says that Churchill asked for his 'assessment of the operations carried out by the Allied Expeditionary Force in Germany. He was obviously pleased with my praise of the Normandy landing.'

'But I have to disappoint you, Mr Churchill,' added Zhukov.

'In what way,' Churchill asked, suddenly intent.

'I believe several serious blunders were made after the Allied landing in Normandy. And if it were not for the mistake in appraising the situation made by the German Command, the Allied advance after the landing might have been held up considerably.'

Zhukov says that Churchill made no objections. He adds: 'It was obviously not in his interest to delve deeply into the matter.'

Historian D.F. Fleming, in the book, *The Cold War and Its Origins* (1961) mentions Eisenhower's invitation to Zhukov to visit the United States shortly after the war and the cancellation of Zhukov's visit 'because of illness'. (It is generally believed it was a 'diplomatic illness'. Zhukov's two eldest daughters confirmed this to the author. Fleming says that New York City authorities had begun to erect reviewing stands for the visit which never took place.) A dozen years later, according to John Gunther, the Kremlin sounded out Washington as to the possibility of a visit by Marshal Zhukov to America. But Secretary of State Dulles is said to have rejected the idea.

Eisenhower wrote his best-known memoir, *Crusade in Europe*, a few years before the 1955 Geneva Conference, and before he became President. In the book he looks back on his membership with Marshal Zhukov in the Allied Control Council and at the successes that were possible in helping create a new Germany.

Here is how Ike described that era:

> A great responsibility devolved upon us in Berlin. We were in daily and hourly contact with problems on which unanimous agreements had to be reached – and we felt that a record of local achievement would have a happy and definite effect upon the whole question of whether [East and West] would find a way to get along together in the same world. Consequently, in personal as well as in official relationships, we spared no pains or trouble to demonstrate good faith, respect, and friendly intent.

On 10 June 1945 Field Marshal Sir Bernard Montgomery delivered a blunt pre-recorded radio message to the German people – the subject was the issue of fraternization. (The broadcast was made on the same day that he and Eisenhower were decorated with the Russian Order of Victory by Marshal Zhukov at a gala ceremony at Ike's headquarters in Frankfurt-am-Main.) Monty's message contained a novel idea: that people must be responsible for their leaders. The message explained why British soldiers were ordered not to fraternize with the German population although 'We [British] are by nature a friendly and kindly people.' The Field Marshal mentioned Berlin's responsibility for the two world wars and the repudiation of the Versailles treaty. He said, 'When your [Nazi] leaders were successful you were jubilant, you celebrated and laughed.' Now, he said, 'Our soldiers have seen their comrades shot down, their homes in ruins, their wives and children hungry. They have seen terrible things in many countries where your rulers took the war.' The core of his message was contained in this sentence: 'The German people and this nation is responsible for its leaders.' But in his conclusion, Monty hinted that the non-fraternization policy would not last long because 'we are a Christian nation that gladly forgives'.

Montgomery's reputation as a teetotaller was widely known and even Zhukov knew of it. But on one occasion, according to British Major-General Sir Francis de Guingand, Zhukov asked Montgomery if he would dispense just once with his habit and join in a toast to his Supreme Commander-in-Chief, Stalin. Montgomery, it is said, in a generous spirit of Allied unity agreed to break his habit and drained a half tumbler of vodka.

Earlier, Monty had invited another well-known Russian marshal, K.K. Rokossovsky, to his own headquarters to be decorated. But before Rokossovsky set out, he was unofficially 'briefed' on Monty by a group of veteran journalists. The British Field Marshal, they said, was autocratic and vain, was a good listener but didn't think much of other people's opinions, was aloof even with those who were close to him, had no sense of humour, did not drink and could not stand anyone near him who was drunk, and did not smoke and couldn't stand smokers. (Taking issue with this image of Montgomery, Johnny Henderson, who was his aide-de-camp, told the author in December 2002: 'Autocratic and vain, perhaps. But Montgomery was certainly not aloof – and he had a good sense of humour. I was his ADC for four years and I would not have continued with the duty if he hadn't.' Henderson also recalled the monthly meetings of the Allied Control Council, saying that Marshal Zhukov was 'always very friendly and relaxed'. In Berlin, he said fondly, Zhukov had the habit of serving a generous buffet lunch with plenty of caviar and vodka.)[9]

After being filled in on Monty, Marshal Rokossovsky laughed and turned to his generals, telling them with a mischievous smile: 'When you talk to the field marshal don't smoke, and at dinner go easy on the drinks. We shall drink only to victory and the friendship of comrades-in-arms.'

Hearing this, a Russian journalist cut in: 'And to the King ... This is a must at the end of the dinner.'

'Good!' said Rokossovsky. 'Let's see to it that there will be some wine left in the glasses for this toast, as it's the custom in Britain.'

Zhukov met Montgomery for the first time in Berlin on 5 June 1945 at the ceremony for signing the Declaration Regarding the Defeat of [Nazi] Germany. The marshal has summed up his impressions of Monty, but at the same time he takes issue with the idea, presented by Monty, that two great battles of the Second World War, Stalingrad and El Alamein, were both turning points in that conflict.

> During the war [says Zhukov] I had closely followed the actions of British troops under his command. In 1940 the British Expeditionary Force had suffered a disastrous setback at Dunkirk. Later, British troops under Montgomery's command had routed the German corps under General Rommel at El Alamein. Montgomery had skilfully commanded the Allied Forces during their crossing of the English Channel, landing in Normandy and their advance up to the Seine.
>
> Montgomery was above medium height, very agile, smart in a soldierly

way and produced an impression of a lively and intelligent person. He began talking about the operations at El Alamein and at Stalingrad. In his opinion the two operations were of equal significance. I did not want to belittle the deserts of the British troops, but still I was obliged to explain to him that the El Alamein operation was carried out on an army scale while at Stalingrad the operation involved a group of Fronts and was of large-scale strategic importance. It resulted in the rout of a major grouping of the forces of Germany and her allies in the area of the Volga and the Don rivers and, subsequently, in the North Caucasus. It is common knowledge that it was an operation that actually signalled a radical turning-point in the war and triggered the driving of the German forces out of our country.

Notes

1. Eisenhower called the museum's jewellery, diamonds, jewel-encrusted costumes and exhibits of every description 'a magnificent display'. He said that when the time came for the visit almost the entire American Embassy staff joined his group as 'aides-de-camp' that day. US Ambassador Averell Harriman and General J.R. Deane accompanied Zhukov to the reviewing platform. A. W. Harriman and E. Abel, *Special Envoy to Churchill and Stalin, 1941–1946*, London, 1976.
2. See *The Memoirs of Field Marshal The Viscount Montgomery of Alamein*, London, 1958.
3. Eisenhower records that he was astonished when Zhukov once told him that his armies attacked through minefields as if the mines weren't there. For Ike there was always the tedious business of using technicians to destroy as many of the mines as possible. But Zhukov said that the losses from the mines were 'only equal' to those that would result from machine guns and artillery if the enemy chose to defend that particular area. Eisenhower thereupon reflects on what would happen to any American or British commander who pursued the same tactics.
4. Franz Halder, *The Halder Diaries*, Washington DC, 1950.
5. Albert Axell, *Russia's War, 1941–45*, London, Constable, 2001.
6. The world will probably never know the full extent of the private, detailed talks that Eisenhower and Zhukov had together, but the following remarks by Ike help to give some idea of their scope. In July 1957 at a press conference in Washington, an ABC correspondent asked President Eisenhower if he might invite Georgi Zhukov to visit the United States. Here is Eisenhower's lengthy reply:

> Certainly the [recent] changes in the Kremlin are the result of some fundamental pressures within the country. Now, apparently the group that went out were those that could be called the traditionalists. They were the hard core of the Old Bolshevik doctrine, whereas those that stayed and seem now to be in the ascendancy are apparently those who have been responsible for decentralization of industrial control, all that sort of thing.

Therefore, the idea that they are trying to be flexible, to meet the demands, the aspirations, requirements of their people, I think seems to be sound. Now, you referred to General [*sic*] Zhukov, and I must say that during the years that I knew him I had a most satisfactory acquaintance and friendship with him.

We had many long discussions about our respective doctrines. I think one evening we had a three-hour conversation. We each tried to explain to the other just what our two systems meant to the individual, and I was very hard put to it when he insisted that their system appealed to the idealistic, and we completely to the materialistic, and I had a very tough time trying to defend our position, because he said: 'You tell a person he can do as he pleases, he can act as he pleases, he can do anything. Everything that is selfish to man you appeal to him, and we Russians tell him that he must sacrifice for the state.'

We have a very hard programme to sell. So what I am getting at is, I believe he was very honestly convinced of the soundness of their doctrine and was an honest man.

7. A.M. Rosenthal, The *New York Times*, 10 February 1957.

8. Rickenbacker, *Rickenbacker: His Own Story*, New York, 1967.

9. A conversation with the author in December 2002.

10. One of the reasons for Russia's rapid advance into Hitler's Germany was to seize German scientists, not only for the atom bomb but also ballistic missiles which were another concern. And, informs Professor Sir Joseph Rotblat, a noted British physicist, the Russians succeeded in this but only to a limited degree, because the most important of the German nuclear scientists were interned by the West. 'But I don't think that Stalin thought this would enable him to make his atom bomb quicker; Soviet intelligence knew of the failure of the German project and its closure in 1942. The main help for the Russian project came from the United States via Klaus Fuchs.' Sir Joseph told the author that he did not agree that shortage of uranium was a delaying factor in replicating America's Manhattan project. He said the separation of uranium-235 was much more responsible for this delay.

19

WIVES AND DAUGHTERS

Mother knew what an interesting man our father was and how the women
would run after him ... In addition war has its own rules.

Interview with Zhukov's daughter, Ella

Outwardly stern as befits a commander of millions of men, Marshal
Zhukov always remained a loving father. When Zhukov was summoned from the front line to Supreme Headquarters in Moscow for a
day or two on official business, as often happened, he sometimes managed short visits to his wife and young daughters, Era and Ella.
Historian Nikolai Yakovlev, who knew the Zhukov family, says that
between battles Zhukov's thoughts were always with his family; that
when he visited his home in Moscow he could talk about trifles for
hours. Or, with an accordion on his lap, he could amuse his wife and
daughters 'with a mock-serious air'. He was a self-taught musician and
the family's opinions of his talent differed. Ella, who was six in 1943,
would tell her father with a child's frankness what she thought of his
performance.

Era was born in 1928 and Ella in 1937 when Zhukov was married
to Alexandra Dievna. Another daughter, Maria, was born in 1957 after
Zhukov met his second wife, Galina Semyonova, 30 years his junior
and a colonel in the medical service. Still another daughter, Margarita,
was born outside of marriage in 1929.

In a newspaper interview with Ella in 1996 this question and answer
appeared:

Q. Was your father not upset because he had only girls?

Ella: Never. Even when friends joked about this, saying he was a bad
workman – wouldn't he like a son? He always answered: 'Boys always
get into trouble, they even become hooligans. Girls are quieter.'

Both girls said they could count on their fingers how many times they
saw their father during four years of war, even though he was often in

Moscow on official business. But he kept in touch with letters, telling in broad terms about the progress of the war, and also his health, while asking about their schoolwork.

Here are two letters from Zhukov to his first wife, Alexandra Dievna, written after the victories at Stalingrad and Kursk:

5 October 1943:

Darling,

I send you my greetings and tender kisses. Give my love to the kids. We are still doing not too badly, here . . . The Germans want to hold out on the Dnieper river at all costs, but they will not succeed. I am still on the move, inspecting the armies . . . Probably it is in my nature to yearn to be in the field, with the troops; I feel in my element there.

Physically, I'm fine except that my hearing is poor. I ought to have my ear attended to again, but haven't arranged treatment so far. Get slight head- and foot aches sometimes. That's about all I've got to tell you.

Wish you and the kids the best of health. Love.

Georgi

23 October 1943:

Dear Shurik,[1]

Things are going well here at the front. True, there are hitches on some sections but that is perhaps inevitable after such a big advance. I wanted the Kiev operation to be completed as soon as possible, and then go to Moscow, but, unfortunately, progress is slow so far.

As usual my health goes up and down. Have got that dull footache again. I want to go to Moscow for treatment. My hearing remains as before – the noises are still there. Evidently as one grows old [Zhukov was 46 at the time] all one's ills come to the surface.

If everything goes according to plan, I hope to get to Moscow in eight days or so, if the Chief [Stalin] permits. That's about all for today. Love,

Georgi

Zhukov's letters, says Yakovlev, 'breathe infinite weariness'. The war, he says, drained people of all their strength.

Ella recalls her mother's concern when her husband was suddenly called to Moscow in 1939, in the years when such an unexplained summons often meant a visit to Beria's torture chambers. It was a time when many generals kept a small bag of clean clothes next to their bed in case of arrest in the middle of the night.

'I remember one day,' says Era, 'when we were accompanying father to Mongolia. Mama couldn't hold back and she burst out crying. Later in a letter to us he said mother's tears had greatly affected him. He pleaded with her to restrain herself in the future so that he didn't have to worry about the family and could devote himself entirely to his work.'

Zhukov didn't like to see tears, say the daughters, and such weakness was frowned upon at home.

Ella and Era remember Zhukov as being self-confident, kind and cheerful, as someone who liked good jokes, good food, books, loyal friends. 'At home, he paid a lot of attention to us,' says Era. 'Of course we didn't see him on the battlefield but we know he was tough, maybe severe. He was a real captain.'

Of course [adds Era] I saw him mostly at home. And this is mainly how I viewed him. But I know that he was always confident of his capabilities, even at the beginning of the war. Even in 1941 he was confident that we would destroy the Germans and capture Berlin. Even in the very hard first year of war, 1941, he was sure about this. And even before that. When he was at Khalkin Gol fighting against the Japanese in Mongolia he wrote letters home saying that he was sure of their success and utter defeat of Japan's invading army. That was in 1939 when he was far away from being a marshal. And what were his inner thoughts in reality? – this nobody knows. Maybe there were times when he also had some doubts.

Era continued: 'He always had the aim of influencing all those around him, especially military commanders and lower ranks, and to make sure that they would also believe in final victory.'

According to Ella and Era, their father was 'the complete Russian man'. By this they mean he loved the countryside, loved Russian folk songs, loved Russian military bands, went mushroom-picking as often as possible, loved horses, was fond of hunting and fishing – and this was 'part of his inner longing' to be close to the natural beauty of Mother Russia. He enjoyed classical and folk music, dancing and singing. He himself played the accordion and, during lulls in the fighting, he would borrow an instrument and play the Russian tunes that he knew. For him Russian food was tastiest of all.

Ella says he admired the Russian classics and constantly urged his daughters to read such authors and poets as Pushkin, Ostrovskii, Tolstoi, Turgenev and Chekhov. One of the modern authors he liked was Mikhail Sholokhov who wrote incisively about the Don Cossacks and won a Nobel prize for literature in 1965. But Zhukov concentrated on military authors, including Napoleon, Clausewitz, Schlieffen, Fuller and Liddell Hart. Ella, who was born in Belorussia in 1935, said she regretted that she did not catalogue their father's library of some 20,000 books. The daughters said that they and their father once read a translation of an American novel, *Seven Days in May,* about an attempted coup in the USA by military men. They relate that their father poked fun at the book because in his opinion the author's understanding of professional military officers was not true to life.

Era and Ella do not accept the image some people have of their father as a coarse, intolerant, pitiless commander. They contend that those who portray Zhukov in this way either show no understanding of him as a man, or fail to recognize the limitless demands that a savage war makes on the lives of commanders. Such demands, they say, could be fulfilled only by an uncompromising attitude towards slackers and incompetents on the one hand and panic-mongers and cowards on the other.

Ella and Era remember their family as being close knit, doing everything together whenever possible. 'Once,' says Era, 'I went hunting with father for wild duck. It was after the war. Maybe I hit the duck. Anyway father implied I did although we both shot at the same time. I really think father hit the target.'

Ella adds:

We had a rule: Wherever they sent father the family had to be with him. Mother loved father so much that it didn't enter her head to live without him. In 10 years, for example, Era had to change school 11 times. Father even wanted us to go with him to Mongolia in 1939 when the fighting against the Japanese troops had not yet officially ended. But after the victory there, the Mongolian Government invited all of us to come to Ulan Bator, and the entire family went there and we stayed with him for some time in the Mongolian capital.

'I remember,' said Era, 'that during Hitler's invasion of Russia we even went to the front at the end of 1941, by night, in a special plane. In August they had evacuated us all to Kuibyshev [in Siberia] and in the new year as the front line moved closer to Moscow the command post was in Perkhushkovo.'

This was one of the highlights in the young lives of Ella and Era –

that brief visit to the headquarters of the Western Front to be with their father and celebrate the New Year, 1942. The family was flown to Perkhushkovo from Kuibyshev, where they lived since evacuation from Moscow. (They did not leave Kuibyshev to return to Moscow permanently until 1943.)

Era remembers that on a short visit home at that time her father decorated a Christmas tree and prepared a table which had a lot of food and unusual sweets. 'Nobody forbade us to eat as much as we wanted and it was very jolly,' says Era. 'The sensation of joy and celebration stays with us to this day ... Then mother went to join father near the front, for 10 days. When mother couldn't visit father at the front she sent baskets of cabbages, berries, mushrooms and dried fruit for her husband's mess.'

Zhukov's daughter Maria was born after the war and was 16 at the time of her father's death in June 1974. The daughter of Galina Semyonova, she and her maternal grandmother were living at Sosnovka at the time and were required to return the dacha by the government. During his later years Maria's education and subsequent career were a worry to the old soldier as he felt his end approaching, but she finished at an institute and subsequently married. Maria has been active in maintaining her father's reputation and keeping his memory alive. She has preserved and provided her father's previously unpublished manuscript materials to the press and was applauded by Novosti Press Agency for materials she supplied for the tenth edition of Zhukov's memoirs *(Vospominania i Razmyshlenia)*. She has also been an honoured guest at memorial ceremonies commemorating wartime events in which her father played a leading role.

Zhukov's daughters have been forthcoming in speaking about their father. Not only Ella and Era, but also Maria and Margarita. (The author interviewed Ella and Era in Moscow in June 2002.) What follows are items about Marshal Zhukov's extraordinary life taken mainly from these interviews:

On Zhukov's first wife, Alexandra Dievna:

> Ella: They met in 1920 in the Voronezh region, south of Moscow, where my mother was born and my father was fighting against the Antonov gang. One day mother was having a dispute with a Red Army man and father came over to defend her. They liked each other at first glance and were never separated thereafter. Mother started going everywhere with father in a broken-down carriage, called a britchka. They lived in unheated huts. This was in the 1920s. Mother sewed soldiers' shirts into skirts. She took

the Tsarist soldiers' old-style blouses and sewed them into skirts and army shirts . . . As a result of this nomadic life she lost her first child (a boy). They advised her not to have any more children because of her delicate health. But she took a different decision in December 1929, and two daughters were born eight years apart in Belorussia.[2]

On the divorce:

Era: Perhaps mother didn't have enough endurance. Overall it was a tragedy for the whole family. As a result papa left for ever and in January 1965 applied for a divorce. He was then 69 and mama 65. Mama had indeed given her entire life to father. Her love for him lasted all those years. It was an intolerable wound.

On Zhukov's second wife, Galina Semyonova:

Ella: I once had a conversation with her when we were in the south where father had invited us all to have a break together. She herself began it. She said everything that happened was not at her initiative, and if father hadn't decided himself then nothing would have happened. I think this is true. Formerly father had given all of his energies to his work. After his downfall after the war he had nothing to give his energies to. So she [Galina] unfortunately served this purpose. Era adds: Alhough there was a big difference in their ages – some 30 years – Galina undoubtedly loved my father. When he fell ill and needed to go away, she gave up her job in the hospital, the well-known Burdenko Hospital in Moscow, and surrounded her husband with care.

On Zhukov and Eisenhower:

Era: Zhukov often talked about his friendship with General Eisenhower. He liked him very much and he called him 'my good friend'. When we visited the USA in 1996 we visited Eisenhower's birthplace in Kansas. We also attended a ceremony at Arlington National Cemetery and there we met Eisenhower's son, John, who visited Moscow after the war with his father.

When Eisenhower invited Zhukov to visit the USA:

Ella and Era: At first Stalin agreed, but then when it came time to go, Stalin ruled against it. Father wanted very much to visit America and talk to his wartime friends. Especially Generals Eisenhower and Clay. But suddenly somebody stopped the visit. We think Stalin did it.

On Zhukov and Montgomery:

Ella: Field Marshal Montgomery and Marshal Zhukov were very different in character. Zhukov considered Montgomery a bit dry, very reserved. That's why there were no warm relations between the two. The Zhukov–Eisenhower relationship was different.

On Zhukov and Stalin:

Ella: There was no closeness between the two, no sympathy. Many times they were arguing about this or that operation, or this or that decision by Stalin. Of course Zhukov sometimes had to accept Stalin's point of view. Of course it was wrong on some notable occasions. Zhukov wrote somewhere that in the initial period of the war Stalin interfered unwisely in front-line operations ... Stalin was very smart in knowing the merits of Zhukov. Stalin respected those who stood up to him if they were knowledgeable. But he always remembered this and he had a long memory.

On Stalin's jealousy:

Era: Zhukov was too popular for Stalin's taste. And it seems he never wanted others to share his glory as wartime Supreme Commander. So when the war ended he 'exiled' the highest army commanders to different places in the Soviet Union ... You see it's usually a question of power. Those in power are always afraid that someone could rise up and take over the reins of power, and especially a man like Zhukov who had great influence; and also the army is a formidable power. So, in order to diminish the influence and threat from persons like him, they try to collect as much negative information as possible and make it public. Thus, they tried to diminish the standing of Zhukov. And, later, Khrushchev did the same.

On Zhukov and Khrushchev:

Ella and Era: Khrushchev was afraid of Zhukov. And Khrushchev was scared when General Eisenhower became President of the United States of America and no doubt thought Zhukov would follow Eisenhower's steps and seek the top party job in Soviet Russia. Of course if you were in Khrushchev's place you would probably imagine the same ... During the war Zhukov never spoke about Khrushchev because Khrushchev was not significant in the chain of command. When Zhukov was Khrushchev's Minister of Defence, of course he placed his trust in him.

On Lavrenti Beria:

Ella and Era: Father told us some of the details of how they arrested Beria. It is public knowledge now. Of course, he did not treat Beria with respect. He knew that Beria was after him and was seeking an opportunity to arrest him. Beria was constantly looking for compromising material, attempting to gather this from various sources. Beria tried to get information on all spheres of life to implicate Zhukov. For example, the slander that Zhukov was actively plotting against Stalin . . .[3]

On Antony Beevor's *Berlin, the Downfall 1945* (2002):

Era: The book appears to be an attempt to prove a false premise – that our Russian armies and those of Hitler's Germany were equally wicked. To educated people these differences are as obvious as night and day. Here are just two examples, taken from the Nuremberg International Tribunal: One of Hitler's generals [his name was Heusinger] told the Tribunal that the Nazi party and the German General Staff had as their policy the systematic extermination of Slavs. That of course includes Russians. And Hitler had his death camps in Germany, Poland and elsewhere. The head of the Auschwitz death camp, told the same Tribunal (by the way, the trial records are available in many languages) that children of tender years, because they were unable to work, were flung alive into the flaming furnaces of the crematorium. The chief himself admitted killing over 2,500,000 people in the same ovens.[4]

On casualties of war:

Some critics say Zhukov and Stalin wasted too much manpower. 'It's a very complicated issue,' says Ella. 'To say that Zhukov shed a lot of blood is not a proper approach. There were a lot of different factors which determined the casualties in the war . . . We know that the country initially was not prepared to do battle with such a powerful enemy, that the army did not have enough arms. Father was called in to take charge of many operations where the situation was critical; where perhaps others had blundered. And he had to pluck victory out of what looked like a defeat. And that's the reason why a lot of casualties are attributed to these operations in which Zhukov participated. But there are some experts who have calculated the actual casualties suffered under the top commanders like Zhukov, Konev and Rokossovsky; and surprisingly the average figure was the same for each of them. And sometimes other commanders lost more lives on the battlefield than Zhukov. But the general impression is that the majority of casualties were suffered under Zhukov. It is, however well known that Zhukov was always very meticulous in planning military operations, and those who blame him for not doing it properly and losing too many lives are either not knowledgeable enough or have ulterior motives; or out of perversity. More than that, you see a lot of people are criticizing him for squandering lives, but there are also serious articles which prove the contrary. And it must not be forgotten that he was attentive to preventing unnecessary loss of life, that he had been a soldier himself, and he wanted his soldiers to stay alive.' Era adds: 'He was a soldier during the First World War and he went through thick and thin and, therefore, he knew the hardships and perils of war as much as anybody; and he learned that commanders have to protect their soldiers' lives and he did so himself after he became commander. The war records testify to this; there are many instances when he repeatedly advised officers under him not to expend lives needlessly. He also argued with Stalin at times against a certain strategy which, if carried out, would lead to unnecessary casualties.'

On some accusations against Zhukov:

(During Marshal Zhukov's lifetime there were accusations that he had 'misappropriated' a number of items like antiques, cutlery, furs and hunting rifles, and that his wife had a 'certain little black suitcase filled with valuables.')

Era: Denunciations against father were a part of Beria's plot against the marshal to tarnish his memory. They simply put together a case of alleged pillaging. So our dacha was secretly searched. But we had receipts for everything. And there was no case at all ... In regard to that little suitcase, it was of course untrue. It was in reality a small bag containing mother's creams, powders, brushes, etc. The other things are pure invention.

On the Marshal Zhukov Foundation:

This Foundation is cared for by Zhukov's daughter, Margarita. There has been a travelling exhibition dedicated to the memory of Marshal Zhukov that has visited Greece, Egypt, Cyprus, Israel and Turkey where many expatriate Russians and others who took part in wartime resistance movements continue to have considerable interest in the war and Zhukov's role in it. Apparently the Foundation has contacts with the American Eisenhower Centres in London and Paris.

On Solzhenitsyn and Zhukov:

Ella: It seems that writers like Alexander Solzhenitsyn have regarded Zhukov as being merely a part of the system which brought them such unpleasantnesses. This is probably correct. But is that really fair? My father was not a servant of the government or of any leading groups. He was a servant of his country, as far as he understood it. In my opinion we must look at Zhukov the person, and also as a man who was part of Russia and of its people – and belonging to an era that has gone.

On education:

Ella: Georgi Konstantinovich always attached lots of importance to education. In her youth mother spent a long time helping father to improve his Russian. She gave him dictations. Father had only completed a church preparatory – or parish school. Nevertheless he was always trying to improve himself. Previously there were many mistakes in his letters. And then they ceased to have errors. In this sphere mother gave him a great deal.

On Zhukov's travels:

Ella and Era: Zhukov once told a writer the following, 'You know, recently I went up to a map, ran my eye across it, and the thought struck me that there was hardly a place in Russia, Germany, and in Eastern Europe that I had not been to. My driver, Buchin, a good racing motorcyclist, calculated that we covered a total of 175,000 kilometres during the war. How many times around the globe is that? And he wasn't the only driver I had! Add to that the hundreds of hours I spent in the air, wearing out three airplanes. And there was Mongolia, too.'

On the nomadic life:

Both Era and Ella have written about their father and mother in loving terms. Era, the elder, born in 1928, has described their nomadic family life in the years between the World Wars. She emphasizes the support Alexandra Dievna gave their father as he moved up the command ladder, making a home for the family in the harsh conditions of prewar garrisons.

Notes

1. Zhukov (like all Russians), often used affectionate diminutive names, such as 'Shurik' for Alexandra.
2. More from Era about Zhukov's first wife:

   'After the divorce, mother was in a very bad way. With my father's departure the meaning of life left her. For this reason for a long time my sister and I could not forgive our father. We didn't contact him for about a year, although mother thought we should. Then, some form of contact was established. In December 1967 mother had a heart attack and she died the following day. Father was already seriously ill himself at the time and could not attend the funeral. But of course he helped organize everything. Otherwise mother would never have been buried in [Moscow's exclusive] Novodevichy Cemetery.'

3. See also chapter 16.
4. General Adolf Heusinger was Operations Chief of the German General Staff. Rudolf Hoess was the commandant of Auschwitz. He is not to be confused with his near-namesake, Rudolf Hess.

20

FALLING IN LOVE – THE SECOND TIME

Everybody remarked on her individuality.

MARIA ZHUKOVA

Twenty years after Zhukov died, his youngest daughter, Maria, said she wanted to let people know 'how it was exactly' between her mother and the marshal. In June 1994, in an article for a Moscow newspaper, Maria described her mother, Galina Semyonova,[1] who was Zhukov's second wife. Maria told of the very close relationship that existed between her mother and father. She included a few of the marshal's intimate letters to Galina.

'Probably if my mother was alive she herself would have written about life with father,' said Maria. 'You see there've been so many inaccurate and wicked words said about their relations, but mother, alas, is no more, and it's only her daughter who is able to tell the truth.'

Maria revealed how her parents met. It was in the Siberian city of Sverdlovsk (Yekaterinburg) in 1950. Zhukov was then in command of the remote Urals Military District, where Galina worked after graduating from the Kazan Medical Institute. Georgi wrote in his diary that at his first meeting with Galina he didn't pay special attention to her. He had fallen ill and Galina had come to treat him at home. When he recovered he began to take an interest in Galina's life, her family and her hobbies. Maria says he liked her modesty and particularly, he admitted, her 'beautiful warm, green eyes – eyes in which there seemed to always hide some unexplained sadness'. Maria adds that perhaps her mother had a premonition that she was fated to die young.

Maria provided a thumbnail description of her mother's appearance:

'Mother was fit and was always a well-balanced person,' says Maria. She had 'a rich spiritual, internal world, an unusual goodness, a beautiful face, and a fine figure. She had a light gait and a unique way of talking. Everybody remarked on her individuality. Father of course looked younger then, his face was fresher, more lively, his eyes shone and he had – overall – good bearing.'

At the outset, says Maria, her mother didn't encourage Zhukov's attention. She avoided meetings but her father was persistent and Galina 'became the strongest love of his life, albeit late'.

She remembers, when she was a child, asking her father why he fell in love with her mother and not with some other woman. She says his answer is 'seared' in her memory:

'I've met many beautiful women and some more beautiful than mom. But there is no one quite like her. She's like the sun.'

And that, says Maria, was the whole truth.

She writes (in 1994) that people who knew her mother or who had met her, still remember, twenty years after her death, that warmth that she gave to others. 'She became a doctor by vocation and never regretted it. From her youth her mind was exercised by the question of the battle of medicine with terrible epidemics, the plagues that threatened mankind: cholera, typhus and small pox. She praised the courage of doctors who sacrificed themselves for the pursuit of truth. And (sometimes) infected themselves with dangerous diseases.' Maria says she posed this question for herself: 'In what way can I be useful to the world?'

Their love letters, says Maria were only passed on to her after both her parents were gone. She concludes: 'Having read them I was struck by how much anxiety, grief, worry for one another was contained in them. And even poetry.'

4 September 1952

Galina my dear,

I'm in Gurzuf [a town in the Crimea] for four days now. I'm still under the spell of our last enchanting meeting. My Galusenka [an endearment for Galina], I would have very much liked to have preserved your look and general image for a much longer time. But that depends only on you, my beloved.

The weather in the Crimea has become very good. The sky is blue, the sea is bluish-green, warm and welcoming in its embrace. My dear what a pity that you're not with me. I can't get enough of you and I'm bored without you. Let my love and my dreams of you keep you safe.

[signed] G

In 1953 they were both in Moscow. It was the beginning of the year and Mother had been taking a course for doctors for raising their qualifications. And unexpectedly Zhukov was summoned to the capital. After the death of Stalin he was appointed First Deputy Minister of Defence. Having finished her course Galina started working at the Burdenko Hospital as a specialist in infectious diseases and, later, as a therapist. During their days of separation they wrote to one another. Maria says that

> practically in all of these letters they said they wished to see each other soon and expressed caring and tender thoughts. Father confided in his relatives what was in his soul. Knowing mother's purity and loyalty, he trusted her with his thoughts, those thoughts which he couldn't entrust to anyone else. One day in a letter he wrote down a terrible nightmare in which he saw himself fishing at sea. Having caught a few fish he realized there was a snake among them. It sprang on to his chest and wrapped around his neck. Waking up, he couldn't get the unpleasant feeling out of his head and, wondered what this snake represented, what was meant by the attempts to bite him. In the letter father reasoned that he didn't believe in dreams, but when he saw the snake he started to believe that somebody intended some sort of despicable plot against him.

The letter ended with this paragraph:

Well, we will live to see. I'm not used to dealing with bastards and plotters. I'm only writing this to you. Forgive me, Galyusha. Excuse me for spoiling your holiday mood. However, I don't have anybody else so close to whom I can tell my innermost thoughts.

G.

2 Nov. 1955

And then there was this short letter from Zhukov which carried the dateline, 23 August 1956:

My dear one, I want to see you so much. Fly to me soon. I miss you more than ever. What can it mean? What will you say, my dear philosopher? I'm sorry I'm writing badly because I'm writing at sea which looks today rather like your eyes when you're being thoughtful.'

In September 1956 Georgi and Galina holidayed together in Varna, Bulgaria. Judging from the stories they told later the holiday was excellent, their first holiday together. Zhukov had at his disposal a palace of the former Tsar Boris with its beautiful park, and the warm sea.

> One could say [Zhukov wrote in his notebook] that neither I nor Galina had ever holidayed before in such splendid surroundings. I was pleased that Galina was happy with her short work-break and our trips around Bulgaria.

But unfortunately the time flew too quickly and as the end of the holiday approached, Galina became gloomy ... We flew to Moscow together on my aircraft. On arrival in Moscow Bulganin phoned me and said that Nikita [Khrushchev] remarked rather rudely in the Presidium of the Central Committee [the Party's highest body] that I had been holidaying in Varna with Galina. This bothered me and I answered hotly with a string of sharp words about Nikita which Bulganin straightway passed on to Khrushchev, with whom I soon had a conciliatory conversation. Nikita said: 'I'm not against Galina but I recommend that you don't hurry in bringing things to a conclusion.' At the time I didn't understand that he, with his 'well wishing', wanted to see in my face a true friend who would support him in the battle for power.

When they arrived in Moscow Zhukov found out that Galina was pregnant. 'He was proud as he was 60 at the time,' says Maria. 'He had dreamt of a son, remembering and pitying the son not born in 1951. He was touching in his care for mother, looked after her health and made sure that she drank only natural juices and ate fruit. I was born in June 1957.'

A short letter has survived that was sent to the maternity unit in those days when the June Plenum of the Central Committee of 1957 was being held.

22 June 1957

Galusha, my dearest,

For five days a terrible battle has been waged. The result is positive at the moment. But it seems the work will continue for another four or five days as the questions are very complex.

How is your health? How is our baby? Who is she like? And bear in mind in my childhood I had dark hair with ash streaks. Is she anything like that? How much does she weigh, how tall, et cetera. I ask you not to come home for 10 or 12 days, as the little one might fall ill and not be strong enough.

Well, I'll close now. For the fourth day running I'm only getting four or five hours sleep and that's only low quality sleep ... I kiss you and our daughter,

Your Georgi

Maria says the birth was a hard experience for Galina. ('I was a rather sickly infant.') Her mother wrote Zhukov a note full of despair:

For the second day now I feel terrible. Our daughter has jaundice, and she is listless – not active. Today the doctors expressed some doubt, and they are worried for her life. I'm so scared of losing her. On my insistence they brought her to show me today. She's quiet, occasionally opening her grey eyes. The birth was traumatic. She could have been stillborn. How I'm suffering for the little one! I don't even know where to turn. I'm really losing control.

Zhukov sent an immediate reply.

26 June 1957

Galusha my dear,

Today I didn't sleep all night having received your letter about the state of your health and our daughter. How could it happen? I really worry about you. You don't have me beside you nor anybody else who is close.

I beseech you. Pull yourself together and don't buckle under the force of fate. Try to control yourself, even if the circumstances are tough because life is still ahead, and it must be psychologically fulfilling. I have in mind that in such circumstances, weak people don't always come out victorious from the battle. I hope that as a doctor you will understand that in such instances nothing will help. Even a mother's love for her first child.

Galusha, I believe that I will see our baby nice and healthy. It just can't be that the doctors would not save her. In the hope of meeting soon in happier circumstances with you and our daughter, be strong and I send you a strong kiss and one for our daughter,

Your G

At the end of October 1957, father made an official visit to Yugoslavia and Albania. Those were tough times for him. Behind his back, there were those who were plotting against him and undermining his position.

26 October 1957, from the plane

My dear one,

I'm flying over Hungary, it's now 12:15. At 2 p.m. I'm arriving at Vnukovo airport. Behind me I will have 10,000 kilometres, of which more than 2,500 were by sea.

I'm very tired. I'd very much like to rest from this tiring trip but it seems major work lies ahead.

I'm anxious over the happy feeling of meeting you and our daughter. I missed you both terribly. Probably Mashenka has grown and become even sweeter. I would like her to be more like me, but of course with your eyes which I love so very much.

Your Georgi

Later, Russia's foremost war hero became a victim of intrigue, jealousy, Party stringency. Straightway, upon his arrival in Moscow Zhukov was taken from the aircraft to a meeting of the Central Committee Presidium. The October plenum of the Central Committee was in full swing and there were many accusatory speeches and defamatory remarks made about the hero of Moscow, Stalingrad and Leningrad. He was sacked from the post of Minister of Defence, and was removed from membership in the Presidium.

> Father, still full of energy, was ready to serve his beloved motherland and the people, yet he was left without work. He was even struck off the list of general inspectors, something given to all marshals. It was a bitter experience to feel betrayed by friends, and it was the beginning of his loneliness and inactivity. If it were not for his love of mother and the baby then I don't think father could have survived. It wasn't easy for him to stay at home, having seen his wife off to work – a man who was used to constant businesslike activity. Mother saw that and was anxious as well, but insisted that father write his memoirs, and so occupy himself instead of dwelling on stupid negative thoughts.

Starting in 1960 the whole family regularly travelled in summer to Gagra, on the Black Sea coast. Zhukov was offered the second floor of a huge white manor house in the mountains, next to a famous dacha where they filmed *The Happy Lads*. Everywhere he went he was recognized. Many mistook Galina's mother for his wife and thought he was holidaying with his daughter and granddaughter. There were those who stopped the marshal on the street long enough to talk to him about the war, or the weather, while some even remarked, 'What a beautiful granddaughter you have.' Then Zhukov would get annoyed and proudly answer: 'That's my daughter.'

Georgi Zhukov took many amazing photographs at those times: by the colonnades in the park, by the lake, feeding black swans on the beach, in the sea, and so on. 'Father quite literally was never to be parted from his German wide-angle camera,' says Maria, who adds that during their holidays in Gagra he took so many photos that some of the films were never even developed.

Note

1. Maria Zhukova, *Literaturnaya Rossiya*, 17 June 1994.

21

IN MEMORIAM

An irretrievable loss.

(From the official obituary)

With his beloved wife Galina gone, Zhukov's health declined rapidly. On the very eve of entering the Kremlin hospital he corrected and signed the last chapter of his memoirs. On 18 June 1974, Russia's greatest soldier since Suvorov died. Less than a week later his two-volume memoirs were sent to the press. In the words of a loyal friend, 'It was the last great feat of Georgi Konstantinovich Zhukov.'

On 19 June the Soviet Union officially announced the death of its greatest Second World War hero, Marshal Georgi Konstantinovich Zhukov. The announcement carried by Tass, the official press agency, confirmed that the 77-year-old military leader died the previous day 'after a long illness'.

At least some Western newspapers buried the story in their inside pages. In a decision that surprised many, the *New York Times* published the news of Zhukov's death, in eight columns of print on page 46. Apparently the paper's editors did not consider the event deserving enough for page 1.

Adding more details, the obituary said that unofficial sources in reporting Zhukov's death had attributed it to the last in a series of heart attacks in that year (1974).

The obituary was signed by the country's leadership, including Leonid Brezhnev, Aleksei Kosygin and Nikolai Podgorny, as well as senior military officers. The obituary hailed the marshal as 'a striking example of selfless devotion' and called his death 'an irretrievable loss for the people and its armed forces'.

Two men who had recently caused Zhukov considerable grief – Suslov and Yepishev – also affixed their signatures. On the afternoon of 21 June Brezhnev led other pallbearers who carried the urn bearing

Zhukov's ashes to the Kremlin where it was placed in a niche in the red brick wall. An honour guard of two soldiers flanked a photo of the marshal and a display of his many awards.

Stalin and Khrushchev, who had attempted to tarnish Zhukov's reputation, and in the process caused heartache to him and his daughters, have no place in the Kremlin wall. Stalin, who died in 1953, was at first mummified and laid to rest in the mausoleum beside Lenin. At the 22nd Party Congress in October 1961, D.A. Lazukina, a Party member for over half a century, rose to tell the delegates that on the previous evening she had 'consulted' Lenin who told her: 'It is not pleasant for me to lie next to Stalin, who caused so much harm to the Party.' In any case, a resolution was passed to remove Stalin from the mausoleum which was carried out immediately.

Behind the mausoleum a deep pit was dug for Stalin's coffin and a granite plaque was placed on the grave with the name, 'J.V. Stalin' [but in the Cyrillic alphabet].

Nikita Khrushchev fell victim to a heart attack in September 1971. He was interred in Moscow's Novodevichy Monastery.

Marshal Klimenti Voroshilov, who had not raised a hand to help his fellow Red Army officers in the Great Purge, died several years before Khrushchev.

Zhukov's family had another bitter pill to swallow. On the day after his funeral a delegation arrived at Zhukov's dacha and at his Moscow flat to cart off his personal archives and other papers.

After the early 1990s as the Soviet Union disintegrated, Party control of the armed forces was removed. The Russian people, who had endured Party tyranny, could now openly revere the memory of the man who did much to bring victory to the nation. A statue of the marshal was erected in front of the Ministry of Foreign Affairs. A bust was also unveiled at the Ministry of Defence.

In its front-page obituary on Zhukov, the *Guardian* newspaper, calling him the 'saviour of Moscow', recalled that his pre-eminence had come to an abrupt end in October 1957 when it was announced that he would leave his post at the Ministry of Defence. It also said that an article in the party paper, *Pravda*, by Marshal Ivan Konev drew attention to Zhukov's 'attempts to restrict Party influence' in the military. At that time a critical resolution was passed by the Central Committee which expelled Zhukov from membership.

Thus, it continued, the marshal's effective career was ended. He was said to have gone on a three-months' holiday, which, in fact, lasted about eight years. At least a partial rehabilitation came in April 1965 when Konev described him as being, in spite of his 'shortcomings', 'a great military leader'. Zhukov also made a formal appearance in the May Day parade in Moscow in May 1965, when he was invited to stand on the mausoleum's reviewing platform.

When Premier Khrushchev visited America in 1959 he told President Eisenhower: 'Don't worry about your old friend, Zhukov. He's enjoying his retirement and is writing his memoirs.'

The *Annual Register of World Events* in its obituary on Zhukov summed up the life of the marshal in a few concise sentences. It said:

> The marshal's most famous victories were the defence and relief of Moscow (1941), and of Stalingrad (1942–43), followed by the relief of Leningrad (1943). Later he commanded a group of armies (a Front) in the capture of Berlin (1945) and after the German surrender became Commander-in-Chief of the Russian zone in Germany and Soviet member of the Allied Control Council. In 1946 he was recalled and consigned to obscurity, allegedly because of Stalin's jealousy. Restored to favour as First Deputy Defence Minister (1953–55), he became Minister of Defence of the USSR (1955–57) and member of the Presidium. He was again cast into the shadows, this time by Nikita Khrushchev, under the taint of Bonapartist ambition, but was rehabilitated, though not in office, from February 1965. He was honoured during his military career with four awards as Hero of the Soviet Union, and received a host of other government awards as well as foreign decorations.

Perhaps the best epitaph for Zhukov was written by an Indian diplomat, K.P. Menon, in a different context, years before the marshal died, when Zhukov was being hounded by sycophants and ideologists under Nikita Khrushchev, so that officially he had become a so-called non-person.

Menon wrote: 'No star shone in the Russian firmament after Stalin's death with greater lustre than Zhukov's.'

EPILOGUE: A GRATEFUL POSTERITY

I felt that Marshal Zhukov would be a great man in any country.

WALTER BEDELL SMITH, US General (later Ambassador)

I took a great shine to Marshal Zhukov.

KATHLEEN HARRIMAN, daughter of US Ambassador to Moscow

Had Zhukov been given the freedom of action which our government allowed Eisenhower, I believe all our [German] problems could have been solved easily.

JOHN R. DEANE, US General

The greatest conflict in history had ended and Hitler, Goebbels and Himmler had committed suicide, cheating the hangman's rope (as did Goering later, in 1946, after appearing as principal defendant at Nuremberg – escaping execution by a few hours). Now on 10 June 1945 Eisenhower, Zhukov and Montgomery, the Allied victors in the recent war, were gathered in Frankfurt-am-Main for a ceremonial occasion. The atmosphere was lively with genuine bonhomie, mutual respect and joviality. As befits those who had taken part in un-precedented warfare, the smartly uniformed commanders had many recollections to share. Despite the language difference, there was a special closeness between Eisenhower and Zhukov who were often seen together, talking, toasting, joking. It seemed to many observers that nothing could drive a wedge between these Allies who, when fighting a war, had more than once shared top secret information and coordinated their strategies. Later, in memoirs and interviews, there was a consensus among Western diplomats, generals and journalists who met Zhukov: not only was he a matchless military leader but also an outstanding representative of the Russian people.

Zhukov received red carpet treatment after flying into Frankfurt-am-Main, and the meeting between him, General Eisenhower and Field Marshal Montgomery promised to be unforgettable. *The Times* newspaper said Zhukov was 'royally received' at Eisenhower's head-quarters which was housed in the I.G. Farben building, a large modern edifice set amidst green gardens. It was one of the few build-ings that escaped the bomb damage that marked much of the city of Frankfurt. Zhukov's party arrived early, soon after Monty had flown in from his own headquarters in his Dakota aircraft and driven from the airfield. Equal military honours were accorded Zhukov and Montgomery, including the firing of salutes and the presence of an immaculate composite guard of troops from the best British and American contingents. Besides a staff of 20, Zhukov was accompanied by his crusty aide, Andrei Vyshinsky, sent along by Stalin to be his pol-itical mentor. Vyshinsky had been Stalin's chief prosecutor at the Great Purge Trials in 1937–39 – also known as the Great Terror for the numberless victims it devoured. (He'd also been Moscow's first ambassador to the United Nations.) But in the eyes of observers Vyshinsky's presence did not crimp Zhukov's style of impromptu chats and genial toasts with his British and American counterparts.[1] (During one of these chats, Zhukov told Eisenhower about the high cost of Russia's victory. Ike relates that Zhukov told him that so many women, children and old men had been killed by Hitler's marauding armies that the Russian government would never be able to estimate the precise total.)

The first thing Zhukov did after greeting his hosts was to bestow decorations on Eisenhower and Montgomery, giving them Russia's 'super-super award' – the Order of Victory.[2] After the three com-manders had exchanged autographed photos of their earlier meeting in Berlin, Zhukov presented the decorations, uttering the simple words, 'I congratulate you from my heart,' and then the three chatted for a time about the war in the Pacific and Asia, with the Russian mar-shal recollecting memories of the defeat he had meted out to a size-able Japanese invasion force in Mongolia in the summer of 1939. It was this stunning victory that first brought him to Stalin's attention.

As Zhukov presented the decorations, Ike and Monty stood side by side rigidly at attention. Then Zhukov delivered a speech stressing the need for unity among the former Allies in the post-war world. More than half a century before the world came face-to-face with inter-national terrorism, the marshal said – and he later spelled it out in pri-vate talks with Eisenhower – that solidarity among the powers could prevent future outbreaks of violence. It is noteworthy that each year on Victory Day in Moscow (9 May) the Russian president who is the

Supreme Commander-in-Chief of the Armed forces, invariably uses words which echo Marshal Zhukov's recommendations for Allied unity in 1945.

Here, for example, is what President Vladimir Putin said on 9 May 2002:

> The world has changed since 1945. But it remains highly vulnerable. The forces of evil and violence surface again and again. They have different names but old habits ... Victory Day is a lesson and a warning ... We can resist these threats only by joining the efforts of states and the will of nations. The anti-Hitler coalition is a reliable proof of this ... Today we have pooled efforts or are pooling efforts against a common threat called terrorism.

The opulent Order of Victory presented to Eisenhower and Montgomery for their outstanding success in the war, is a five-pointed red, blue and gold platinum star encrusted with 135 diamonds and five rubies. In the centre of the star was a small enamelled image of the Kremlin. Eisenhower says in his memoirs: 'The decorations presented to Montgomery and me were among the few I have seen that have great intrinsic rather than exclusively sentimental and symbolic value.' Only five non-Russians were awarded the medals: Eisenhower, Montgomery, Marshal Josip Broz Tito, Polish Marshal Mikhail Rola-Zymierski, and King Michael of Romania. (A few days before the Frankfurt meeting, Eisenhower had flown to Berlin to present an American medal to Zhukov – the Order of the Legion of Merit Commander in Chief), awarded to the marshal by the US government. Montgomery had also presented a British decoration to Zhukov – the Knight Grand Cross of the Order of Bath.

After the Order of Victory was presented to Eisenhower and Montgomery, the three commanders clinked glasses in a toast to the victory of the United Nations. It was a beautiful summer day, recalls Eisenhower, and after pre-luncheon refreshments and wines, and then a grand luncheon, there was a series of toasts. Zhukov was an accomplished speaker, says Eisenhower, and the sentiments he expressed during a luncheon speech 'were complimentary to the Allies and hopeful of success in our co-operative purposes'.

In his speech Zhukov used no notes. Probably if he had made the same remarks a year, or even a few months later, he would have got a stiff reprimand from Moscow for being too lavish in praising the Allies. He began:

Everyone knows that our people have carried the mass of the weight of the war on their shoulders. The people of the Soviet Union have suffered the greatest losses of the war and their country has been burned and ravished more than the countries of any other of the belligerent powers. But our people believed that they would not be alone in battle and in the righteousness of their cause. They fought cleanly and honestly, so that now they can look into the eyes of their allies.

Zhukov then spoke candidly about wartime help from London and Washington: 'Great Britain and the United States supported the Soviet Union when such support was hard to give. Our people will never forget that help. In future, all of us will have to carry out their obligations in regard to the protection of the world of tomorrow from further acts of aggression.'

Afterwards, Zhukov's toast to Eisenhower showed admiration for his genial American friend: 'Here is a man with the heart of a soldier and the mind of a diplomat – the man who has been able to organize the many different nationalities under his command and lead them to victory.'

In reply, Eisenhower said: 'It seems fitting on this occasion for me to say that I have had the advantage of the help of the most skillful soldiers and diplomats that two great nations could provide. To them I owe an immeasurable debt of gratitude. I cannot name them today, because to single out any would not be fair, but I know what they want – they want peace.'

Meanwhile, Ike came up with one of his pithy formulations: 'Speaking for the Allied forces, I say we mean to have peace even if we have to fight for it.'

'Speaking for myself,' he added, 'I believe that there is no man around this table who would not give up all the honors, all the publicity, and everything else this war has brought him if he could have avoided the misery and suffering brought to the populations by reason of this war. This was a holy war and had to be won regardless of cost.'

After Eisenhower's words, everybody at the luncheon who wanted had their turn at offering a toast – British, Americans, Russians and French. Earlier, Montgomery spoke formally when he was presented with the Order of Victory by Zhukov: 'I regard it as a high honour to receive this award from such a renowned marshal of the Soviet Union as Marshal Zhukov.' But later, Monty, in an expansive mood, was seen slapping Zhukov on the back, reportedly telling him, 'You've got to come around [to British headquarters], old boy!'

The Frankfurt ceremony was a huge success. Zhukov had been

completely relaxed and appeared to enjoy himself to the hilt, especially during the entertainment that followed the luncheon, when he and Eisenhower sang songs together despite the difference in language. (Eisenhower had learned, meanwhile, that all too often, before Zhukov at his post in Berlin could act on minor details, including making personal visits, or answering the simplest questions from his Allied counterparts, he had to ask for instructions from Moscow. However, Ike says that Zhukov showed more 'independence in action' after he told him: 'If I sent such small details to Washington for decision I would be fired and my government would get someone who would handle these things himself.')

In Eisenhower's book, *At Ease,* published in 1967, he makes an interesting observation about Zhukov: 'The Marshal had scant patience with political men. Once, when I told him that I wanted to talk about a military matter and had not brought along my political adviser [Robert Murphy], I added that he could have his present if he liked. "No," he replied, "if you're not going to have yours, I'm going to throw mine out." He turned to Andrei Vyshinsky, his adviser, and said, "Get out, I don't want you here".' Historian Stephen Ambrose tells how Eisenhower sized up Zhukov as a commander. Ike told Montgomery that the Russian marshal was in a class all by himself, that his account of his campaigns (and he was always present at the critical point) plus his reasons for each action that he took, including his use of weapons in which he had a superiority, his concern for the weather, and his care in providing the organization and equipment before he delivered his blow, 'all added up to making him a standout'.

Actually, the Eisenhower–Zhukov singing duet was sparked by the arrival of a troupe of black singers from America who had volunteered to perform for the Allied ceremony in Frankfurt. Fond of spirituals, Eisenhower had broken the ice and he and Zhukov joined with the professionals, harmonizing to the guitar strains of 'Old Black Joe', 'Old Folks at Home' and 'Ol' Man River'. (Two months later, when Eisenhower and his staff, with Ambassador Harriman, were guests in Moscow, and Japan's unconditional surrender was announced at a gala reception at the Grand Palace in the Kremlin, Eisenhower – as well as the other guests – overcome by the spontaneous gaiety – sang the 'Song of the Volga Boatman'. Adding to the merriment, recalls Eisenhower's deputy, Lieutenant-General Lucius Clay, were the never-ending toasts accompanied by the clinking of glasses of vodka which the attendants, adds Clay, were pouring out assiduously.)

Following the awards ceremony and luncheon there was a parade and an air show. Under the approving eye of British Air Chief Marshal Sir Arthur Harris, guests craned their necks to watch a fly-past in close formation of 1,700 Anglo-American fighters and bombers. Zhukov, says Eisenhower, seemed much impressed. Afterwards, Zhukov made more awards presentations, handing out to 20 British and American officers the Order of the Red Banner or the Medal for Battle Merit.

Two months after the Frankfurt meeting, Ike accepted an invitation from Zhukov to visit Moscow. President Truman's aide, Harry Hopkins, had told Eisenhower of Stalin's anxiety to have him come to Moscow on 24 June (the day of the Victory Parade, but if that was not convenient, any time before the Potsdam Conference (17 July–2 August) or immediately after it. Eisenhower told Hopkins that he had been invited to Moscow sometime earlier but that the US War Department refused him permission to make the trip, although he had been anxious to go. Eisenhower thought it a mistake that he did not go when he was asked. He also told Hopkins that if he was to go to Moscow then Zhukov should be invited to the United States. Later, Hopkins took this matter up with President Truman who was 'all for the idea'.

During Ike's visit to Moscow, when he and Zhukov were introduced at a soccer game, the cheers 'surpassed anything I had ever heard', Ambassador Harriman said. Eisenhower was seen as a living symbol of Soviet–American cooperation, and Harriman sensed a yearning among the people, if not their leaders, to see it continue.[3]

Another witness to the response of the soccer crowd was US General John R. Deane who says that when the game ended and Ike and Zhukov rose to leave, the crowd gave them an ovation that grew ever larger in volume. Finally in a gesture of friendliness, Eisenhower threw his arm over Zhukov's shoulder, and Zhukov responded by embracing Eisenhower. With that, says Deane, there was pandemonium in the stands. Eisenhower and Zhukov waved to the crowd, and the only way they could bring the cheering to an end was by leaving the box, which they did after it had gone on for ten minutes. Deane says there was nothing rehearsed about the demonstration, that it had nothing to do with ideologies or politics. It was simply a sincere outpouring of feeling by a cross-section of Russian people, of their deep affection for Americans as embodied in Eisenhower. 'It was heartwarming,' says Deane, and 'reassuring to us Americans who were there.'

Deane records Ike's first meeting with Stalin, saying he knew Ike made a great impression on the Russian dictator by saying very little and refraining from any of the flattering remarks that Stalin was accustomed to hear from foreigners. The two stood together for five hours on the Lenin Mausoleum (to watch a sports parade) but because of the language problem they did not have any lively conversations.

Eisenhower was apparently so infected by the buoyant mood of the Russians he met that he told Harriman he was confident his friend Zhukov would succeed Stalin as leader and usher in a new era of Russian–American friendship. He mentioned that, in frequent toasts to peace, he and Zhukov had often linked arms in public. But the ambassador sought to cool Ike's hopes, saying they were 'unrealistic', that military leaders were the last to realize that the former wartime cooperation was over. In Harriman's eyes, the greater the hopes, the greater the eventual disillusionment. 'Like General Marshall,' he later wrote, 'Eisenhower was slow to understand the crucial importance of the Communist Party in making Soviet policy.'

Although Eisenhower wrote his memoirs during the Cold War, he speaks warmly of his friendship with Zhukov, saying that it continued to grow until the moment he left Europe for home. He says candidly: 'That friendship was a personal and individual thing and unfortunately was not representative of a general attitude.' (It would be ten years before the two met again – at the Geneva Big Four Summit in 1955 – but that would be a time when personal friendship took a back seat to Big Power politics, when Ike was now the President of the United States and Zhukov, Russia's Defence Minister. Some observers would say Zhukov's place in the Russian delegation to Geneva was mere 'window-dressing'.)

Eisenhower's successor in Germany, Lucius Clay, noted, perhaps wistfully, that while Zhukov and Eisenhower were in Berlin the relations between the two countries were good; but that after both men departed, these relations began to sour. Clay commented that he too was very friendly with Zhukov, and also with General Sokolovsky. 'This is,' he says, regretting the slide into the Cold War, 'one of the reasons I think we could have avoided the worst of what followed. Because it looked at the beginning as though we were going to get along. That is why I think that the Soviet behavior grew out of events, rather than having been predetermined.' He adds, 'Then, Zhukov left and ... we began to find that we just couldn't deal with them.'[4]

Clay afterwards told Eisenhower that Zhukov was particularly affected by his departure from Berlin. He says Eisenhower truly believed that cooperation with the Russians was possible. Some years later he said: 'I think Eisenhower felt very strongly about his friendship with Zhukov . . . I really believe Zhukov wanted to be friends.'[5]

After a year of dealing with the Russians in Berlin, US General Walter Bedell Smith, Eisenhower's Chief of Staff – later Ambassador to Moscow – summed up his own personal feelings towards Zhukov and his successor in Berlin, V.D. Sokolovsky: 'Our principal contacts were with Marshal Zhukov and General Sokolovsky, both of whom we admired very much, and who, I felt, would be great men in any country.' He said that, in spite of the language barrier and the post-war problems dividing the two countries, 'These two men . . . impressed us not only by their ability, but by their frank and straight-forward attitude.' (This goodwill seemed also to carry over into Anglo–Russian ties. When Zhukov met the British member of the Allied Control Council, General Ronald Weeks, he said that after one meeting they had achieved a great deal. Weeks agreed, causing Zhukov to remark: 'I think we will go on achieving a great deal so long as the politicians keep out.')

On 20 April 1955 Zhukov sent a personal message to Eisenhower and indirectly invited the President to negotiate an end to the Cold War. Ten days later in another personal message to the President, Zhukov again stressed the need for talks to settle Big Power discord. Ike acknowledged the messages from Zhukov but he himself did not reveal their content. The *New York Times* and other papers did. Zhukov alleged that Washington was brandishing the atomic bomb. He also urged the USA to close down foreign military bases and 'silence the advocates of war'. There was no dearth of these advocates in America.[6]

But Eisenhower was far from being an out-and-out hawk. In November 1954 it was reliably reported that Ike found 'the mass killing required in a knock-out blow against Soviet Russia profoundly morally abhorrent'.[7]

Many authors say that when Eisenhower was at the 1955 Geneva Summit he was anxious to see Zhukov again, not only to find out what had happened to him, but (in the words of historian Stephen Ambrose) 'to explore the possibility of re-establishing the working partnership of the two that had been created in Germany after the war'. Many of these authors quote John Eisenhower as saying that at Geneva he and his father no longer saw in Zhukov the 'cocky little rooster' they remembered at the end of the war. Instead, Zhukov seemed, reserved, cowed, pathetic, even frightened. But Zhukov, who had been in the middle of some of history's most awesome shoot-outs was unlikely to be frightened. What is more likely is Zhukov's despondency concerning the backdrop to the 1955 Summit, which is not mentioned by these authors. To wit: A bitter war had been fought on the Korean peninsula; Vietnam and Formosa (Taiwan) were contemporary focal points of Big Power rivalry in the Far East; the arms race appeared to be getting out of hand – in April 1954 it was announced that the United States planned to spend US$ 427 million more in the next year to push ahead with 'greatly increased production of thermonuclear weapons'; in the USA staunchly anticommunist lawmakers had all but silenced liberal dissent in America.[8]

Charles Bohlen, the Russian-speaking US ambassador to Moscow, says at that time the Soviets had brought 'old soldier' Zhukov along to Geneva, apparently as a gesture of friendship towards Eisenhower. The two lunched privately one day at the President's villa. The only other persons present were a Russian interpreter and Bohlen. Bohlen had first met Zhukov at the end of the war when Harry Hopkins and he had visited Berlin. Zhukov, he says, looked like a soldier – stocky, 'sturdy as a Russian oak', a man with a slightly ruddy complexion and clear blue eyes. Although Zhukov had a pleasant smile, he was very reserved, particularly with foreigners. Zhukov was a Bolshevik who undeviatingly followed the Party line, but Bohlen modifies this remark by saying Zhukov was first of all a Russian patriot. The marshal believed in the independence of the army and, says Bohlen, one of the reasons for his eventual downfall was his attempt to throw off the political commissar system. (Newly published materials suggest that the party bosses were upset not only with Zhukov's independence of views, but his persistent allegations that the hands of high-ranking Party members were not clean in connection with the Stalinist Terror of the late 1930s.) There was, says Bohlen, a fresh spirit about Zhukov that contrasted sharply with the deviousness of other Bolshevik leaders. Furthermore, he conveyed tolerance, even respect for America, and there was no doubt in Bohlen's mind that his affection for Eisenhower was genuine and 'not put on for occasions'.

At the close of the luncheon, Eisenhower asked Zhukov what he was going to do for a vacation. Zhukov said he was going to the southwest of European Russia for trout fishing. The two discussed the merits of fishing equipment, and Eisenhower promised to send

Zhukov an American rod and reel. About a month after Bohlen's return to Moscow, the Embassy received through the diplomatic bag a rod and reel with a letter from President Eisenhower to Marshal Zhukov. The letter was sent unsealed, presumably out of courtesy to the Embassy. It contained nothing more than a friendly greeting and a mention that the rod and reel were being shipped under separate cover.

Some years earlier, when Ike took up his duties at the Pentagon, Zhukov sent him some presents, including a large white bearskin rug. Ike informed Zhukov that the rug had found a good place in his study at home. Ike wrote the marshal, saying he remembered the friendly military and philosophical talks they had in Berlin, Frankfurt and Moscow as among the most memorable of his life.[9]

It was during their first meeting in Frankfurt in 1945 that Eisenhower gave his high evaluation of Zhukov's role in the war:[10]

> In Europe [the war] has been won and to no man do the United Nations owe a greater debt than to Marshal Zhukov who, being an modest man, no doubt underrates the standing he holds in our hearts. One day when all of us are gathered to our fathers there is certain to be another [Russian] Order – that will be the Order of Zhukov which will be prized by every man who admires courage, vision, foresight and determination in a soldier.

Eisenhower's prediction came true but only half a century later. In 1996 at a ceremony to mark the 100th anniversary of Zhukov's birth, a new Russian decoration was introduced – the coveted Order of Zhukov. Newspaper columns said a grateful posterity was acknowledging at last the nation's considerable debt to a worthy native son.

Notes

1. Eisenhower recorded that in subsequent meetings, usually held in Berlin, Zhukov discarded the practice of having his political adviser constantly at his side, and that he and Zhukov would sometimes meet alone with only an interpreter present.
2. 'The super-super award' – these are the words of General John Deane, who was head of the US Military Mission in Moscow.
3. Some details of Ike's visit to Moscow are covered in chapter 18.
4. Of course, Moscow said the opposite, blaming Washington for all difficulties.
5. Lucius Clay, *Decision in Germany*, London, 1950.
6. Some of the war advocates: US Admiral Robert Carney, Chief of Naval Operations, who said the United States would shortly have to 'fight to the finish with Russia' (29 May 1954). US Major-General James Saliba told an

American Legion meeting that America could erase Red Russia 'overnight' (3 December 1954). When 1954 ended it was reported in Britain that some of the more provocative statements made by US generals, admirals and politicians were 'regarded with horror' (The *New York Times*, 6 December 1954).

7. The *Nashville Tennesseean*, 28 November 1954.

8. The multi-volume *Great Soviet Encyclopedia*, although harshly critical of Eisenhower as President, said his administration 'took some realistic steps in the area of international relations'. 'Eisenhower terminated military actions in Korea in July 1953 ... and in 1955 took part in the Geneva Conference attended by the heads of the USA, USSR, Great Britain and France.' It also said, 'Taking into account the growing opposition to McCarthyism, the Eisenhower administration and the Congress dissociated themselves from that movement's most odious methods, which presented the American system in an unfavourable light to the entire world. In December 1954 the Senate adopted a resolution censuring McCarthy.' The *Encyclopedia* added: 'In 1959 [Premier Nikita Khrushchev] accepted an invitation from Eisenhower and paid a state visit to the USA.'

9. The Geneva Summit of 1955 had a number of beneficial results, especially in the field of cultural exchanges. Not least of which was the arrival in Russia of the American cast of the hit show, *Porgy and Bess*, very amusingly described in vivid detail by author Truman Capote who accompanied the troupe.

10. An official report by another high-ranking US General, George C. Marshall, highly evaluated the war role of the British and Russians. Marshall said: 'The heroic stands of the British and Russian peoples saved the United States a war on her own soil.' (*The War Reports of Marshall*, New York, 1947.)

SELECT BIBLIOGRAPHY

Allenbrooke, Field Marshal Lord, *War Diaries, 1939–1945*, London, 2001.

Ambrose, Stephen, *Eisenhower and Berlin: The Decision to Halt at the Elbe*, New York, 1967.

Ambrose, Stephen, *Eisenhower the President*, London, 1984.

Andrew, Christopher and Gordievsky, Oleg, *KGB: The Inside Story*, London, 1990.

Axell, Albert, *Stalin's War: Through the Eyes of His Commanders*, London, 1997.

Axell, Albert, *Russia's Heroes*, London, 2002.

Becker, Carl, *Modern History*, New York, 1931.

Beevor, Antony, *Berlin, the Downfall 1945*, London, 2002.

Beevor, Antony, *Stalingrad*, London, 1998.

Beria, Serge, *Beria, My Father: Inside Stalin's Kremlin*, London, 2001.

Bernadotte, Count Folke, *The Curtain Falls*, New York, 1945.

Bohlen, Charles E., *Witness to History*, New York, 1973.

Bradley, Omar, *A Soldier's Story*, London, 1951.

Bullitt, William C., *The Bullitt Mission to Russia*, New York, 1919.

Chaney, Otto Preston, *Zhukov*, Norman, Oklahoma, 1996.

Chuikov, Vasily, *The End of the Third Reich*, London, 1967.

Churchill, Winston, *History of the Second World War*, 6 vols., London, 1948–54.

Clark, Alan, *Barbarossa: The Russian–German Conflict, 1941–1945*, London, 1965.

Clay, Lucius, *Decision in Germany*, London, 1950.

Cohen, Stephen, *Bukharin and the Bolshevik Revolution, 1888–1938*, New York, 1974.

Cohen, Stephen, *Commissars, Commanders and Civilian Authority: The Structure of Soviet Military Politics*, Cambridge, Massachusetts, 1979.

Collier, Richard, *The War That Stalin Won: Tehran–Berlin*, London, 1983.

Connolly, Cyril, *The Missing Diplomats*, London, 1952.

Conquest, Robert, *The Great Terror: Stalin's Purges of the Thirties*, London, 1968.

Crossman, Richard, *The God That Failed*, London, 1950.

Dallin, Alexander, *German Rule in Russia, 1941–44*, London, 1957.

Dallin, Alexander (ed.), *The Khrushchev and Brezhnev Years*, New York, 1992.

Davies, Norman, *White Eagle, Red Star*, London, 1972.

Deane, J.R., *The Strange Alliance*, London, 1947.

de Guingand, Sir Francis, *Generals at War*, London, 1972.

Deutscher, Isaac, *Stalin: A Political Biography*, New York, 1982.

Douglas, William O., *Russian Journey*, New York, 1956.

Dragunsky, David, *A Soldier's Life*, Moscow, 1977.

Dulles, Allen, *Germany's Underground*, New York, 1947.

Eisenhower, Dwight, *Crusade in Europe*, New York, 1948.

Eisenhower, John, *Strictly Personal*, New York, 1969.

Erickson, John, *The Road to Berlin*, London, 1999.

Farrago, Ladislas, *Patton: Ordeal and Triumph*, London, 1966.

Feis, Herbert, *The Atomic Bomb and the End of World War II*, Princeton, 1966.

Fest, Joachim, *The Face of the Third Reich*, London, 1988.

Fest, Joachim, *Hitler*, London, 1980.

Fischer, John, *Why They Behave Like Russians*, New York, 1957.

Fischer, Louis, *The Road to Yalta: Soviet Foreign Relations, 1941–1945*, London, 1972.

Gaddis, John L., *We Now Know: Rethinking Cold War History*, Oxford, 1997.

Gehlen, Reinhard, *The Gehlen Memoirs*, London, 1972.

Getty, J. Arch, *Origins of the Great Purges*, Cambridge, 1985.

Gilbert, G.M., *Nuremberg Diary*, London, 1948.

Gilbert, Martin, *Winston S. Churchill*, 8 vols., London, 1966–1988.

Gilbert, Martin, *Road to Victory*, London, 1986.

Gilbert, Martin, *The Second World War*, London, 1989.

Glantz, David, *Zhukov's Greatest Defeat*, 1999.

Glantz, David, and House, Jonathan, *When Titans Clashed*, Kansas, 1995.

Goebbels, Josef, *The Goebbels Diaries, 1942–3*, London, 1949.

Görlitz, Walter, *Paulus and Stalingrad*, London, 1963.

Grabsky, Phil, *The Great Commanders*, London, 1993.

Gromyko, Andrei, *Memories*, London, 1989.

Guderian, Heinz, *Panzer Leader*, New York, 1952.

Gunther, John, *Inside Russia Today*, London, 1957.

Halder, Franz, *Hitler as Warlord*, London, 1950.

Harriman, W. Averell and Abel, Elie, *Special Envoy to Churchill and Stalin: 1941–1946*, New York, 1975.

Henderson, Sir Neville, *Failure of a Mission*, London, 1940.

Hosking, Geoffrey, *A History of the Soviet Union*, London, 1990.

Hyland, William, *The Fall of Khrushchev*, New York, 1968.

Isaacson, Walter and Thomas, Evan, *The Wise Men: Acheson, Bohlen, Harriman, Kennan, Lovett, McCloy*, London, 1986.

Jukes, Geoffrey, *Stalingrad: The Turning Point*, New York: 1968.

Keegan, John, *The Second World War*, London, 1989.

Keitel, Wilhelm, *The Memories of Field Marshal Keitel*, London, 1965.

Kennan, George F., *Russia and the West Under Lenin and Stalin*, New York, 1960.

Khrushchev, N.S., *Khrushchev Remembers: The Glasnost Tapes*, Boston, 1990.

Khrushchev, Sergei, *Khrushchev on Khrushchev: An Inside Account of the Man and His Era*, Boston, 1990.

Knight, Amy, *Beria: Stalin's First Lieutenant*, Princeton, 1993.

Konev, I.S., *Year of Victory*, Moscow, 1984.

Lauterbach, Richard E., *These Are the Russians*, New York, 1944.

Le Tissier, Tony, *Zhukov at the Oder: The Decisive Battle for Berlin*, London, 1996.

Liddell Hart, B.H. (ed.), *The Soviet Army*, London, 1956.

Lockhart, R.H. Bruce, *Memoirs of a British Agent*, New York, 1932.

Lynch, Michael, *Stalin and Khrushchev: the USSR, 1924–1964*, London, 1990.

McCauley, Martin, *Stalin and Stalinism*, New York, 1995.

McCauley, Martin, *Russia, America and the Cold War*, London, 1998.

Medvedev, Roy A., *Let History Judge*, London, 1972.

Medvedev, Roy A. and Zhores A., *Khrushchev: The Years in Power*, New York, 1978.

Menon, K.P.S., *Delhi–Chungking*, Oxford, 1947.

Miller, Merle, *Plain Speaking: Conversations with Harry S. Truman*, London, 1974.

Naimark, Norman M., *The Russians in Germany: A History of the Soviet Zone of Occupation, 1945–1949*, Cambridge, Massachusetts, 1995.

Overy, Richard, *Why the Allies Won*, London, 1995.

Overy, Richard, *Russia's War*, London, 1998.

Papen, Franz von, *Memoirs*, London, 1952.

Pares, Sir Bernard, *A History of Russia*, New York, 1965.

Reitlinger, Gerald, *The Final Solution*, London, 1953.

Ribbentrop, Joachim von, *The Ribbentrop Memoirs*, London, 1954.

Rickenbacker, Eddie, *Rickenbacker: His Own Story*, New York, 1967.

Roberts, Geoffrey, *The Unholy Alliance: Stalin's Pact With Hitler*, Bloomington, Indiana, 1989.

Roberts, Geoffrey, *Victory at Stalingrad*, London, 2002.

Rokossovsky, K.K., *A Soldier's Duty*, Moscow, 1970.

Schellenberg, Walter, *The Schellenberg Memoirs*, London, 1956.

Schlabrendorff, Fabian von, *Revolt Against Hitler*, London, 1948.

Seaton, Albert, *The Russo–German War, 1941–45*, London, 1971.

Sethi, A.L., *Marshal Zhukov, the Master Strategist*, New Delhi, 1988.

Sherwood, Robert E., *Roosevelt and Hopkins*, New York, 1948.

Shirer, William L., *A Berlin Diary*, London, 1941.

Shirer, William L., *The Rise and Fall of the Third Reich*, London, 1960.

Shtemenko, S.M., *The Last Six Months*, New York, 1977.

Shukman, Harold (ed.), *Stalin's Generals*, London, 1993.

Spahr, William J., *Zhukov: The Rise and Fall of a Great Captain*, 1993.

Steinbeck, John, *A Russian Journal*, London, 1949.

Strasser, Otto, *Hitler and I*, London, 1940.

Taylor, A.J.P., *The Second World War*, London, 1975.

Tell, Rolf (ed.), *Nazi Guide to Nazism*, Washington DC, 1942.

Trevor-Roper, H.R., *The Last Days of Hitler*, London, 1950.

Troyat, Henry, *Daily Life in Russia under the Last Tsar*, Stanford, California, 1961.

Tucker, Robert C., *The Soviet Political Mind; Stalinism and Post-Stalin Change*, New York, 1971.

Volkogonov, Dmitri, *Lenin: New Biography*, tr. by Harold Shukman, New York, 1994.

Volkogonov, Dmitri, *Stalin: Triumph and Tragedy*, tr. by Harold Shukman, London, 1991.

Ward, Chris, *Stalin's Russia*, London, 1994.

Ward Price, G., *I Knew These Dictators*, London, 1937.

Warlimont, Walther, *Inside Hitler's Headquarters, 1939–1945*, London, 1964.

Werth, Alexander, *Russia at War*, London, 1964.

Westphal, Siegfried, *The German Army in the West*, London, 1951.

Wheeler-Bennett, J.W., *The Nemesis of Power: The German Army in Politics, 1918–45*, London, 1953.

Wolf, Markus, *Man Without a Face, The Autobiography of Communism's Greatest Spymaster*, New York, 1997.

Zhukov, Georgi, *Reminiscences and Reflections*, Moscow, 1985.

INDEX

ABC News, 211
A Lifelong Cause, 78
A Soldier's Story, 137
Abakumov, Viktor, 7, 157
Aberdeen, 3
Airborne Division (US 82nd), 160
Albania, 227
Alanbrooke, Field-Marshal, 1
Allied Control Council, 7, 168
Allied Expeditionary Force, 132, 201, 208
Allied Intervention, 34
Allied Supreme Command HQ, 204
Ambrose, Stephen, 236
Anfilov, Viktor, historian 1, 156
Anglo-Russians relations, 239
Annual Register, 30, 45, 231
Antipenko, Gen. Nikolai, 148
Antonov, Gen. A.I., 117, 126, 205
Antonovites, 39, 41
Archangelsk–Astrakhan Line, 100
Ardennes, 204
Army Group Centre, 78, 111, 124
Assumption Cathedral, 15
At Ease, 236
Atlantic Wall, 202
Atomic bomb, 208
Auschwitz, 222
Austria, 21, 66
Axis forces, 114

Badiakin, N., 2
Bagramyan, Gen. Ivan, 172
Bagration, Operation, 122
Baldwin, Hanson W., 6
Baltic Fleet, 92
Baltic region, 34
Barbarossa, Plan, 65

Barents Sea, 102
Battle of Belorussia (Bagration), 122–134
Battle of Berlin, 135–149
Battle of Kursk Bulge, 113–121
Battle of Moscow, 78–89
Battle of Stalingrad, 100–112
Beaverbrook, Lord, 87
Beevor, Antony, 5, 138, 220
Belgium, 66
Belarus (Belorussia), 34, 73, 122–134
Beloborodov, Gen. Afanasy, 124
Belov, Gen. Mikhail, 12
Benes, Edvard, 46
Bergholts, Olga, 95
Beria, Lavrenti, 7, 157, 184–190
Berlin, 7, 8, 9, 10, 198, 209
Berlin Garrison, 145
Berlin Operation, 136, 135–149
Bernadotte, Count Folke, 141
Berzarin, Gen. Nikolai, 10
Big Brother, 5
Black Hundreds, 19
Black Sea, 37, 45, 117
Black Sea Fleet, 117
Blumentritt, Gen. Gunther, 76
Blyukher, Marshal Vasily, 45
Bohlen, Charles, 240–241
Bolsheviks, 32
Bonapartism, 166
Bormann, Martin, 136, 151
Borovitsky Gate, 186
Bradley, Gen. Omar, 136, 204
Brauchitsch, Field Marshal Walter v., 76
Braun, Eva, 150–155
Brest, 122
Brezhnev, Leonid, 168, 193, 194, 196

British Expeditionary Force, 210
Bulganin, Marshal Nikolai, 157
Britain, 65
British General Staff, 134
Budenny, S.M., 3, 80
Burdenko Hospital, 218
Busch, Field Marshal Ernst v., 124

Caldwell, Erskine, 82
Capote, Truman, 242
Carney, Admiral Robert, 241
Carpathians, 204
Casualties, Russian, 74, 220–221, 233
Cathedral of the Saviour, 15
Caucasus, 103, 112, 115
Cavalry units, 21–29, 34
Central Committee, 157
Chamberlain, Neville, 62
Chamberlain, William Henry, 34
Chaney, Otto P., 6
Chekhov, Anton, 215
China, 54, 164
Choibalsan, Marshal K., 60
Chuikov, Gen. Vasili, 142, 146
Churches of Moscow, 84
Churchill, Winston, 65, 67, 101, 112,
    114, 120, 137, 199, 202, 207,
    208
Ciano, Count, 64, 83
Civil War, 34, 35
Clausewitz, Karl Maria v., 216
Clay, Gen. Lucius, 156, 197, 236,
    238
Cold War, 137, 238
The Cold War and Its Origins, 208
Combat Engineers, 135
Concentration camps, 9
Considine, Bob, 167
Cossacks, 3, 35, 190
Crimea, 37, 224
'Cradle of the Revolution,' 179
Crusade in Europe, 137
Cult of Personality, 191
Czechoslovak Corps, 34
Czechoslovakia, 66

Dakota aircraft, 233

Danzig (Gdansk), 64
Deane, Gen. John, 148, 237
Decision in Germany, 241
de Gaulle, Charles, 8
de Guingand, Gen. Sir Francis, 4, 209
Demonstrations in 1905, 18, 20
Dnieper river, 175
Doctors' Plot, 162
Doerr, Gen. Hans, 109
Dolmatovsky, E., 146
Dragunsky, Gen. David, 149
Dulles, John Foster, 163, 208
Dunkirk, 204, 210
Dvina river, 72

East Prussia, 132
Edelweiss, Plan, 103
Eden, Anthony, 164, 180
Egypt, 164
Eisenhower, Dwight, 1, 8, 9, 136,
    168, 197–212, 218–219
Eisenhower, John, 4, 197, 206, 218,
    239
Eisenhower, Mamie, 206
El Alamein, 210, 211
Elbe, 136
English Channel, 202, 210
Entente, 37
Eremenko, Gen. Andrei, 102, 103,
    105

Far East, 34
Feis, Herbert, 65
Feklenko, N.F., 51
Fest, Joachim, historian, 5
Festung Europa, 113
Finnish troops, 91, 96, 179
Fleming, D.F., 64, 208
France, 66, 102
Frankfurt-am-Main, 209, 232, 235,
    241
French Armed Forces, 67
Friedeburg, Admiral of the Fleet
    H. G. v., 148
Fritzsche, Hans, 76, 152
Frunze, Mikhail, 35
Fuller, J.F.C., 216

Gallup-type poll, 137
Gamarnik, Jan, 46
Geneva, 163
Geneva Summit Conference,
    205–206, 209, 239
Georgia, 168, 184
German Condor Squadron, 53
German General Staff, 67
German POWs, 9
German people, 9
Germany, 4, 102
Gestapo, 44
Giap, Vo Nguyen, 8
Glantz, David, 8
Gleiwitz, 63
Glinka's 'Glory', 182
Goebbels, Joseph, 63, 67, 78, 106,
    145, 147, 232
    Propaganda Ministry, 151
Golikov, Gen. Filipp, 47, 68
Gorky, Maxim, 121
Gorshkov, Admiral Sergei, 167, 169
Grabsky, Phil, 8, 13
Great Soviet Encyclopedia, 161
Great Terror, 233, 240
Grechko, Gen. A.A., 118
Griffith, Hubert, 64
Gritsevets, S.I., 61
Gromyko, Andrei, 44, 205
The Guardian, 230
Guderian, Gen. Heinz, 1, 8, 79, 83,
    109, 121
Gunsche, Otto, 154
Gunther, John, 4, 208

The Halder Diaries, 211
Halder, Gen. Franz, 3, 72
Harriman, Averell, 87, 89, 211, 236
Harriman, Kathleen, 232
Harris, Air Chief Marshal Sir Arthur,
    237
Henderson, Johnny, 210
Hermitage Museum, 91
    Madonnas, 99
Hess, Rudolf, 222
Heusinger, Gen. Adolf, 87, 220, 222
Higher Cavalry School, 42

Himmler, Heinrich, 141, 150
Hitler, Adolf, 3, 78
    Directive 41
    generals, 85
    his doubles, 153
    invasion of Russia, 63–77
    on Napoleon, 76
    Secret order, 15 April 1943
    suicide, 146, 232
Hollywood, 203
Hopkins, Harry, 207
Hoth, Gen. Hermann, 72
Hungary, 164
Hungarian crisis, 167

Imperial Chancellery, 153
India, 166
Institute of Military History, Russian,
    73
International Military Tribunal, 64 (see
    also Nuremberg Tribunal)
Israel, 164
Isakov, Admiral Ivan, 92
Ivan the Terrible, 162

Jalil, Mussa, 149
Japan, 8, 202
Japanese Army in Vladivostok, 34
Japanese in Mongolia, 215, 233
Jews, 162
Jodl, Gen. Alfred, 76, 141

Kaganovich, Lazar, 166
Kaiser Wilhelm II, 21
Kalinin Front, 85
Kalinin, Mikhail, 174
Karasin, Ambassador Grigory, 5
Karelian Isthmus, 91
Karpov, Vladimir, 166, 193
Katyusha rockets, 173
Kazan Medical Institute, 223
Keegan, John, 8
Keitel, Field Marshal Wilhelm, 87,
    136
Kelly, Sir David, 3
Kesselring, Field Marshal A., 69
Khalkin Gol (Mongolia), 46, 215

Kharkov, 25
Khrushchev, Nikita, 1, 7, 156,
    and Beria, 185–188
    secret speech, 163
    visit to USA, 168
    and Zhukov, 219
Kiev, 73, 175
Kiev Military District, 67
Kiev operation, 214
Klin, 180
Kluge, Gen. Gunther v., 76, 113
Kolchak, Admiral A.V., 35
Konev, Marshal Ivan, 80, 140, 159
Konotop, 10
Korfes, Gen. Otto, 109
Kotlyar, Nikolai, 153
Korean peninsula, 240
Korean War, 162, 242
Kosygin, Aleksei, 229
Kozhedub, Ivan, 120
Krasnaya Zvezda, 2
Kravchenko, G.P., 61
Krebs, Gen. Hans, 146
Kremlin, 4, 159
Kremlin Museum, 198
Kremlin Palace of Congresses, 168,
    236
Kulaks, 34
Kuban Cossacks, 37
Kuibyshev, 216
Kulik, Marshal G.I., 56, 94
Kurchatov, Igor, 208
Kursk, Battle of, 113–122, 181
Kutuzov, Mikhail, 1, 169
Kuznetsov, Admiral of the Fleet
    Nikolai, 157

Lake Baikal, 52
Lake Ladoga, 91
Lapin, Gen. A.Y., 46
de Lattre de Tassigny, Gen. Jean, 148
Lazukina, D. A., 230
Lebensraum, 63
Lefortovo barracks, 37
Lefortovo Prison, 157
Leipzig–Dresden area, 136
Lena goldfields, 19

Lend–Lease, 114, 121, 204
Leningrad (St Petersburg), 5, 79
    blockade, 90
Leningrad Front, 125
Leningrad orchestra, 90
Lenin Mausoleum, 6, 157
Levine, Alan J., 112
Liddell Hart, B.H., 133, 216
London, 3, 5
The Longest Day, 203
Lord Moran, 139
Lost Victories, 72
Luftwaffe, 64, 82
Lvov Region, 132

MacArthur, Gen. Douglas, 1, 8, 199
McCarthyism, 242
Main Political Administration, 162,
    167
Malenkov, Gen. Georgi, 166
Malinin, Gen. M.S., 116
Manstein, Field Marshal Erich v., 1, 107
Maresyev, Alexei, 120
Marshall, Gen. George C., 242
Mediterranean sector, 202
Medvedev, Roy, 7
Mein Kampf, 65
Mekhlis, Gen. L.Z., 175
Menon, Krishna, 168
Mensheviks, 31
Meretskov, Marshal Kirill, 172, 195
Messerschmitt planes, 180
Michael, King of Romania, 234
Minsk, 122, 129
Minsk Opera House, 129
The Moabit Notebooks, 149
Moabit Prison, 145
Molotov, V. 130, 161, 173
Mongolia, 8, 50–62, 215, 233
Montgomery, Field Marshal B., 1, 8,
    200, 218–219
Montreal, 113
Morozov, Vasily, 1
Moscow, 6, 8, 13, 112
Moscow News, 184
Moscow's Churches, 84
Moskalenko, Gen. K.S., 185, 189

Mozhaisk Defence Line, 80
Munich Pact, 65
Murphy, Robert, 236
Mussolini, Benito, 65
MVD (Ministry of Internal Affairs), 185
My New Order, 76
Myagkov, Dr. Mikhail, 8

Napoleon, armies of, 75
Napoleon (Bonaparte), 216
Nashville Tennesseean, 242
National Anthem, 23
National Socialist Party, 65
NATO, 163
Nazi crimes, 9
Nazi Germany, 2, 120
Nazi Propaganda Ministry, 67
New Delhi, 166, 206
New York City, 3
New York Times, 6, 21, 229, 239
Nineteenth Party Congress, 161
NKVD (forerunner of KGB), 48
Nizhny Novgorod, 16
'Nomonhan Incident', 61
Non-aggression Pact of 1939, 192
Non-fraternization policy, 209
Normandy (Second Front), 122, 202, 203, 208
North Caucasian Front, 194
Novikov, Gen. A.A., 158
Novodevichy Monastery, 222
Novorossisk, 117
Nuremberg International Tribunal 64, 92

Obersaltzburg, 150
October Revolution, 32
Odessa, 7
Odessa Military District, 157
OGPU (secret police), 45
Oktyabrsky, Admiral Filipp, 75
'Old Black Joe,' 236
Old Testament, 138
Operation Mars, 8
Operation White, 64
Order of Victory, 209, 233

Order of Zhukov, 241
Orel, 102
Orenburg, 35
Orwell, George, 5, 191
Overseas Press Club of America, 163
Overy, Richard, 47, 133, 135

Panzer Leader, 121
Partisans, 122–134
Party Chancellery, 150
Party statistics, 42
Patton, Gen. George, 1, 8, 200, 203, 204
Paulus, Field Marshal Friedrich, 109
Pavlov, Gen. D.G., 74–75
Pavlovsky, Gen. I.G., 12
Pearl Harbor, 50, 202
Peter the Great, 91
Piskarevskoye Cemetery, 98
Plan Barbarossa, 65
Plenum of Central Committee, 226
Pletzensee Prison, 145
Podgorny, 229
Pogroms, 20
Pogue, F.C., 203
Poland, 63–64, 164
Polish Home Army, 133
Porgy and Bess, 242
Portugal, 66
Potsdam Conference, 201, 208
Poznan, 170
Pravda, 157
Prohkorovka, tank battle, 118
Propaganda, 63, 138, 151
Pushkin, Alexander, 78
Pushkin Family Museum, 96
Putin, President Vladimir, 234
Pyatakov, Yuri, 45

Queensberry Rules, 3

Radio Leningrad, 95
Red Army, 32
Red Guards, 32
Red Square, 6, 182
Red Terror, 34
Reichenau, Field Marshal Walter v., 155

Reichstag, 138, 146
Reminiscences and Reflections, 7,
  191–196
Remizov, S.N., 16
Reserve Front, 176
Rheims, 147
Rhine, 203
Ribbentrop, Joachim von, 64
Rickenbacker, Capt. Eddie, 207
Ritter, Prof. Gerhard, 76
Romanian forces, 105–106
Rommel, Gen. Erwin, 1, 8
Rokossovsky, K.K., 3, 195
  on Stalingrad battle, 89
Roosevelt, Franklin D., 131
Rosenthal, A.M., 212
Roslavl, 177
Rostov-on-Don, 34
Rotblat, Prof. Sir Joseph, 208, 212
Rotmistrov, Gen. P.A., 2
Rudenko, Air Marshal Sergei, 7, 149
Russell, Bertrand, 165
Russian cavalry, 34
Russian Defence Ministry, 107
Russian Foreign Ministry, 230
Russian Mirror, 156
Russian songs, 4, 18
Rybalko, Gen. Pavel, 159
Rzheshevsky, Prof. Oleg, 8, 111
Rzhev, 111

St Petersburg, 20
Saliba, Gen. James, 241
Samara, 35
San Francisco, 113
Savichev, Tanya (diarist), 98
Schlabrendorff, Fabian v., 89
Schlusselburg, 98, 179
Second Front, 101
Second World War, 64
Seelow Heights, 144
Serbia, 21
Sethi, Col. A.L., 8
Seven Days in May, 216
Shatilov, Gen. Vasili, 138
Shaposhnikov, Marshal B.M., 93, 176
Shaw, George Bernard, 148

Shcheglov, Dmitry, 149
Shirer, William L., 63
Shkaravsky, Faust, 150
Sholokhov, Mikhail, 216
Shostakovich, Dmitri, 90, 96
Shtemenko, Gen. S.M., 90, 96
Shtern, G.M., 58
Siberia, 19
Siberian gulag, 47
Simonov, Konstantin, 54, 148
Smith, Gen. Walter Bedell, 239
Smolensk, Battle of, 75, 174
Smorodinov, Gen. Ivan, 51
Smushkevich, Y.V., 53
Snow, Edgar, 142
Socialist-Revolutionaries, 33
Sokolovsky, Gen. V.D., 81, 146, 156
  on Stalingrad battle, 89
Song of the Falcon, 121
'Song of the Volga Boatman,' 236
Sorge, Dr Richard, 67
South America, 154
Spaatz, Gen. Carl, 148
Spahr, William J., 6, 43
Spain, 45, 66
Spanish Civil War, 58
Spassky Gate, 182
Sputnik, 135
Stalin, Josef, 1
  death, 184
  Great Terror, 39, 53
  jealousy, 219
  paranoia, 67
  purge of military, 53
  and Zhukov, 171–183
Stalin, Vasily, 7
Stalingrad, Battle of, 3, 8, 100–113
State Defence Committee, 130
Steppe Front, 181
Stewart, George, 43
Strelkovka, 13
Suez Crisis, 164
The Supreme Command, 203
Suslov, Mikhail, 193–194
Suvorov, Alexander, 10
Sverdlovsk (Ekaterinburg), 161
Sweden, 66

Taiwan (Formosa), 240
Taman grouping, 117
Tedder, Air Marshal Arthur, 147
Telegin, Gen. K.F., 158
The Times, 46, 52, 151
T-34 tanks, 9
Third Reich, 106
Timoshenko, Marshal S.K., 68, 173
Tippelskirch, Gen. Kurt v., 85
Tito, Marshal, 164, 234
Tolstoi, Leo, 215
Tominaga, 'Kamikaze' Gen. Kyoji, 51
Trans-Siberian Railway, 13, 52
Trotsky, Leon, 44, 45
Troyanovsky, Oleg, 163
Truman, Harry, 207
Tsar Boris, 225
Tsar Nicholas II, 18, 21
Tsarist Army, 21–29,
Tukhachevsky, M.N., 39, 46, 72
Turgenev, Ivan, 215
Turkey, 66
Twentieth Party Congress, 163
Twenty-fourth Party Congress, 196

Uborevich, I.P., 39
Ukraine, 29, 79, 175, 193
United Nations, 1, 163, 234
Urals, 35, 85
Urals Military District, 223
Uranus, 12
US Military Mission in Moscow, 241
US Senate, 242
US Strategic Air Command, 199

Varna, 225
Vasilevsky, Marshal A., 78, 106, 109,
    110, 117, 195
Vatutin, Gen. N.F., 68, 109
Versailles Treaty, 209
Victory Day, 151
Victory Parade, 6
Vietnam War, 240
VJ Day, 200
Vnukovo Airport, 227
Volga river, 17
Volkogonov, Dmitri, 45

Volga region, 34
Volga river, 73
Voronezh, 115
Voronov, Gen. Nikolai, 109
Voroshilov, Marshal K.Y., 49, 92
Vyazma, 111
Vyshinsky, Andrei, 233, 236

Warsaw, 133
Washington, 141
Wavell, Field Marshal A.P., 1, 101
Weeks, Gen. Ronald, 239
Wehrmacht, 1, 95
Weidling, Gen. Helmuth, 145
Western Front, 85, 174
White Armies of Russia, 43
White Guards, 34, 39
White Sea, 100
World War One, 19
World War Two, 3, 64
Wrangel, Baron P.N., 37

Yagoda, G., 190
Yakovlev, Nikolai, 120
Yelnya bulge, 175
Yelnya–Smolensk railway, 177
Yezhov, N., 190
Yugoslavia, 164

Zhdanov, Andrei, 92
Zheltov, Gen. A.S., 167, 169
Zhilin, Dr. Pavel, 67
Zhukova, Ella, 16, 213–222
Zhukova, Era, 16, 213–222
Zhukova, Maria, 1, 2, 194–195
Zhukov Foundation, 221
Zhukov, Georgi, 1
    criticisms of, 48, 221,
    on education, 222
    Eisenhower and Zhukov, 197–212
    first wife, 161
    his library, 16
    daughter Margarita, 213
    meetings with Stalin, 171–183
    and Montgomery, 210
    obituary, 229, 231
    personal message to Ike, 239

second wife, 165
on Stalingrad battle, 88
on travels, 222
visit to India, 166
war memoirs, 4, 191–196

WW I decorations, 29
wounded, 36
Zolotarev, Dr. Vladimir, 73
Zub, Col. I.G., 187